SAUL BELLOW

GARLAND REFERENCE LIBRARY
OF THE HUMANITIES
(VOL. 679)

SAUL BELLOW
An Annotated Bibliography, Second Edition

Gloria L. Cronin

Blaine H. Hall

GARLAND PUBLISHING, INC. • NEW YORK & LONDON
1987

15487197

© 1987 Gloria L. Cronin and Blaine H. Hall

$49—

Library of Congress Cataloging-in-Publication Data

Cronin, Gloria L., 1947–
Saul Bellow : an annotated bibliography.

(Garland reference library of the humanities ;
vol. 679)
Includes index.
1. Bellow, Saul—Bibliography.   I. Hall, Blaine H.
II. Title.   III. Series: Garland reference library of
the humanities ; v. 679.
Z8087.8.C76   1987   016.813'52   87-7607
[PS3503.E4488]
ISBN 0-8240-9421-2 (alk. paper)

Printed on acid-free, 250-year-life paper
Manufactured in the United States of America

Contents

Acknowledgments

The authors would like to thank the following institutions and people for their invaluable professional services and support: Brigham Young University English Department, Harold B. Lee Library, the Interlibrary Loan Department of the Harold B. Lee Library, Melvin Smith of the Humanites Research Center, Brigham Young University, technical assistants Kristina Eby, Cecilia Farr, Brian Merrill, Mark Bennet, Tory Anderson, Julianna Argyle, translators Gerhard Bach, Thomas E. Lyon, Madison Sowell, Cinzia Donatelli Noble and Sandy Mangum.

Introduction

Saul Bellow's stature in the postwar period of American literature can only be compared to that of Hemingway or Faulkner in the earlier part of the century. Nobel Laureate and winner of numerous prestigious fiction awards, Bellow has commanded serious attention from a large range of reviewers and critics at home and abroad for forty years. By now he is undoubtedly the most written about novelist of the contemporary American period.

This bibliography reflects this scholarly interest in Bellow as accurately and comprehensively as possible through 1985 with a significant number of titles from 1986. By intent, however, we have not included everything he wrote or that has been written about him. The early critical reactions to Bellow consist of little more than book notices and sketchy reviews. Later as he becomes more generally recognized, more scholarly works appear. With few exceptions, any review or article with substantive critical commentary has been listed and annotated. Brief book notes or announcements providing little more than a plot summary, however, have generally been omitted. We have included all of his major works--novels, short fiction, plays, essays, and some miscellaneous writings. However, we have not included some early short publications that later appeared in revised form as parts of longer works.

In the annotations we have taken care to reflect the author's tone and choice of language. Annotations contain main ideas or summarize directions of thought but do not attempt to paraphrase the course of the article or its argument. Some articles, of course, lend themselves better to this approach than do others. Generally, the annotations are descriptive rather than evaluative, but occasionally we have noted major articles. The length of the annotation sometimes indicates the entry's importance. More often it reflects a clearly focused and organized article. We have not annotated the works by Bellow nor the reviews of the novels, short fiction, and plays. The citations to reviews are listed without annotation immediately following the annotated articles in each subsection of **Criticism and Reviews.**

ix

Reviews providing substantial critical insight have been annotated and listed with the critical articles.

We have attempted to obtain copies of all the items included and to verify each citation, but there are some exceptions. In instances where, after three tries, we were unable to obtain a copy, we have listed it with a note showing in what bibliographic source it was cited. This is particularly true of some foreign language publications. In other instances, we received a copy of an item without any indication of source. If these citations could be verified in every detail in two or more bibliographic sources, i.e. *MLA Bibliography, Abstracts of English Studies, American Literary Scholarship, Annual Bibliography of English Language and Literature*, or one or more of the bibliographies listed in the section on **Bibliographies and Checklists**, we considered them verified citations.

The bibliography is divided into two main divisions: **Primary Sources** and **Secondary Sources**. In the first section we have categorized Bellow's works as **Novels, Short Fiction, Plays, Essays, Miscellaneous Writings, and Interviews**. The primary sources appear without annotations.

In listing the novels we have tried to discover and list all editions of each work, both English and foreign translations, hardbound and paperback. This listing has been compiled from the *Library of Congress, National Union Catalog, Cumulative Book Index, Books in Print, Paperbound Books in Print, British Books in Print, British Museum Catalog*, and the *British National Bibliography*, with additional information from the RLIN (Research Libraries Information Network) and OCLC shared cataloging online databases. The foreign language translations show only the publishing information, not the translated titles.

Under **Short Fiction** we have included only those titles that can be considered distinct short stories. We have excluded "short stories" that were reprinted parts of novels or that later became parts of novels in revised form. We have included both original sources of publication as well as reprint sources in short story collections since the latter will often be much more readily available to readers.

Bellow's dramatic writings were few, but we have treated them in much the same way as the short fiction, providing original publication sources as well as reprint sources.

Bellow's nonfiction works originally published in magazines, newspapers, journals, and books by other authors were more problematic. Generally we placed his longer, more substantial works in **Essays**, including his one nonfiction book, *To Jerusalem and Back.* We have also included as essays some major addresses later published as articles. The remainder of his nonfiction works have been categorized in **Miscellaneous Writings**. These include most of his book and movie reviews, forewords and introductions to the works of other authors, and shorter magazine and newspaper articles.

We categorized the interviews as primary sources on the basis that their main value to scholars is likely to be Bellow's own comments and ideas rather than those of the interviewers.

The **Secondary Sources** section has been arranged under the following headings: **Bibliographies and Checklists, Books and Monographs, Special Journal Issues, Biographical Sources, Criticism and Reviews,** and **Doctoral Dissertations**. Only the criticism has been annotated.

The **Books and Monographs** section includes three types of works: (1) works by a single author dealing with Bellow only, some based on doctoral dissertations, (2) works by a single author dealing with Bellow and one or more other authors, and (3) edited collections of essays, many of them reprinted from other sources,. The books have not been annotated, but each of the essays in the edited collections has been listed and annotated in the appropriate subsection of **Criticism and Reviews**. There the citations for reprinted essays first show the original source publication with reprint sources following chronologically. We have also provided reprint and original source information for previously published parts of the works in the two single-author categories when appropriate.

In the absence of a published biography of Bellow, we have included a list, without annotations, of the articles from a wide variety of magazines, newspapers, and journals that provide information about Bellow's life. Users should also be aware that in some instances the interviews with Bellow also provide this kind of information as do some of the reviews and critical articles. Generally, we have included under **Biography** those items that focus primarily on Bellow rather than on his works. The critical sources with significant biographical content can be found indexed under "biography" in the index.

In the **Criticism and Reviews** section, the sources have been listed in subsections devoted to each of Bellow's major works, his plays and short stories. **General Articles, Chapters, and Reviews** includes those sources not limited to a discussion of a single major work, the

plays, or the short stories. The index, however, provides references
to the specific works discussed in these sources.

Doctoral Dissertations includes only those cited in the *Comprehensive
Dissertation Index* and *Dissertation Abstracts International* that
specifically name Bellow or one of his works in the title. We have
not cited the abstract source. These are readily available in the
abstracting sources themselves.

A word about the **Author and Subject Index**. We have regularized
author's names to a single form when multiple citations showed
variations in the published sources. Interestingly, unpublished
dissertations by these authors generally included full names, while
most published sources used only initials for one or more given
names. We have adopted the form with initials as the standard,
unless a majority of published sources showed a preference for the
full name or for eliminating initials.

The names of all authors are included in the index except for the
authors of unannotated reviews. Anyone wanting to find reviews of
specific works can do so by consulting the appropriate subsection
under **Criticism and Reviews** where the reviews follow the annotated
articles in a separate subsection. This decision was based on the
belief that users of the bibliography would find the index more
useful if it listed only substantive items.

Users will also find the index a useful adjunct to the classified
section on a specific work, referring them to relevant sources in the
other sections of the bibliography, particularly the annotated articles
under **General Articles, Chapters, and Reviews**.

The subject terms have been purposely limited since this was
designed as a simple index and not as an exhaustive concordance.
Some terms, such as "theme," "character" or "characterization" have
not been included, since they represent the critical commonplaces of
Bellow scholarship and would have unreasonably cluttered the index.
However, some specific themes have been included under such terms
as "death," "alienation," and "love." This is not a title index, but the
titles of all Bellow's novels, short stories and short story collections,
plays, and *To Jerusalem and Back* are included as subject terms.

The foreign sources presented several serious problems: (1) finding
references and obtaining copies, (2) obtaining translations, (3)
evaluating their importance, and (4) handling diacritics. In many
instances, our interlibrary loan service was unable to verify the
source publications or to obtain them. For some foreign language

items, we therefore resorted to including only the citation with a
note as to the source of the bibliographic information. Also, to
facilitate preparation of the manuscript, we have arbitrarily eliminated
all diacritics from names and titles.

We have not included in the bibliography an inventory of the
manuscript or other special collections containing Bellow items. The
major repositories of Bellow materials have limited access, generally
requiring Bellow's direct permission. Those wishing further information should contact the libraries listed below directly for information
about the contents and availability of their collections.

The major collection of Bellow manuscripts, typescripts, correspondence, notes, reviews, translations, foreign editions of some works,
galley proofs, and other papers have been deposited at the Regenstein
Library at various times since 1963 by Mr. Bellow. The library has
published no register of the collection, but a working list of
holdings is available in the library, an earlier version of which was
published in Nault's *Saul Bellow: His Works and His Critics, An
Annotated International Bibliography.* (See Item 162 below.) Since
Nault's publication in 1977, however, the library has obtained
additional material and has rearranged some of the earlier collection,
making Nault's list incomplete and inaccurate.

The Humanities Research Center at the University of Texas,
Austin, has a small collection of manuscripts, typescripts and galley
proofs, some showing the author's revisions and emendations.
Bellow's permission is required to examine the manuscripts.

In addition, some Bellow documents, letters, correspondence to
Bellow, and memorabilia are included in the following libraries and
special collections. Most of these collections consist of fewer than
five items.

American Academy of Arts and Letters Library. [New York]
    Manuscript Collections, 1881- . Letters relate primarily to the
    Academy and the National Institute of Arts and Letters.
Boston University Mugar Memorial Library
Columbia University Libraries.
    Richard Volney Chase Papers, 1930-1967.
    Herbert Gold Papers, 1959-1969.
    Benjamin Nelson Papers, 1925-1977.
Cornell University John. M. Olin Library
Ford Foundation Library [New York]
Harvard University Houghton Library
Library of Congress.

Louis Aston Marantz Simpson Papers, 1943-1969.
Middlebury College Abernathy Library [Vermont]
Northwestern University Library
Rutgers University Library
University of California, San Diego Library
University of Illinois Archives [Urbana]
University of Massachusetts at Amherst Library.
  Harvey Swados Papers, 1936-1982.
University of Michigan Library
University of Pennsylvania Van Pelt Library
University of Virginia [Charlottesville] Library.
  Robert Wooster Stallman Papers, 1935-1962. Part of the library's
  Barrett Collection of American Literature.
University of Wyoming, Archives-American Heritage Center.
  Harry Barnard Papers, 1925-1977.
Vassar College Library
Washington University [St. Louis, MO] Library
  Modern English and American Literary Papers, 1950-1968.

This bibliography was prepared using Pro-Cite bibliographic soft-
ware from Personal Bibliographic Service. This program formatted
the citations according to *The MLA Style Manual* (1985), numbering
the items consecutively throughout the bibliography and supplying
terms for the index. Within each section and subsection the arrangement is alphabetical, except for the listings of editions of the novels,
short stories and plays and the listings of reprint sources, where a
chronological arrangement was obtained by inputting data in that
order.

  Inevitably users will discover omissions, oversights, and perhaps some
errors in citations. We would be grateful for any corrections,
comments or suggestions that would help us improve this bibliography
in a later edition.

          Gloria L. Cronin
          Blaine H. Hall
          Brigham Young University
          February 1987

Chronology

1915	Born July 10 in Montreal, Canada, the fourth child of Abraham Bellow and Liza Gordon Bellow who had immigrated from St. Petersburg, Russia in 1913.
1924	Family moves to Chicago permanently.
1933	Graduates from Tuley High School (on Chicago's Northwest Side) and enters University of Chicago.
1935	Transfers to Northwestern University.
1937	B.A. from Northwestern. Honors in sociology and anthropology.
1938	Returns to Chicago. Works on WPA Writers' Project.
1939	Supports himself with teaching, odd jobs and work on the Index (*Synopticon*) of *Great Books* series and generally leads a bohemian existence.
1941	"Two Morning Monologues," first publication.
1942	"The Mexican General."
1943	Working on *Dangling Man*.
1944	*Dangling Man*, first novel.
1946-48	Teaches at the University of Minnesota in Minneapolis.
1947	*The Victim*.
1948	Guggenheim Fellowship.
1948-50	Writes and lives in Paris. Travels in Europe. Begins work on *The Adventures of Augie March*, and publishes segments in various magazines.
1949	"Sermon of Dr. Pep."
1950	Returns to U.S.A. for the next ten years and lives in New York City and Duchess County, New York. Teaches evening courses at New York University, Washington Square. Reviews books, writes articles. Works on novels and short stories.
1951	"Looking for Mr. Green"; "By the Rock Wall"; "Address by Gooley MacDowell to the Hasbeens Club of Chicago."
1952	National Institute of Arts and Letters Award. Creative Writing Fellow, Princeton University.
1953	*The Adventures of Augie March*; National Book Award; translates Isaac Bashevis Singer's "Gimpel the Fool" from

	the Yiddish.
1955	"A Father-to-Be"; Guggenheim Fellowship.
1956	*Seize the Day*; "The Gonzaga Manuscripts."
1958	"Leaving the Yellow House"; Ford Foundation grant.
1959	*Henderson the Rain King.*
1960-62	Co-edits *The Noble Savage*; Friends of Literature Fiction Award.
1962	Honorary Doctor of Letters, Northwestern University; joins Committee on Social Thought at the University of Chicago. "Scenes from Humanitis," an early version of the play *The Last Analysis.*
1963	Edits *Great Jewish Short Stories*; Honorary Doctor of Letters, Bard College. Returns to Chicago in the fall.
1964	*Herzog*; James L. Dow Award; National Book Award; Fomentor Award; *The Last Analysis* opens on Broadway.
1965	International Prize for *Herzog*; three one-act plays: "Out from Under," "Orange Souffle," "A Wen," staged in April off-off Broadway by Nancy Walker, for a private showing at the Loft.
1967	"The Old System"; reports on the Six-Day War for *Newsday* magazine, then published by Bill Moyers.
1968	*Mosby's Memoirs and Other Stories*; Jewish Heritage Award from B'nai B'rith; French *Croix de Chevalier des Arts et Lettres.* Begins work on *Mr. Sammler's Planet.*
1969	Early version of *Mr. Sammler's Planet* appears.
1970	*Mr. Sammler's Planet.*
1971	National Book Award for *Mr. Sammler's Planet.*
1974	"Zetland: By a Character Witness."
1975	*Humboldt's Gift.*
1976	*To Jerusalem and Back: A Personal Account*; Nobel Prize for Literature.
1978	"A Silver Dish."
1982	*The Dean's December.*
1984	*Him with His Foot in His Mouth and Other Stories.*

Abbreviations

AM	*The Adventures of Augie March*
DM	*Dangling Man*
DD	*The Dean's December*
HRK	*Henderson the Rain King*
HWFIM	*Him with His Foot in His Mouth and Other Stories*
H	*Herzog*
HG	*Humboldt's Gift*
LA	*The Last Analysis*
MSP	*Mr. Sammler's Planet*
MM	*Mosby's Memoirs*
SD	*Seize the Day*
TJ	*To Jerusalem and Back*
TV	*The Victim*

PRIMARY SOURCES

Novels

1. *The Adventures of Augie March.*

> New York: Viking, 1953, 1965.
> London: Weidenfeld and Nicolson, 1954, 1958, 1968.
> New York: Popular Library, 1955.
> Toronto: Macmillan, 1956.
> London: World Distributors, 1959.
> Greenwich, CT: Fawcett, 1960, 1965, 1967, 1970, 1973, 1974.
> New York: Compass-Viking, 1960.
> New York: Modern Library, 1965.
> New York: Random House, 1965.
> Harmondsworth: Penguin, 1966, 1984.
> New York: Penguin, 1977.
> New York: Avon, 1977.

> Translations
> Turin: Einandi, 1962.
> Zagreb: Zora, 1965.
> Milan: Mondadori, 1967

2. *Dangling Man.*

> New York: Vanguard, 1944, 1971.
> London: Lehmann, 1946.
> New York: Compass-Viking, 1960.
> New York: Meridian, 1960.
> New York: Weidenfeld and Nicolson, 1960 (2nd ed.), 1972.
> Cleveland: World, 1963.
> Harmondsworth: Penguin, 1963.
> New York: New American Library, 1965, 1974.
> New York: Avon, 1975.
> New York: Penguin, 1977.

3

Bath: Lythway, 1978. (Large Print ed.)
Translations
   Rio de Janeiro: Bloch, 1967
   Santiago: Zig-Zag, 1968.
   Cologne: Rowohlt, 1971.

3. *The Dean's December.*

New York: Harper, 1981. (Book Club ed.)
New York: Harper, 1982.
Franklin Center, PA: Franklin, 1982. (Limited ed.)
Boston: Hall, 1982. (Large Print ed.)
London: Secker and Warburg, 1982.
New York: Pocket Books, 1983.
Harmondsworth: Penguin, 1983.

Translations
   Milan: Rizzoli, 1982.
   Taipei: Crown, 1982.
   Barcelona: Plaza y Janes, 1982.

4. *Henderson the Rain King.*

New York: Viking, 1959.
London: Weidenfeld and Nicolson, 1959, 1968.
Toronto: Macmillan, 1959.
Greenwich, CT: Crest-Fawcett, 1959, 1965, 1969, 1974.
New York: Avon, 1959.
New York: Popular Library, 1960.
New York: Compass-Viking, 1965, 1975.
Harmondsworth: Penguin, 1966.
New York and Harmondsworth: Penguin, 1976.
New York: Avon, 1976.
New York: Penguin, 1984.

Translations
   Stockholm: Bonniers, 1960.
   Paris: Gallimard, 1961.
   Mexico: Moritz, 1964.
   Munich: Deutscher Taschenbuch, 1964.
   Belgrade: Minerva, 1967.
   Budapest: Europa, 1970, 1972.
   Tel Aviv: Sifriyat-Poalim, 1976.

5. *Herzog.*

> New York: Viking, 1964.
> London: Weidenfeld and Nicolson, 1965.
> Toronto: Macmillan, 1964, 1967.
> New York: Compass-Viking, 1964, 1967.
> Greenwich, CT: Fawcett, 1965.
> Harmondsworth: Penguin, 1966, 1969.
> New York: Penguin, 1972, 1976, 1984.
> New York: Avon, 1976.
> New York: Viking, 1976. (*Herzog: Text and Criticism.* Ed. Irving Howe.)

> Translations
> Milan: Feltrinelli, 1965.
> Cologne: Kiepenheuer, 1965.
> Tel Aviv: Sifriyat-Poalim, 1965.
> Oslo: Aschehoug, 1966.
> Lisbon: Estudios Cor, 1966.
> Zagreb: Hrvatska, 1966.
> Paris: Gallimard, 1966.
> Ljubljana: Cankarjeva Zalozba, 1966.
> Budapest: Europa, 1967.
> Bratislava: Tatran, 1968.
> Prague: Odeon, 1968.
> Amsterdam: Bezige Bij, 1969.
> Tokyo: Hayakawa Shobo, 1970.
> Bucharest: Kriterion, 1970.
> Hong Kong: Chin Jih Shih Chieh, 1971.
> Milan: Feltrinelli, 1971.
> Warsaw: Czytelnik, 1971.
> Copenhagen: Schonbergske, 1971.
> Tallinn: Kirjastus, 1972.
> Barcelona: Destino, 1976.

6. *Humboldt's Gift.*

> New York: Viking, 1975.
> London: Secker and Warburg, 1975.
> New York: Avon, 1976.
> Hamondsworth: Penguin, 1977.
> Franklin Center, PA: Franklin, 1980 (Limited ed.)
> New York: Penguin, 1984.

Translations
  Milan: Rizzoli, 1976.
  Cologne: Keipenheuer, 1976.
  Helsinki: Kustannusosakeyhtio Tammi, 1976.
  Tel Aviv: Sifriyat-Poalim, 1978.
  Bucharest: Univers, 1979.
  Barcelona: Plaza y Janes, 1984.

7. *Mr. Sammler's Planet.*

  New York: Viking, 1964, 1970, 1976.
  New York: Viking, 1970. (Book Club ed.)
  London: Weidenfeld and Nicolson, 1970.
  Harmondsworth: Penguin, 1972, 1977, 1984.
  New York: Compass-Viking, 1973.
  Greenwich, CT: Crest-Fawcett, 1971, 1974, 1976.
  New York: Penguin, 1977.

Translations
  Helsinki: Kustannusosakeyhtio Tammi, 1970.
  Copenhagen: Gyldendal, 1970.
  Amsterdam: Meulenhoff, 1970.
  Stockholm: Bonniers, 1970.
  Oslo: Aschehoug, 1971.
  Cologne: Kiepenheuer, 1971.
  Milan: Feltrinelli, 1971.
  Tel Aviv: Sifriyat Poalim, 1971.
  Paris: Gallimard, 1972.
  Barcelona: Destino, 1972.
  Hamburg: Rowohlt, 1973.

7a. *More Die of Heartbreak.*

  New York: Morrow (To be published June 1987).

8. *Seize the Day.*

  New York: Viking, 1956, 1965.
  Toronto: Macmillan, 1956.
  London Weidenfeld and Nicolson, 1957, 1968.
  New York: Compass-Viking, 1961, 1964, 1974.
  Greenwich, CT: Fawcett, 1965, 1968, 1970, 1973.

Harmondsworth: Penguin, 1966, 1976.
New York: Penguin, 1974, 1984.
New York: Avon, 1977.
Rpt. in *The Portable Saul Bellow*. Comp. Edith Tarcov. The
  Viking Portable Library 79. New York: Viking, 1974,
  Penguin, 1978.

Translations
Helsinki: Kustannusosakeyhtio Tammi, 1956.
Paris: Gallimard, 1962.
Copenhagen: Glydendal, 1966.
Rio de Janeiro: Bloch, 1967.
Barcelona: Barral, 1968, 1976 [2nd ed.].
Tallinn: Kirjastus, 1968.
Barcelona: Edicions 62, 1970.
Rio de Janeiro: Bloch, 1972.
Tokyo: Kawade Shobo Shinsha, 1972.
Amsterdam: Meulenhoff, 1972.

9. *The Victim.*

New York: Vanguard, 1947.
London: Lehmann, 1948.
New York: Compass-Viking, 1956, 1962, 1964.
Toronto: Macmillan, 1956.
London: Weidenfeld and Nicolson, 1965.
New York: New American Library, 1965, 1974.
Harmondsworth: Penguin, 1966.
New York: Avon, 1975.
New York: Penguin, 1977.

Translations
Paris: Gallimard, 1964.
Rio de Janeiro: Bloch, 1966.
Milan: Feltrinelli, 1966.
Cologne: Kiepenheuer, 1966.
Bratislava: Tatran, 1967.
Oslo: Aschehoug, 1967.
Santiago: Zig-Zag, 1969.
Belgrade: Prosveta, 1973.
Seoul: Munye Chupansa, 1976.

Short Fiction

10. "Address by Gooley MacDowell to the Hasbeens Club of Chicago."
    Hudson Review 4.2 (1951): 222-27. Rpt. in *Nelson Algren's
    Own Book of Lonesome Monsters.* Ed. Nelson Algren. New
    York: Geis, 1963.

11. "Burdens of a Lone Survivor." *Esquire* Dec. 1974: 176-85, 224,
    226, 228, 230, 232.

12. "Cousins." *Him with His Foot in His Mouth and Other Stories.*
    New York: Harper; London: Secker and Warburg, 1984.

13. "Dora." *Harper's Bazaar* Nov. 1949: 118, 188-90, 198-99.

14. "A Father-to-Be." *New Yorker* 5 Feb. 1955: 26-30. Rpt. in *Seize
    the Day.* New York: Viking, 1956; *Mosby's Memoirs and
    Other Stories.* New York: Viking, 1968; London: Weidenfeld
    and Nicolson, 1969; *Story: An Introduction to Prose
    Fiction.* Eds. Arthur Foff and Daniel Knapp. 2nd ed.
    Belmont, CA: Wadsworth, 1971. *Stories from the New
    Yorker.* New York: New Yorker, [n.d.].

15. "The Gonzaga Manuscripts." *Discovery.* No. 4. New York:
    Pocket Books, 1954. Rpt. in *Seize the Day.* New York:
    Viking, 1956; London: Weidenfeld and Nicolson, 1957; *Prize
    Stories, 1956, The O. Henry Awards.* Eds. Paul Engle and
    Constance Urdang. Garden City, NY: Doubleday, 1957;
    Contemporary American Short Stories. Comp. Douglas Angus
    and Sylvia Angus. Greenwich, CT: Fawcett, 1967; *Mosby's
    Memoirs and Other Stories.* New York: Viking, 1968; London:

9

Weidenfeld and Nicolson, 1969; *Fifty Years of the American
Short Story from the O. Henry Awards, 1919-1970.* Ed.
William Abrahams. Vol. 1. Garden City, NY: Doubleday, 1970.
The Design of Fiction. Eds. Mark Harris, et al. New York:
Crowell, 1976; *The Arbor House Treasury of Nobel Prize
Winners.* Eds. Martin Harry Greenburg and Charles G.
Waugh. New York: Arbor, 1983..

16. "Him with His Foot in His Mouth." *Atlantic* Nov. 1982: 114-19,
    122, 125-26, 129-32, 134-35, 137-42, 144. Revised version rpt.
    in *Him with His Foot in His Mouth and Other Stories.* New
    York: Harper; London: Secker and Warburg, 1984.

17. *Him with His Foot in His Mouth and Other Stories.* New York:
    Harper, 1984; London: Secker and Warburg, 1984; New York:
    Pocket, 1985. Translations: Milan: Mondadori, 1984; Taipei:
    Huang Kuan, 1984; Cologne: Kiepenheuer, 1985.

18. "Leaving the Yellow House." *Esquire* Jan 1958: 112-26. Rpt. in
    Short Stories Classic, Modern, Contemporary. Eds. Marcus
    Klein and Robert Pack. Boston: Little, Brown, 1967; *Mosby's
    Memoirs and Other Stories.* New York: Viking, 1968; London:
    Weidenfeld and Nicolson, 1969; *The Portable Saul Bellow.*
    Comp. Edith Tarcov. The Viking Portable Library 79. New
    York: Viking, 1974, Penguin, 1978.

19. "Looking for Mr. Green." *Commentary* Mar. 1951: 251-61. Rpt.
    in *Seize the Day.* New York: Viking, 1956; London:
    Weidenfeld and Nicolson, 1957; *Mosby's Memoirs and Other
    Stories.* New York: Viking, 1968; London: Weidenfeld and
    Nicolson, 1969; *The Realm of Fiction.* Ed. James B. Hall.
    2nd ed. New York: McGraw, 1970; *Short Stories: A Critical
    Anthology.* Eds. Ensaf Thune and Ruth Prigozy. New York:
    Macmillan, 1973; *Major American Short Stories.* Ed. A.
    Walton Litz. New York: Oxford UP, 1975; *The Short Story:
    An Introduction.* Eds. Wilfred Stone, et. al. New York:
    McGraw, 1976.

20. "The Mexican General." *Partisan Review* 9.3 (1942): 178-94.

21. "Mosby's Memoirs." *New Yorker* 20 July 1968: 36-42, 44-49.
Rpt. in *Mosby's Memoirs and Other Stories.* New York:
Viking, 1968; London: Weidenfeld and Nicolson, 1969. *Stories
from the Sixties.* Ed. Stanley Elkin. Garden City, NY:
Doubleday, 1971; *The Portable Saul Bellow.* The Viking
Portable Library 79. Comp. Edith Tarcov. New York: Viking,
1974, Penguin, 1978.

22. *Mosby's Memoirs and Other Stories.* New York: Viking, 1968.
London: Weidenfeld and Nicolson, 1969; Greenwich, CT:
Fawcett, 1969; Harmondsworth: Penguin, 1971; New York:
Penguin, 1977, 1984. Translations: Cologne: Kiepenheuer,
1968; Amsterdam: Meulenhoff, 1969; Barcelona: Destinos,
1969; Stockholm: Bonniers, 1970; Copenhagen: Gyldendals,
1970; Oslo: Aschehoug, 1970.

23. "The Old System." *Playboy* Jan. 1968: Rpt. in *Mosby's Memoirs
and Other Stories.* New York: Viking, 1968; London:
Weidenfeld and Nicolson, 1969; *Twentieth Anniversary
Playboy Reader.* Ed. Hugh M. Hefner. Chicago: Playboy
Press, 1974; *The Portable Saul Bellow.* Comp. Edith Tarcov.
The Viking Portable Library 79. New York: Viking, 1974,
Penguin, 1978; *Jewish American Stories.* Ed. Irving Howe.
New York: New American Library, 1977.

24. "Sermon by Dr. Pep." *Partisan Review* 16.5 (1949): 455-62. Rpt.
in *Best American Short Stories, 1950-1954.* Ed. Martha
Foley. Vol.1. Boston: Houghton, 1954. 5 vols.; *Fiction of the
Fifties: A Decade of American Writing.* Comp. Herbert Gold.
Garden City, NY: Dolphin-Doubleday, 1959. 69-75.

25. "A Silver Dish." *New Yorker* 25 Sept. 1978: 40-50. Rpt. New
York: Albondaconi Press, 1979 [Limited ed.]; *The Best
American Short Stories 1979.* Eds. Joyce Carol Oates and
Shannon Ravenel. Boston: Houghton, 1979; *Prize Stories
1980: The O. Henry Awards.* Ed. William Abrahams. Garden
City, NY: Doubleday, 1980; *Prize Stories of the Seventies
from the O. Henry Awards.* Ed. William Abrahams. Garden
City, NY: Doubleday, 1981; *The Treasury of American Short
Stories.* Comp. Nancy Sullivan. Garden City, NY: Doubleday,
1981.

26. "The Trip to Galena." *Partisan Review* 17.8 (1950): 779-94.

27. "What Kind of a Day Did You Have?." *Vanity Fair*. Rpt. in *Him with His Foot in His Mouth and Other Stories*. New York: Harper; London: Secker and Warburg, 1984.

28. "Zetland: By a Character Witness." *Modern Occasions 2*. Ed. Philip Rahv. Port Washington, NY: Kennikat, 1974. 9-30. Rp in *Him with His Foot in His Mouth and Other Stories*. New York: Harper; London: Secker and Warburg, 1984.

Plays

29. *The Last Analysis*. New York: Viking, 1965; London: Weidenfeld and Nicolson, 1966; New York: Compass-Viking, 1966, 1972. Translations: Milan: Feltrinelli, 1966; Cologne: Kiepenheuer, 1968. Rpt. in *Best American Plays 1963-1967*. Eds. John Gassner and Clive Barnes. 6th Series. New York: Crown, 1971; *Comedy: A Critical Anthology*. Ed. Robert W. Corrigan. Boston: Houghton, 1971; *Broadway's Beautiful Losers*. Ed. Marilyn Stasio. New York: Delacorte, 1972.

30. "Orange Souffle." *Esquire* Oct. 1965: 130-36. Rpt. in *The Discovery of Drama*. Thomas S. Sanders. Glenview, IL: Scott, Foresman, 1968; *The Best Short Plays of the World Theatre*, 1968-1973. Ed. Stanley Richards. New York: Crown, 1973. Chicago Radio Theatre Presentation of Saul Bellow's "Orange Souffle" and "The Wrecker." Sound Recording. Chicago: All-Media Dramatic Workshop, 1978.

    One of three one-act plays performed on Broadway and in London in 1966 as *Under the Weather*.

31. "Out from Under." Unpublished in English. Italian translation "Ce Speranza del Sesso." Milan: Feltrinelli, 1967

    One of the three one-act plays performed on Broadway and in London in 1966 as *Under the Weather*.

32. "Scenes from 'Humanitis--A Farce'." *Partisan Review* 29.3 (1962): 327-49.

    Part of an early version of *The Last Analysis*.

13

33. "A Wen." *Esquire* Jan. 1965: 72-74, 111. Rpt. in *Traverse Plays.*
    Ed. Jim Haynes. London, 1966; French translation "Un Grai
    de Beaute" in *Saul Bellow.* Pierre Dommergues. Paris:
    Grasset, 1967.

    One of three one-act plays performed on Broadway and in
    London in 1966 as *Under the Weather.*

34. "The Wrecker." *New World Writing.* No. 6. New York: New
    American Library, 1954. 271-87. 10 vols. 1952-1956. Rpt. in
    Seize the Day. New York: Viking, 1956; London: Weidenfeld
    and Nicolson, 1957.

Essays

35. "Are Many Modern Writers Merely Becoming Actors Who Behave Like Writers?" *Chicago Sun-Times Book Week* 15 Sept. 1968: 1, 10.

36. "Cloister Culture." *New York Times Book Review* 10 July 1966: 1. Rpt. in *Page 2: The Best of "Speaking of Books" from The New York Times Book Review*. Ed. Francis Brown. New York: Holt, 1969. 3-9.

37. "Culture Now: Some Animadversions, Some Laughs." *Modern Occasions* 1 (1971): 162-78.

38. "Deep Readers of the World, Beware!" *New York Times Book Review* 15 Feb. 1959: 1, 34. Rpt. in *Opinions and Perspectives from the New York Times*. Ed. Francis Brown. Boston: Houghton, 1964. 24-28.

39. "Distractions of a Fiction Writer." *The Living Novel: A Symposium*. Ed. Granville Hicks. New York: Macmillan, 1957. 1-20. Rpt. in *New World Writing*. New York: New American Library, 1957.

40. "Facts that Put Fancy to Flight." *New York Times Book Review* 11 Feb. 1962: 1, 28. Rpt. in *Opinions and Perspectives from the New York Times*. Ed. Francis Brown. Boston: Houghton, 1964. 235-40

41. Foreword. *Recovery/Delusions, etc.* John Berryman. New York:

Delta/Dell, 1974. ix-xiv.
42. "How I Wrote Augie March's Story." *New York Times Book Review* 31 Jan. 1954: 3, 17.

43. "Keynote Address Before the Inaugural Session of the 34th Session of the International Congress of Poets, Playwrights, Essayists, and Editors, 13 June 1966." *Montreal Star* 25 June 1966: Special Insert, 2-3.

44. "Literature." *The Great Ideas Today.* Eds. Mortimer Adler and Robert M. Hutchins. Chicago: Encyclopaedia Britannica, 1963. 135-79.

45. "Machines and Storybooks: Literature in the Age of Technology." *Harper's* Aug. 1974: 48-59. Rpt. as "Literature in the Age of Technology." *Technology and the Frontiers of Knowledge.* Frank K. Nelson Doubleday Lecture Series, 1972-73. New York: Doubleday, 1975. 1-22.

46. "A Matter of the Soul." *Opera News* 11 Jan. 1975: 26-29. Address to the Fourth International Congress of the Institute of Verdi Studies.

47. "The Nobel Lecture." *American Scholar* 46 (1977): 316-25. Also published Stockholm: U.S. Information Service, 1977; New York: Targ, 1979. [Limited ed.]

48. "The Sealed Treasure." *Times Literary Supplement* 1 July 1960: 414. Rpt. in *The Open Forum: Essays For Our Time.* 2nd ed. New York: Harcourt, 1965. 15-22.

49. "Skepticism and the Depth of Life." *The Arts and the Public: Essays by Saul Bellow.* Ed. James E. Miller, Jr. and Paul D. Herring. Chicago: U of Chicago P, 1967. 13-30.

50. "Some Notes on Recent American Fiction." *Encounter* Nov. 1963: 22-29. Also published as *Recent American Fiction: A Lecture Presented Under the Auspices of the Gertrude*

Clarke Whittall Poetry and Literature Fund. Washington, DC:
Library of Congress, 1963. Rpt. in *Literary Lectures:
Presented at the Library of Congress.* Washington, DC:
Library of Congress, 1973; "Recent American Fiction."
American Studies International 15.3 (1977): 7-16.

51. "Starting Out in Chicago." *American Scholar* 44.1 (1974-75):
71-77.

52. *To Jerusalem and Back: A Personal Account.* New York: Viking;
London: Secker and Warburg, 1976; Boston: Hall, 1977 (Large
Print ed.); New York: Avon, 1977; London: Prior, 1978 (Large
Print ed.); Harmondsworth: Penguin, 1978, 1985; New York:
Penguin, 1985. Translations: Jerusalem: Idanim Mahadurat,
1977; Barcelona: Plaza y Janes, 1977.

53. "The University as Villain." *Nation* 16 Nov. 1957: 361-63. Rpt.
and slightly changed as "The Enemy is Academe." *Publishers
Weekly* 18 July 1966: 34.

54. "The Uses of Adversity." Rev. of *Five Families*, by Oscar
Lewis. *Reporter* 1 Oct. 1959: 42-45.

55. "Where Do We Go From Here: The Future of Fiction." *Michigan
Quarterly Review* 1.1 (1962): 27-33. Rpt. in *To the Young
Writer: Hopwood Lectures, Second Series.* Ed. Arno L. Bader.
Ann Arbor, MI: Ann Arbor Paperbacks/U of Michigan P,
1965. 136-46; *Saul Bellow and the Critics.* Ed. Irving Malin.
New York: New York UP, 1967. 211-20.

56. "A World Too Much With Us." *Critical Inquiry* 2.1 (1975): 1-9.

57. "The Writer as Moralist." *Atlantic* Mar. 1963: 58-62.

58. "A Writer from Chicago." *The Tanner Lectures on Human
Values.* Ed. Sterling M. McMurrin. Vol. 3. Salt Lake City,
UT: U of Utah P; Cambridge, Eng.: Cambridge UP, 1982.
175-219.

Miscellaneous Writings

59. "Americans Who Are Also Jews." *Jewish Digest* Apr. 1977: 8-10.
Cited in *Index to Jewish Periodicals*, Jan.-June 1977.

60. "Beatrice Webb's America." Rev. of *Beatrice Webb's American Diary* (1898), ed. David A. Shannon. *Nation* 7 Sept. 1963: 116.

61. "Bellow on Himself and America." *Jerusalem Post Magazine* 3 July 1975: 11-12; 10 July 1975: 12.

62. "Dreiser and the Triumph of Art." Rev. of *Theodore Dreiser*, by F. O. Matthiessen. *Commentary* May 1951: 502-03. Rpt. in *The Stature of Theodore Dreiser: A Critical Survey of the Man and His Work*. Eds. Alfred Kazin and Charles Shapiro. Bloomington, IN: Indiana UP, 1955. 146-48.

63. "The Evil That Has Many Names." Rev. of *The Hive* by Camila Jose Cela. *New York Times Book Review* 27 Sept. 1953: 5.

64. Foreword. *The Boundaries of Natural Science*. Rudolf Steiner. Trans. Frederick Amrine and Konrad Oberhuber. Spring Valley, NY: Anthroposophic, 1983.

65. Foreword. *The Revolt of the Masses*. Jose Ortega y Gasset. Notre Dame, IN: U of Notre Dame P, 1985. ix-xiii.

66. Foreword. *An Age of Enormity: Life and Writing in the Forties and Fifties*. Isaac Rosenfeld. Ed. Theodore Solotaroff. Cleveland, OH: World, 1962. 11-14.

67. "The French as Dostoevsky Saw Them." *New Republic* 23 May
    1955: 17-20. Rpt. in slightly revised version as Foreword.
    Winter Notes on Summer Impressions. Feodor M. Dostoevsky.
    New York: Criterion, 1955. 9-27.

68. "Gide as Writer and Autobiographer." Rev. of *The Counterfeiters*
    with *Journal of the Counterfeiters,* by Andre Gide. *New
    Leader* 4 June 1951: 24.

69. "Gimpel the Fool." Isaac Bashevis Singer. Trans. Saul Bellow.
    Partisan Review 20.3 (1953): 300-13. Rpt. in *A Treasury of
    Yiddish Stories.* Eds. Irving Howe and Eliezer Greenberg.
    New York: Viking, 1954; Isaac Bashevis Singer. *Gimpel the
    Fool and Other Stories.* New York: Farrar, 1957; London:
    Owen, 1958. *Great Jewish Short Stories.* Ed. Saul Bellow.
    New York: Dell, 1963, 1985; London: Valentine, 1971.

70. "Hemingway and the Image of Man." Rev. of *Ernest Hemingway,*
    by Philip Young. *Partisan Review* 20.3 (1953): 338-42.

71. "Illinois Journey." *Holiday* Sept. 1957: 62-63, 102-07.

72. "In the Days of Mr. Roosevelt." *Esquire* Dec. 1983: 530-32,
    35-36, 39-40.

73. Introduction. *Great Jewish Short Stories.* Ed. Saul Bellow. New
    York: Dell, 1963.

    Includes his translation of Isaac Bashevis Singer's "Gimpel
    the Fool."

74. "Isaac Rosenfeld." *Partisan Review* 23.4 (1956): 565-67.

75. "Italian Fiction: Without Hope." Rev. of *The New Italian
    Writers: An Anthology from Botleghe Obscure,* ed. Marguerite
    Caetani. *New Leader* 11 Dec. 1950: 21-22.

76. "The Jewish Writer and the English Literary Tradition: A Symposium, Part II." *Commentary* Oct. 1949: 336-67.

    Bellow's contribution to a symposium by Jewish writers on the question "What can we do about Fagin?"

77. "Jewish Writers are Somehow Different." *National Jewish Monthly* Mar. 1971: 50-51.

78. "Laughter in the Ghetto." Rev. of *The Adventures of Mottel and the Cantor's Son*, by Sholom Aleichem. *Saturday Review* 30 May 1953: 15.

79. "Literary Notes on Krushchev." *Esquire* Mar. 1961: 106-07. Rpt. in *Esquire* Oct. 1973: 194-95, 412, 414; *First Person Singular: Essays for the Sixties*. Ed. Herbert Gold. New York: Dial, 1963. 46-54.

80. "Man Underground." Rev. of *Invisible Man*, by Ralph Ellison." *Commentary* June 1952: 608-11. Rpt. in *Ralph Ellison: A Collection of Critical Essays*. Ed. John R. Hersey. Twentieth Century Views. Englewood Cliffs, NJ: Prentice, 1974.

81. "The Mass-Produced Insight." *Horizon* Jan. 1963: 111-13.

82. "Mind over Chatter." *New York Herald Tribune Book Week* 4 Apr. 1965: 2.

    Revised version of his remarks at National Book Award ceremonies, Mar. 9, 1985, where he received 1964 award for *Herzog*.

83. "Movies: Adrift on a Sea of Gore." Rev. of *Barabbas*." *Horizon* Mar. 1963: 109-11.

84. "Movies: Bunuel's Unsparing Vision." *Horizon* Nov. 1962: 110-12.

85. "Movies: The Art of Going It Alone." *Horizon* Sept. 1962:
   108-10.

86. "My Man Bummidge." *New York Times* 27 Sept. 1964: sec. 2: 1,
   5.

87. "My Paris." *New York Times Magazine* Part 2, *The Sophisticated
   Traveler* 13 Mar. 1983: 36-37, 130-35.

88. Rev. of *Barefoot Boy: A Precocious Autobiography*, by Yevgeny
   Yevtushenko, trans. Andrew R. MacAndrew. *New York
   Review of Books* 26 Sept. 1963: 8-9.

89. "New York--at a Comfortable Distance: 'World-Famous Impossi-
   bility.'" *New York Times* 6 Dec. 1970: 1A, 12A.

90. "On Jewish Storytelling." *Jewish Heritage* 7.3 (1964-65): 5-9.

91. "On John Cheever." *New York Review of Books* 17 Feb. 1983:
   38. Speech to the American Academy of Arts and Letters.

92. "An Open Letter to General Jaruzelski." *New York Review of
   Books* 27 June 1985: 8.

   Nobel Laureates sign letter protesting imprisonment of Polish
   dissident leaders.

93. "Paris Falling." *New Republic* 13 Sept. 1943: 367.

94. "A Personal Record." Rev. of *Except the Lord*, by Joyce Cary.
   New Republic 22 Feb. 1954: 20-21.

95. "Rabbi's Boy in Edinburgh." Rev. of *Two Worlds*, by David
   Daiches. *Saturday Review* 24 Mar. 1956: 19.

96. "A Revolutionist's Testament." *New York Times Book Review* 21 Nov. 1943: 1, 53. Rpt. in *Arthur Koestler: A Collection of Critical Essays*. Twentieth Century Views. Ed. Murray A. Sperber. Englewood Cliffs, NJ: Prentice, 1977. 30-33.

97. "Saul Bellow on America and American Jewish Writers." *Congress Bi-Weekly* Part I, 23 Oct. 1970: 8-11; Part II, 4 Dec. 1970: 13-16.

98. *Saul Bellow on Art, Literature, and American Life*. Audio cassette. Danbury, CT: Grolier, 1982. Vital History Cassettes 3.

99. "Spanish Letter." *Partisan Review* 15.2 (1948): 217-30.

100. "The Swamp of Prosperity." Rev. of *Goodbye, Columbus*, by Philip Roth. *Commentary* July 1959: 77-79.

101. "A Talk with the Yellow Kid." *Reporter* 6 Sept. 1956: 41-44.

102. "The Thinking Man's Wasteland." *Saturday Review* 3 Apr. 1965: 20.

   Adapted from a speech accepting the National Book Award for *Herzog*.

103. "A Time for Rethinking." *Newsweek* 27 Dec. 1976: 62.

104. "Two Faces for a Hostile World." Rev. of *Five A.M.*, by Jean Dutourd, trans. Robin Chancellor." *New York Times Book Review* 26 Aug. 1956: 4-5.

105. "What's Wrong with Modern Fiction." *Sunday Times* 12 Jan. 1975: 31A.

106. "The Writers and the Audience." *Perspectives USA* 9 (1954):
     99-102.

Interviews

107. Bellow, Saul. "An Interview With Myself." *New Review* 2.18 (1975): 53-56.

108. Boyers, Robert T. "Literature and Culture: An Interview With Saul Bellow." *Salmagundi* 30 (1975): 6-23. Rpt. in *Salmagundi Reader*. Eds. Robert T. Boyers and Peggy Boyers. Bloomington, IN: Indiana UP, 1983. 366-383.

109. Brandon, Henry. "Writer versus Readers: Saul Bellow." *Sunday Times* 18 Sept. 1966: 24.

110. Brans, Jo. "Common Needs, Common Preoccupations: An Interview With Saul Bellow." *Southwest Review* 62 (1977): 1-19.

111. Breit, Harvey. "A Talk With Saul Bellow." *New York Times Book Review* 20 Sept. 1953: 22. Rpt. in *The Writer Observed*. Harvey Breit. Cleveland: World, 1956. 271-74.

112. Bruckner, D. J. R. "A Candid Talk With Saul Bellow." *New York Times Magazine* 15 Apr. 1984: 52, 54, 56, 60, 62.

113. Carroll, Paul. "Saul Bellow Says a Few Words about His Critics and Himself." *Chicago Sun-Times Book Week* 9 Nov. 1975: 8.

114. Ciocaltea, Georgeta. "An Interview with Saul Bellow." *Luceafarul* 13 Jan. 1979: 8. Cited in *Annual Bibliography of English Language and Literature*, 1979.

115. Clemons, Walter, and Jack Kroll. "America's Master Novelist: An Interview With Saul Bellow." *Newsweek* 1 Sept. 1975: 32-34, 39-40.

116. Coleman, Terry. "Saul Bellow Talks." *Manchester Guardian* 23 Sept. 1966: 11.

117. Cook, Bruce. "Saul Bellow: A Mood of Protest." *Perspective on Ideas and the Arts* 12 Feb. 1963: 46-50.

118. Cromie, Robert. "Saul Bellow Tells (among other things) the Thinking Behind *Herzog*." *Chicago Tribune Books Today* 24 Jan. 1965: 8-9.

119. Davis, Robert Gorham. "Readers and Writers Face To Face." *New York Times Book Review* 9 Nov. 1958: 4, 40-41.

120. Dommergues, Pierre. "An Interview with Saul Bellow." *Delta* [Paris]. 19 (1984): 1-27.

121. Dommergues, Pierre. "Recontre avec Saul Bellow." *Preuves* 191 (1967): 38-47. Also published in *Les U.S.A. a la Recherche de Leur Identite Recontres avec 40 Ecrivain Americains.* Paris: Grasset, 1967 (English with French introduction); abridged version in *Les Langues Modernes* 60.5 (1966): 595-603

122. Ellenberg, Al. "Saul Bellow Picks Another Fight." *Rolling Stone* 4 Mar. 1982: 14-16, 64.

123. Enck, John J. "Saul Bellow: An Interview." *Contemporary Literature* 6.2 (1965): 156-60.

124. Epstein, Joseph. "A Talk With Saul Bellow." *New York Times Book Review* 5 Dec. 1976: 3, 92-93.

125. *Focus on Saul Bellow; The Author of Herzog Discusses the Responsibility of Artists in the U. S..* Audio Cassette. Center for Cassette Studies 0106462, 1971.

   In conversation with historian Eric Goldman, Bellow discusses American politics and culture and the role of the individual in a complex society.

126. Galloway, David D. "An Interview With Saul Bellow." *Audit-Poetry* 3 (1963): 19-23.

127. Genie, Bernard. "Avec Saul Bellow le Franc-tireur." *Quinzaine Litteraire* 380 (1982): 11-12.

128. Gray, Rockwell, et al. "Interview With Saul Bellow." *TriQuarterly* 60 (1984): 12-34. Rpt. in *TQ 20: Twenty Years of the Best Contemporary Writing and Graphics from TriQuarterly Magazine.* Spec. issue of *TriQuarterly* 63 (1985): 632-50.

129. Gutwillig, Robert. "Talk With Saul Bellow." *New York Times Book Review* 20 Sept. 1964: 40-41.

130. Harper, Gordon Lloyd. "The Art of Fiction: Saul Bellow." *Paris Review* 9.36 (1966): 48-73. Rpt. in *Writers at Work: Paris Review Interviews.* Ed. Alfred Kazin. 3rd ser. London: Viking, 1967. 175-96.

131. Henry, Jim Douglas. "Mystic Trade: The American Novelist Saul Bellow Talks of Jim Douglas Henry." *Listener* 22 May 1969: 705-07.

132. Heyman, Harriet. "Q & A With Saul Bellow." *Chicago Maroon* 4 Feb. 1972: 1.

133. Hoge, Alice Allbright. "Saul Bellow Revisited at Home and at Work." *Chicago Daily News* 18 Feb. 1967, Panorama sec.: 5.

134. Howard, Jane. "Mr. Bellow Considers His Planet." *Life* 3 Apr. 1970: 57-60.

135. "Il Dono di Humboldt: Un romanzo comico di impianto tragico." *Uomini e Libri: Periodico Bimestrale di Critica ed Informazione Litteraria* 60 (1976): 37-38.

136. Illig, Joyce. "An Interview With Saul Bellow." *Publishers Weekly* 22 Oct. 1973: 74-77.

137. Kakutani, Michiko. "A Talk With Saul Bellow: On His Work and Himself." *New York Times Book Review* 13 Dec. 1981: 1, 28-31.

138. Kulshrestha, Chirantan. "A Conversation with Saul Bellow." *Chicago Review* 23.4-24.1 (1972): 7-15.

139. Lacium Wu [Wu Lu-chin]. *Sixteen English and American Great Writers.* Taipei: China Times, 1981. 270-93 [In Chinese].

     Saul Bellow explains his appreciation of writers like Dreiser, Hemingway, Fitzgerald, Joyce, D. H. Lawrence and others; evaluates his change of style in writing as the result of his growth and maturity; and confirms the issue of victim as the essential of modern realism, with death as its related subject.

140. "Literature and Culture: An Interview With Saul Bellow." *Salmagundi* 30 (1975): 6-23.

141. Medwick, Cathleen. "A Cry of Strength: The Unfashionably Uncynical Saul Bellow." *Vogue* Mar. 1982: 368-9, 426-427.

142. Mitgang, Herbert. "With Bellow in Chicago." *New York Times Book Review* 6 July 1980: 23.

143. Nachman, Gerald. "A Talk with Saul Bellow." *New York Post Magazine* 4 Oct. 1964: 6.

144. Nash, Jay, and Ron Offen. "Saul Bellow." *Literary Times* [Chicago] Dec. 1964: 10.

145. Pinsker, Sanford. "Saul Bellow in the Classroom." *College English* 34 (1973): 975-82.

146. Ralea, Cantinca. ""Intilnire cu Saul Bellow." [An Interview with Saul Bellow]." *Romania Literara* [Bucharest] 11.52 (1978): 19. Cited in *MLA Bibliography*, 1978.

147. Ralian, Antoaneta. ". . . Sint un observator si un istoric." [. . . I Am after all an Observer and Historian]. *Secolul* 20 (1980): 73-9. Cited in *Annual Bibliography of English Language and Literature*, 1980.

148. Robinson, Robert. "Saul Bellow at 60--Talking to Robert Robinson." *Listener* 13 Feb. 1975: 218-19.

149. Roudane, Matthew C. "An Interview with Saul Bellow." *Contemporary Literature* 25.3 (1984): 265-80.

150. Sanoff, Alvin. "'Matters Have Gotten Out of Hand' in a Violent Society." *U. S. News and World Report* 28 June 1982: 49-50.

151. Saporta, Marc. "Saul Bellow: Une Interview." *Figaro Litteraire* 23 Mar. 1969: 24-25.

152. "Saul Bellow despre literatura, scriitori, public" [Saul Bellow on Literature, Writers and Public]. *Contemporanul* [Bucharest] 19 (1973): 10.

153. Simmons, Maggie. "Free to Feel: Conversation with Saul Bellow." *Quest* Feb.-Mar. 1979: 31-35.

154. "Some Questions and Answers: An Interview with Saul Bellow."
     Ontario Review 3 (1975): 51-61. Cited in *MLA Bibliography*,
     1975.

155. Steers, Nina. "'Successor' to Faulkner?: An Interview with Saul
     Bellow." *Show* Sept. 1964: 36-38.

156. Steinem, Gloria. "Gloria Steinem Spends a Day in Chicago with
     Saul Bellow." *Glamour* July 1965: 98, 122, 125, 128.

SECONDARY SOURCES

Bibliographies and Checklists

157. Cronin, Gloria L. "Saul Bellow Selected and Annotated Bibliography." *Saul Bellow Journal* 4.1 (1985): 80-89.

   This issue lists criticism from 1980. Subsequent issues will each contain selected annotated bibliographical listings for subsequent years until the listings are current with the final issue of each year.

158. Cronin, Gloria L., and Liela H. Goldman. "Saul Bellow." *American Novelists*. Detroit: Gale, 1986. 83-155. Vol. 1 of *Contemporary Authors Bibliographical Series*. 3 vols. to date. 1986-

159. Field, Leslie, and John Z. Guzlowski. "Criticism of Saul Bellow: A Selected Checklist." *Modern Fiction Studies* 25.1 (1979): 149-71.

160. Galloway, David D. "A Saul Bellow Checklist." *The Absurd Hero in American Fiction: Updike, Styron, Bellow, Salinger*. Austin: U of Texas P, 1966. 210-26; Rev. ed. 1970: 220-39.

161. Lercangee, Francine. *Saul Bellow: A Bibliography of Secondary Sources*. Brussels: Center for American Studies, 1977.

162. Nault, Marianne. *Saul Bellow: His Works and His Critics: An Annotated International Bibliography*. Garland Reference Library of the Humanities 59. New York: Garland, 1977.

163. Noreen, Robert G. *Saul Bellow: A Reference Guide*. A Reference Publication in Literature. Boston: Hall, 1978.

164. Schneider, Harold W. "Two Bibliographies--Saul Bellow/William
     Styron." *Critique* 3.3 (1960): 71-91.

165. Sokoloff, B. A., and Mark E. Posner. *Saul Bellow: A Compre-
     hensive Bibliography.* Bibliographies in Contemporary American
     Fiction. Folcroft, PA: Folcroft, 1971, 1974, 1977; Norwood,
     PA: Norwood, 1973; Philadelphia: West, 1978. Updated edition
     by Sokoloff. Belfast, ME: Bern Porter, 1985.

Books and Monographs

166. Bakker, Jan. *Fiction as Survival Strategy: A Comparative Study of the Major Works of Ernest Hemingway and Saul Bellow.* Amsterdam: Rodopi, 1983.

167. Bischoff, Peter. *Saul Bellows Romane: Entfremdung Suche.* Abhandlungen zur Kunst-, Musik- und Literaturwissenschaft 160. Bonn: Bouvier, 1975.

168. Bloom, Harold, ed. *Saul Bellow.* Modern Critical Views. New York: Chelsea, 1986.

169. Bradbury, Malcolm. *Saul Bellow.* Contemporary Writers. London and New York: Methuen, 1982.

170. Braham, Jeanne. *A Sort of Columbus: The American Voyages of Saul Bellow's Fiction.* Athens, GA: U of Georgia P, 1984.

171. Clayton, John J. *Saul Bellow: In Defense of Man.* Bloomington, IN: Indiana UP, 1968. 2nd ed. 1979.

172. Cohen, Sarah Blacher. *Saul Bellow's Enigmatic Laughter.* Urbana, IL: U of Illinois P, 1974.

173. Detweiler, Robert. *Saul Bellow: A Critical Essay.* Contemporary Writers in Christian Perspective. Grand Rapids, MI: Eerdmans, 1967.

174. Dommergues, Pierre. *Saul Bellow.* Paris: Grasset, 1967.

175. Dutton, Robert R. *Saul Bellow.* Twayne's United States Author
     Series 181. New York: Twayne, 1971. Rev. ed. 1982.

176. Fuchs, Daniel. *Saul Bellow: Vision and Revision.* Durham, NC:
     Duke UP, 1984.

177. Galloway, David D. *Absurd Hero in American Fiction: Updike,
     Styron, Bellow, Salinger.* Austin, TX: U of Texas P, 1966.
     2nd rev. ed. 1970.

178. Goldman, Liela H. *Saul Bellow's Moral Vision: A Critical Study
     of the Jewish Experience.* New York: Irvington, 1983.

179. Harris, Mark. *Saul Bellow: Drumlin Woodchuck.* Athens, GA: U
     of Georgia P, 1980.

180. Hasenclever, Walter. *Saul Bellow: Eine Monographie.* Cologne:
     Kiepenheuer, 1978.

181. Kegan, Robert. *The Sweeter Welcome: Voices for a Vision of
     Affirmation: Bellow, Malamud and Martin Buber.* Needham
     Heights, MA: Humanities, 1976.

182. Kulshrestha, Chirantan. *Saul Bellow: The Problem of Affir-
     mation.* New Delhi: Arnold, 1978.

183. Levy, Claude. *Les Romans de Saul Bellow: Tactiques Narratives
     et Strategies Oedipiennes.* Etudes Anglo-Americaines 5. Paris:
     Klincksieck, 1983.

184. Malin, Irving. *Saul Bellow's Fiction.* Crosscurrents/Modern
     Critiques. Carbondale, IL: Southern Illinois UP, 1969.

185. Malin, Irving, ed. *Saul Bellow and the Critics.* New York: New
     York UP, 1967.

186. McCadden, Joseph F. *The Flight From Women in the Fiction of Saul Bellow.* Washington, DC: UP of America, 1981.

187. McConnell, Frank D. *Four Postwar American Novelists: Bellow, Mailer, Barth, and Pynchon.* Chicago: U of Chicago P, 1977.

188. Newman, Judie. *Saul Bellow and History.* New York: St. Martin's; London: Macmillan, 1984.

189. Opdahl, Keith M. *The Novels of Saul Bellow: An Introduction.* University Park, PA: Pennsylvania State UP, 1967.

190. Porter, M. Gilbert. *Whence the Power? The Artistry and Humanity of Saul Bellow.* Columbia, MO: U of Missouri P, 1974.

191. Rodrigues, Eusebio L. *Quest for the Human: An Exploration of Saul Bellow's Fiction.* Lewisburg, PA: Bucknell UP, 1981.

192. Rovit, Earl. *Saul Bellow.* University of Minnesota Pamphlets on American Writers 65. Minneapolis: U of Minneapolis P, 1967. Rpt. in *American Writers: A Collection of Literary Biographies.* Ed. Leonard Ungar. Vol. 1. New York: Scribners, 1974. 144-66. 4 vols. 1974.

193. Rovit, Earl, ed. *Saul Bellow: A Collection of Critical Essays.* Twentieth Century Views. Englewood Cliffs, NJ: Prentice, 1975.

194. Scheer-Schaezler, Brigitte. *Saul Bellow.* Modern Literature Monographs. New York: Ungar, 1972.

195. Schraepen, Edmond, ed. *Saul Bellow and His Work.* Proceedings of a symposium held at the Free University of Brussels (V.U.B.), Dec. 10-11, 1977. Brussels: Centrum voor Taal-en Literatuurwetenschap Vrije Universiteit Brussel, 1978.

196. Scott, Nathan A., Jr. *Three American Moralists: Mailer, Bellow, Trilling.* Notre Dame, IN: U of Notre Dame P, 1973.

197. Shibuya, Yuzaburo. *Bellow: Kaishin no Kiseki.* [Saul Bellow: The Conversion of the Sick Soul]. Eibei Bungaku Sakkaron Sosho 28. Tokyo: Tojusha, 1978.

198. Tanner, Tony. *Saul Bellow.* Writers and Critics. Edinburgh and London: Oliver and Boyd; New York: Barnes, 1965; New York: Chips, 1978.

199. Trachtenberg, Stanley, ed. *Critical Essays on Saul Bellow.* Critical Essays on American Literature. Boston: Hall, 1979.

200. Wilson, Jonathan. *On Bellow's Planet: Readings From the Dark Side.* Rutherford, NJ: Dickinson UP; London and Toronto: Associated University Presses, 1985.

201. Zapf, Hubert. *Der Roman als Medium der Reflexion; eine Untersuchung am Beispiel dreier Romane von Saul Bellow (Augie March, Herzog, Humboldt's Gift).* Europaische Hochschulschriften 14; Angelsachsische Sprache und Literatur 88. Frankfurt am Main: Lang, 1981.

Special Journal Issues

202. *Critique* 3.3 (1960). Special issue on Bellow and William Styron.

203. *Critique* 7.3 (1965).

204. *Delta* [Paris] 19 (Oct. 1984).

205. *Journal of English Studies* [India] 12.1 (1980).

206. *Modern Fiction Studies* 25.1 (1979).

207. *Modern Jewish Studies Annual II* (1978). Joint issue of *Studies in American Jewish Literature* (University Park, PA) 4.2 and *Yiddish* 3.3 (1978).

208. *Notes On Modern American Literature* 2.4 (1978).

209. *Salmagundi* 30 (Summer 1975).

210. *Saul Bellow Journal* 1.2 (1982-). Published twice yearly since 1982.

211. *Saul Bellow Journal* 1.1 (1981). Name changed from *Saul Bellow Newsletter* with issue 1.2 (1982).

212. *Studies in American Jewish Literature* 3.1 (1977). Issue title: *Saul Bellow: The Vintage Years.*

213. *Studies in the Literary Imagination* 17.2 (1984). Issue title:
   Philosophical Dimensions of Saul Bellow's Literary Imagination.

Biographical Sources

214. Anderson, Jon. "Homage to Saul Bellow." *Saul Bellow Journal* 4.2 (1985): 11-13.

215. Asher, Aaron. "An Awed Bystander." *Saul Bellow Journal* 4.2 (1985): 10.

216. Atlas, James. "Unsentimental Education." *Atlantic* June 1983: 78-84, 87-92.

217. Basic, Sonja. "Portret pisca: Saul Bellow" [The Author's Portrait: Saul Bellow]." *Knjizevna Smotra* [Zagreb, Yug.] 1.4 (1970): 68-73. Cited in *Annual Bibliography of English Language and Literature*, 1970.

218. Boroff, David. "Saul Bellow." *Saturday Review* 19 Sept. 1964: 38-39, 77.

219. Clemons, Walter, and Chris J. Harper. "Bellow the Word King." *Newsweek* 1 Nov. 1976: 89.

220. Daniels, Shouri. "The Lie That Tells the Truth." *Saul Bellow Journal* 4.2 (1985): 6-8.

221. Dworkin, Susan. "The 'Great Man' Syndrome: Saul Bellow and Me." *Ms* Mar. 1977: 72-73.

222. Epstein, Joseph. "Saul Bellow of Chicago." *New York Times Book Review* 9 May 1971: 4, 12, 14, 16.

223. Fuchs, Daniel. "Saul Bellow: A Literary Reminiscence." *Saul Bellow Journal* 4.2 (1985): 14-16.

224. Grodzensky, Shlomo. "Firm in the Void." *Jewish Frontier* Mar. 1977: 20-22.

225. Hammer, Joshua. "Saul Bellow Returns to Canada Searching for Phantoms That Shaped His Life and Art." *People* 25 June 1984: 114.

226. Harris, Mark. "Of Cars, Woodchucks and Being Bellow's Boswell." *New York Times Book Review* 4 Nov. 1984: 3, 41.

227. Harris, Mark. "Saul Bellow at Purdue." *Georgia Review* 32.4 (1978): 715-54. An abridged excerpt from his *A Drummlin Woodchuck*.

228. Kazin, Alfred. "My Friend Saul Bellow." *Atlantic* Jan. 1965: 51-54. Rpt. in *Saul Bellow Journal* 4.2 (1985): 26-33.

229. Klinkowitz, Jerome. "Words of Humor." *Wilson Quarterly* 2.1 (1978): 126-42.

230. Kulshrestha, Chirantan. "The Estate." *Miscellany* Jan.-Feb. 1977: 17-29.

231. Lamont, Rosette C. "Bellow Observed: A Serial Portrait." *Mosaic* 8.1 (1974): 247-57. Rpt. in *Saul Bellow Journal* 4.2 (1985): 34-48.

232. "Laureate for Saul Bellow." *Time* 1 Nov. 1976: 91.

233. Marin, Daniel B. "Saul Bellow." *American Novelists Since World War II*. Detroit: Gale, 1978. 39-50. Vol. 2 of *Dictionary of Literary Biography*. 45 vols. to date. 1978- .

234. Neal, Steve. "The Quintessential Chicago Writer." *Chicago Tribune Magazine* 16 Sept. 1979: 14-16, 18, 20, 22, 24.

235. O'Sheel, Patrick. "Laughter from the Styx." *Eco-logos* 23 (1977): 11-14.

236. Pop-Cornis, Marcel. "Premiul Nobel Pentru Literatura 1976: Saul Bellow" [Nobel Prize for Literature 1976: Saul Bellow]." *Orizont* [Romania]. 27.47 (1976): 8. Cited in *Annual Bibliography of English Language and Literature*, 1977.

237. Roosevelt, Karyl. "Saul Bellow." *People Weekly* 8 Sept. 1975: 60-63.

238. Rule, Philip C. "Saul Bellow: Teller of Tales." *America* 13 Nov. 1976: 319-20.

239. "Saul Bellow: Yet Another Nobel for Viking." *Publishers Weekly* 1 Nov. 1976: 22.

240. Silva, Ribeiro da. "Samuel [sic.] Bellow: Nobel da Literatura." *Broteria* 103 (1976): 435-44.

241. Spivey, Ted R. "In Search of Saul Bellow." *Saul Bellow Journal* 4.2 (1985): 17-23.

242. Sprunsinski, Michal. "Nobel 76: Bellow, czyli 'Tajemnica Trwa Wiecznie'" [Bellow and the Secret of Eternity]. *Literatura* [Warsaw] 4 Nov. 1976: 16.

243. Steinberg, Saul. "Saul Bellow in Uganda." *Saul Bellow Journal* 4.2 (1985): 24-25.

244. Stern, Richard. "Bellow's Gift." *New York Times Magazine* 21 Nov. 1976: 42, 44, 46, 48, 50, 52.

245. Stern, Richard. "A Friendship of Thirty Years." *Saul Bellow
      Journal* 4.2 (1985): 4-5.

246. Toynbee, Philip. "To Be a Good Man." *Observer* 24 Oct. 1976:
      13.

247. Tureck, Rosalyn. "Looking Backward." *Saul Bellow Journal* 4.2
      (1985): 9.

248. Weinstein, Ann. "Bellow's Reflections on His Most Recent
      Sentimental Journey to His Birthplace." *Saul Bellow Journal*
      4.1 (1985): 62-71.

General Articles, Chapters, and Reviews

249. Abbott, H. Porter. "Saul Bellow and the 'Lost Cause' of Character." *Novel: A Forum on Fiction* 13 (1980): 264-83.

Establishes the idea that "what is modern about character is neither its trivialization, conversion into words, or other forms of diminishment, but that concern for it would lead to a panel on the topic. . . . character has become a subject." Concentrates largely on *DM* as a discourse on man in search of his character and unable to find it because he suffers from the "disease" of lucidity and alienation. Provides an in-depth examination of subsequent novels from this perspective.

250. Aharoni, Ada. "Bellow and Existentialism." *Saul Bellow Journal* 2.2 (1983): 42-54.

A close look at Bellow's novels reveals a profound link between his introspective mode of fiction and modern European existentialism. This article sees existentialism not just as a philosophy, but as a shift in ordinary human attitudes which has altered every aspect of life in our civilization. Traces Bellow's concern with this shift and with the essence of human existence, and sees them as close to those of the existentialists. European existentialism has influenced Bellow's beliefs; his thought is not derivative. Aharoni concludes that Bellow has intelligently absorbed these sources and developed his own introspective mode, thus enriching both American and world literature.

251. Aharoni, Ada. "The Cornerstone of Bellow's Art." *Saul Bellow Journal* 2.1 (1982): 1-12.

Identifies six main elements in all the novels: 1) protagonist

in existential crisis, 2) encounter with mentor, 3) confrontation with death or danger, 4) epiphany, 5) environment as
a reflection of the character's mind, 6) use of images and
symbols as "agents of the introspective process." After a
detailed discussion of each of these phases with specific
reference to each of the novels, Aharoni ends with a con-
cluding section describing the train journey as the recurrent
image of life in the Bellow novel. The journey metaphor,
she argues, suggests a pilgrimage via the subway, which has
connotations of the human underground of unconscious levels.
The Bellow hero, though not the driver, can miss the right
stations, or, on occasion, take the right opportunities to
alight. Bellow always warns the hero which stop is coming
up. Through using these six cornerstones, claims Aharoni,
Bellow has not only obtained the Nobel Prize, he has "succeeded in reproducing and conveying the most fundamental
texture of subjective reality in its most complex inwardness,
its ambiguity, its ephemerality . . . thus giving us one of
the deepest, and truest insights into modern man. . . ."

252. Aharoni, Ada. "Women in Saul Bellow's Novels." *Studies in
American Jewish Literature* 3 (1983): 99-112.

Defends Bellow from the charge that his women characters
are generally fantastic and unconvincing by arguing that
while Bellow's artistic technique imposes some "limitations
on his portrayal of women," namely that they are usually
perceived through the eyes of men going through existential
crises, nevertheless, Bellow has given us "a vast and rich
gallery of convincing and vivid women."

253. Aldridge, John W. "Nothing Left to Do But Think--Saul
Bellow." *Time to Murder and Create.* John W. Aldridge. New
York: McKay, 1966. 87-94.

Calls for more intellect and more feeling in the contemporary novel. Calls Bellow an "establishment" or "laureate"
writer because of his stylistic and intellectual seriousness as
a "high brow." Sees him as representative of the crisis of
intellect in the contemporary novel.

254. Alexander, Edward. "Saul Bellow: A Jewish Farewell to the
Enlightenment." *The Resonance of Dust: Essays on Holo-*

caust Literature and Jewish Fate. Edward Alexander.
Columbus, OH: Ohio State UP, 1979. 171-93.

Describes Bellow's life-long sense of the inadequacy of
Enlightenment principles and categories as a means of
interpreting modern experience. Alexander argues that in
Bellow's mind the holocaust functions as a metaphysical
refutation of Enlightenment assumptions. He explicates *MSP*
from this perspective.

255. Allen, Michael. "Idiomatic Language in Two Novels by Saul
Bellow." *Journal of American Studies* 1.2 (1967): 275-80.

Discusses the language of *HRK* and *AM*. In the former,
Henderson's language allows strongly literary phrases to be
transformed and energized by the emphatic rhythms of a
slang idiom which might be heard anywhere from the
Eastern Seaboard to the Midwest. It enables Bellow to
characterize Henderson as both Henry Adams and Hemingway
in his state of arrested development. Such language also
keeps a comic balance between his anguish and his irrespon-
sibility. It also conveys the pathos of his incoherence.
Ultimately Bellow's fictional colloquialisms become merely the
variegated language of an idiosyncratic individual. What is
missing is the backing of an oral tradition such as Twain
was able to draw on. In *AM* Bellow's use of language is less
like Twain's and more like Salinger's in its more limited
vitality. All three draw on the tension between an orally
transmitted small community language and the language of
the printed culture. The function of Augie's Jewish idioms
is to heighten, elaborate, and enrich. Commends the
effectiveness of Grandma Lausch's language.

256. Alter, Robert. "The Stature of Saul Bellow." *Midstream* 10
(Dec. 1964): 3-15. Rpt. as "Saul Bellow: A Dissent from
Modernism" in *After the Tradition: Essays on Modern Jewish
Writing.* Robert Alter. New York: Dutton, 1969. 95-115.

Sees *DM* and *TV* not as early examples of alienation fiction,
but as distinct from that genre in that they actually subvert
it. According to Alter, Bellow's methods here are explora-
tory and not obtrusively experimental. *DM* is clearly
influenced by Dostoevsky and Proust, though not derivative
because the style is informal and less strikingly "modern."

Bellow revitalizes pre-revolutionary forms while exploring the awareness and technical resources of the major moderns. He is a master of literary combinations and permutations.

257. Alvarez, Carmen Gago. "The Hero and the Social in Saul Bellow's Fiction." *Estudios Anglo-Americanos* 5-6 (1981-82): 137-44. Cited in *MLA Bibliography*, 1983.

258. Anders, Jaroslaw. "Saul Bellow's Treatment of Ideas in Three Major Works." *Kwartalnic Neofilologiczny* 27.4 (1980): 455-66.

Examines *H, MSP* and *HG* in an effort to determine the place ideas take in the novelistic structure, along with their relation to the general thematic outlines of the novels. Concludes that their final effect is a total change of vision on the part of the protagonists and their eventual silencing as a "contemplative repose."

259. Anderson, David D. "Chicago as Metaphor." *Great Lakes Review* 1.1 (1974): 3-15.

Traces Chicago as a metaphor in the works of several writers from Sherwood Anderson to Saul Bellow. Deals briefly with *AM.*

260. Atlas, Marilyn Judith. "The Figurine in the China Cabinet: Saul Bellow and the Nobel Prize." *MidAmerica* 8 (1981): 36-49.

Describes Bellow's mixed responses to winning the Nobel Prize in 1976. Comments on the judges' reasons for the award in terms of Bellow's ability to create character and critique contemporary culture. Summarizes Bellow's printed responses, Richard Stern's *NYT* essay and all of Bellow's previous awards. Documents Bellow's defensiveness after receiving the award and his refusal to become a cultural "functionary." Analyzes the content of Bellow's Nobel Lecture in terms of his focus on the individual life, his identification with Conrad as a displaced person, and his artistic faith in character. Discusses the chief protagonists briefly and in chronological order in terms of their dimensions as "characters."

261. Axthelm, Peter M. "The Full Perception: Bellow." *The Modern Confessional Novel.* Peter M. Axthelm. Yale College Series 6. New Haven, CT: Yale UP, 1967. 128-77.

262. Ayyan, Poppy. "The Changing Character of the Jew in American Fiction." *Asian Response to American Literature.* Ed. C. D. Narasimaiah. New York: Barnes, 1972. 293-98.

Paper presented at an Asian Seminar on American Literature held in Srinagar, India, 1970.

263. Bach, Gerhard. "Saul Bellow's German Reception. Part I." *Saul Bellow Journal* 5.2 (1986): 52-65. Part II is scheduled for publication in Saul Bellow Journal 6.1 (1987).

Describes in considerable detail American writers and post-war Germany, Bellow publications in German, German readers and reviewers, German critics, and the German position on Bellow. A major article on German scholarship on Bellow.

264. Bailey, Jennifer M. "The Qualified Affirmation of Saul Bellow's Recent Work." *Journal of American Studies* 7.1 (1973): 67-76.

Discusses the ambivalences which exist in Bellow's mid to late period novels as Bellow demonstrates his inability to "balance his protagonist's subjective reality with a convincing version of their social milieu."

265. Baker, Sheridan. "Saul Bellow's Bout with Chivalry." *Criticism* 9.2 (1967): 109-22.

The fantasies and cliches of the chivalric romance appear well into the modern era in the works of both the eighteenth and nineteenth centuries, not to mention such contemporary works as *AM* and *HRK*. Claims part of Bellow's answer to the faithlessness of the age in which we live is provided through these novelistic means.

266. Bakker, Jan. "In Search of Reality: Two American Heroes Compared." *Dutch Quarterly Review of Anglo-American Letters* 4 (1972): 145-61.

Makes an elaborate and detailed comparison of the Heming-
way hero and the Bellow hero, focussing primarily on *DM*.
This work is further elaborated in Bakker's major book
*Fiction as Survival Strategy: A Comparative Study of the
Major Works of Ernest Hemingway and Saul Bellow* (1983).

267. Balbert, Peter. "Perceptions of Exile: Nabokov, Bellow and the
     Province of Art." *Studies in the Novel* 14.1 (1982): 95-104.

     Compares the two writers as precocious sons of persecuted
     Russian minorities, men who in middle life affiliated with
     major US academic institutions, who use academia as a
     recurrent theme and locale, and who initially identify them-
     selves as impoverished Jews with aristocratic heritages, and
     use themes of literary exile. Both had to abandon their
     natural idioms for English. Both avoid political partisanship.
     Both are suspicious of popular clamor. Both see art as
     something to do with arresting people's attention in the
     midst of distraction.

268. Belitt, Ben. "Saul Bellow: The Depth Factor." *Salmagundi* 30
     (1975): 57-65.

     Defines the term "depth" from painting and applies it to
     literature with specific reference to several Bellow novels.

269. Bellamy, Michael O. "Bellow's More-or-Less Human Bestiaries:
     Augie March and *Henderson the Rain King*." *Ball State
     University Forum* 23.1 (1982): 12-22.

     One of the chief methods by which Bellow goes about deter-
     mining in his novels just what exactly is human is by
     "comparing man to his fellow creatures, a device which
     provides a kind of scale of creatures, a chain of living
     beings, against which to measure what truly is human." His
     bestiaries, *AM* and *HRK*, serve another function that is
     equally important in defining what truly is human. The
     enormous number and variety of animals in these two novels
     point us toward Bellow's belief in man's immanence within
     nature. We are reminded by the ubiquity of these creatures
     that man is himself a creature whose nature is to be assessed
     not only over against the animal kingdom, but also within

that kingdom in terms of the way he interacts with his fellow creatures.

270. Bellman, Samuel I. "Two-Part Harmony: Domestic Relations and Social Vision in the Modern Novel." *California English Journal* 3.1 (1967): 31-41.

Describes briefly how *SD* and *H* "point up the shabbiness and brittleness, and emptiness of urbanized society in terms of weak, foolish husbands making messes out of their home lives while their wives trample on them." This discussion is part of a much longer discussion on the general subject of domestic relations in the twentieth-century American novel.

271. Berets, Ralph. "Repudiation and Reality Instruction in Saul Bellow's Fiction." *Centennial Review* 20.1 (1976): 75-101.

Discusses Bellow's fiction within the context of the idea that each central character fluctuates between his own forces and those of reality instructors who present "alternative philosophical perspectives." Berets illustrates that in some works "the same individual is the vehicle for repudiation and redemption, but in most works different characters perform these roles."

272. Berthoff, Warner. *A Literature without Qualities: American Writing Since 1945.* Berkeley, CA: U of California P, 1979. [passim].

273. Bezanker, Abraham. "The Odyssey of Saul Bellow." *Yale Review* 58.3 (1969): 359-71.

Praises Bellow for his "speculative brilliance" and for "assimilating the literary and intellectual traditions of the West and for re-shaping them into rich, vivid, and persuasive characterizations." Describes Bellow's odyssey as a Jewish writer, illuminating several key themes and generalizing about several works as he does so.

274. Bigsby, C. W. E. "Saul Bellow and the Liberal Tradition in American Literature." *Forum* [Houston] 14.1 (1976): 56-62.

Begins with the assumption that the old liberal tradition
may have been lost in contemporary literature, and that
Bellow is busy, along with other contemporary American
novelists, trying to find out what a human being is, if
indeed he is not what he was thought to be a century ago.
Concludes that the liberal tradition is alive and well in the
Bellow novel.

275. Binni, Francesco. "Percorso narrativo di Saul Bellow." *Ponte* 22
(1966): 831-42.

Bellow is not an author of only one book like so many
other American writers. Bellow thinks that the writer must
have a certain influence (weight) on society. He is different
from Hemingway. Concerns himself with isolation and trium
phant individuality. Practices the aesthetics of the "hard
boiled." Describes the dilemma between the will of being
self-sufficient and risk of a social emptiness. Concentrates
on *DM* and *AM*. Compares Bellow with other recent authors.
Comments on Bellow's admiration for the European writers,
and the war of power in America concerning the social
system vs. the writer. Discusses Bellow's importance in
terms of his belief in man's ability and in the search for
self and brotherhood.

276. Bischoff, Peter. "Protagonist und Umwelt in Saul Bellows
Romanen: Ein Forschungsbericht." *Literatur in Wissenschaft
und Unterricht* [Kiel] 8 (1975): 257-76.

277. Borrus, Bruce J. "Bellow's Critique of the Intellect." *Modern
Fiction Studies* 25.1 (1979): 29-45.

While Bellow's thinkers clearly value the process of thought,
they are often incapable of accomplishing anything. Though
aware of the reasons for their alienation from society, they
cannot think their way through to accommodation. "Thinkin
leads only to more thinking--not action. . . .The life of the
mind seems useless outside of the library." Borrus argues
that Bellow toys with the idea that a decrease in self-
awareness might mean greater strength and freedom to act.

278. Bosha, Francis J. "The Critical Reception of Saul Bellow in Japan." *Saul Bellow Journal* 1.2 (1982): 34-46.

Dates the beginning of Japanese interest in Western literature from the Meiji era (1867-1912). Serious Bellow scholarship begins with Motoji Karita's translation of *AM*. Bellow
studies were then stimulated by Bellow's visit to Japan in
1972 and the Nobel Prize in 1976. Most Japanese literary
scholarship is not indexed and circulates only within individual
academies and universities. By 1965 there were many articles
on *H*. The most noted Japanese scholar is Yazaburo Shibuya,
who has translated and annotated a number of novels and
written a book-length study and numerous articles on Bellow.
Describes the 1970's as a prolific period of Bellow scholarship
in Japan. Documents much of the critical opinion of this
period. Discusses Shibuya's *Bellow Kaishin no Kiseki* (1978).
(Item 197.) States that in the 1980's many Bellow novels
appeared on reading lists of Japanese colleges and universities.

279. Boyers, Robert T. "Confronting the Present." *Salmagundi* 54
(1981): 77-97. Cited in *MLA Bibliography*, 1981.

280. Brackenhoff, Mary. "Humboldt's Gift: The Ego's Mirror--A
Vehicle for Self-Realization." *Saul Bellow Journal* 5.2 (1986):
15-21.

Discusses the fact that because his protagonists are frequently
blinded "by their egocentricity they need to distance themselves from their own strong personalities in order to
examine and, hopefully, redirect their lives. To aid his
protagonists, Bellow has frequently employed a narrative
ingenuity or caste of secondary characters to provide mirror
images, alter egos, or reality instructors-points of view that
throw the protagonists' characters into relief."

281. Bradbury, Malcolm. "Leaving the Fifties: The Change of Style
in American Writing." *Encounter* [London] 45.1 (1975): 40-51.

282. Bradbury, Malcolm. "'The Nightmare in Which I am Trying to
Get a Good Night's Rest': Saul Bellow and Changing History."
Saul Bellow and His Work. Ed. Edmond Schraepen. Brussels:
Centrum Voor Taal En Literatuurwetenschap, Vrije Universiteit

Brussel, 1978. Symposium held at the Free University of Brussels (V.U.B.) on 10-11 Dec. 1977. Rpt. as "Saul Bellow and Changing History" in *Saul Bellow.* Ed. Harold Bloom. Modern Critical Views. New York: Chelsea, 1986. 129-46.

Attempts to account for the dark places in the novels and to detail Bellow's European appeal. Discusses also the ambiguous Bellow ending in light of the themes of darkness and the influence of European thinking in the novels. Concludes that the Bellow hero lives in a world where metaphysical measurements cannot be taken, yet where the mind insists that they be taken anyway.

283. Bradbury, Malcolm. "Saul Bellow and the Naturalist Tradition." *Review of English Literature* 4.4 (1963): 80-92.

Links Bellow to the great Russian naturalists and identifies his subject matter primarily as the answer to the question "How should a good man live?" Sees the two early novels as controlled and oppressively moral. Sees the advent of *AM* as a broadening out, even though it and subsequent novels are still concerned with Darwinian ideas, evolution and struggle.

284. Bradbury, Malcolm. "Saul Bellow and the Nobel Prize." *Journal of American Studies* 11.1 (1977): 3-12.

Praises the Nobel Prize committee for its choice of Saul Bellow as candidate for the award. Discusses the propensity of judges to award the prize to writers who deal in moral affirmations, and proceeds to justify the award to Bellow on these grounds and others. A useful thematic overview of the works concludes the article.

285. Braem, Helmut M. "Der Weg Saul Bellows." *Neue Rundschau* 4 (1971): 742-752.

Traces Bellow's development as a novelist of ideas from *DM* to *MSP*. Characterizes Bellow's protagonists as alienated academics who loathe academia, as outsiders whose conflicts with de-individualizing society teach them lessons in self-preservation, compassion and acceptance. Suggests that Bellow has broken with several American traditions, from Faulkner's naturalism to Hemingway's realism, projecting

American literature into a new era, which Braem describes
rather than defines. He sees Bellow's heroes as "dangling"
between the two worlds of ideas and reality. Estranged from
both, their estrangement is not a Marxist alienation but a
voluntary self-denial for the sake of a higher social order.
Searching for their place in the world, they encounter the
world and themselves as suffering but compassionate--basi-
cally "content to be as is willed." They all share Bummidge's
burden of "humanitas" and Sammler's somewhat sentimental
strife for a "sanctified simplicity."

286. Braham, Jeanne. "The Struggle at the Center: Dostoyevsky and
Bellow." *Saul Bellow Journal* 2.1 (1982): 13-18.

Briefly outlines Bellow's debt to Dostoyevsky and the Russian
realists, and points out that while he obviously admires the
Russians tremendously, his own fiction "registers an attempt
at transcendence which remains short of resolution." Like
the Russian novelists, he would like to lead his protagonist
away from the void, but instead he details all the road
blocks. What happens in the Bellow novel is the undercutting
of the protagonists' efforts in such a way that they mock
his beliefs in transcendence. The fiction registers the value
of the continuous process of ethical struggle--not religious
questing. "Transcendence is a means not an end."

287. Brodin, Pierre. "Saul Bellow." *Continuateurs et Novateurs;
Ecrivains americains d'aujourd'hui.* Pierre Brodin. Paris:
Debreise, 1973. 33-38.

288. Bryant, Jerry H. "Ambiguity and Affirmation: The Moral Outlook."
*The Open Decision: The Contemporary American Novel and
its Intellectual Background.* Jerry H. Bryant. New York: Free
Press, 1970. 341-69.

Briefly compares Bellow's thematic concerns with those of
Malamud. Locates the moral issues within the dialogue
between "snarling realism" and transcendence. Bellow is
primarily concerned with examining the machinery of this
issue. Provides a detailed treatment of each novel up to
HRK.

289. Buitenhuis, Peter. "A Corresponding Fabric: The Urban World
     of Saul Bellow." *Costerus* 8 (1973): 13-35.

     Sees Bellow breaking out of his Jewish individuality and
     joining other great writers as he strings his novels on the
     poles between free will and determinism. Ranges across the
     canon and establishes Bellow's progressive identification with
     the widest possible range of human issues.

290. Bullock, C. J. "On the Marxist Criticism of the Contemporary
     Novel in the United States: A Re-Evaluation of Saul Bellow."
     Praxis 1.2 (1976): 189-98.

     Accuses modern criticism of failing to come to terms with
     the "socio-historical specificity of the contemporary American
     novel." The article then proceeds to a methodological exercise
     in Marxist criticism which takes the Bellow hero under
     consideration.

291. Burgess, Anthony. "The Jew as American." *Spectator* 7 Oct.
     1966: 455-56.

     In *TV* he seems to be playing a popular anti-semitic tune
     but with ambivalent counterpoint. Out of the hostile symbiosis
     of Albee and Leventhal these two attempt to define them-
     selves as men, failing for the most part because of self-pity.
     Claims that Bellow is working the *Death of a Salesman* theme
     in his own terms. Applauds the concreteness of descriptive
     language with which Bellow clothes his ideas and abstractions

292. Burns, Robert. "The Urban Experience: The Novels of Saul
     Bellow." *Dissent* 24 (1969): 18-24.

     Bellow concerns himself with how a man surrounded and
     swallowed in "the bowels of the monster metropolis" can
     survive in spirit. Concludes that Bellow portrays such an
     environmental force as bounded and merely objective, while
     the human spirit is not thus bound and static.

293. Calin, Vera. "Ignorarea psihologiei" ["The Ignoring of Psychol-
     ogy"]." *Omisiunea elocventa* [The Eloquent Omission] Bucha-
     rest: Editura enciclopedica romana, 1973. 243-46.

294. Carter, Everett. "Optimism in the Twentieth Century: Saul Bellow." *The American Idea: The Literary Response to American Optimism.* Everett Carter. Chapel Hill, NC: U of North Carolina P, 1977. 249-54.

> Places Bellow in the wake of Henry Adams and James. Deals with his philosophical affirmations in brief summary.

295. Chametzky, Jules. "Notes on the Assimilation of the American-Jewish Writer: Abraham Cahan to Saul Bellow." *Jahrbuch fur Amerikastudien* 9 (1964): 173-80.

> Outlines very briefly the history of American-Jewish writers, mentioning Bellow at the end of the article. Mainly useful for historical perspective.

296. Chapman, Abraham. "The Image of Man as Portrayed by Saul Bellow." *College Language Association Journal* 10 (1967): 285-98.

> Discusses Bellow's first six novels and novella from the point of view of the Odyssean search for self. Illustrates the thesis that "Man Searching is very close to Man Lost, but equally close to Man Found."

297. Chavkin, Allan. "Bellow and English Romanticism." *Studies in the Literary Imagination* 17.2 (1984): 7-18.

> Traces the immense debt to English (and American) Romanticism found throughout the Bellow novels. This is a detailed and erudite analysis. Concludes that the soaring spirit is never far from the "clamoring world." A major article.

298. Chavkin, Allan. "Father and Sons: 'Papa' Hemingway and Saul Bellow." *Papers on Language and Literature* 19.4 (1983): 449-60.

> Bellow's literary relationship with Hemingway, Chavkin claims, was compounded of defensiveness, envy, love and hate. Often he distorted the work of his literary forefather. Chavkin goes on to examine the critique of Hemingway in Bellow's novels. Discusses also the father-son relationship in

the novels in light of the father-son relationship between
Bellow and Hemingway. In the course of this relationship,
Bellow ultimately rejects Hemingway's fatalistic view of the
universe. Both writers grapple with the same problems, but
when they differ the comparison between the two is useful
because each illuminates the other.

299. Chavkin, Allan. "The Problem of Suffering in the Fiction of
Saul Bellow." *Comparative Literature Studies* 21.2 (1984):
161-74.

Rejects Clayton's thesis of Jewish guilt, and pathological
social masochism as being simplistic. Argues that Bellow's
very sophisticated view of suffering derives from Dostoevskian humanism, English romanticism, Jewish comedy and
anti-modernism--or rather, Bellow's interpretation of these
traditions. Provides an overview of the canon from this
perspective. A major article.

300. Christhilf, Mark M. "Death and Deliverance in Saul Bellow's
Symbolic City." *Ball State University Forum* 18.2 (1977):
9-23.

With the exception of *HRK*, the cityscapes in the Bellow
novel function as an inferno which threatens man's sanity
and dignity at each turn. But in addition, Bellow's fictional
city also has mythic, apocalyptic overtones. In the later
works the city, in terms of the physical imagery used to
embody it, undergoes a transformation from a concrete
narrative setting to a higher abstract place. Utilizing various
novelistic forms and techniques, Bellow has dramatized the
city as an extension of the evil potential within man, a
theme he conveys throughout his works.

301. Christhilf, Mark M. "Saul Bellow and the American Intellectual
Community." *Modern Age* 28.1 (1984): 55-67.

Argues that a critique of the American intellectual community informs all of Bellow's work. Discusses his estrangement
from this community. Discusses the middle and later novels
in detail. Concludes with an estimate of Bellow's influence
in this intellectual community.

302. Cohen, Sarah Blacher. "The Comedy of Urban Low Life: From Saul Bellow to Mordecai Richler." *Thalia* 4.2 (1981-82): 21-24.

Cohen examines the fascination of the Bellow hero with low-life Chicago types like Cantabile and shows how both characters are determined to profit instantly from their association with each other. The humor arises with the sudden shifting of planes up or down and the undercutting of intellectual pretension by bodily needs. However, as in the dynamics of conventional comedy, that which is deviant and threatening is ultimately banished and conservative norms of social order restored. Cohen compares and contrasts the humor of both Richler and Bellow and concludes that the prudish intellectual Bellow produces humor that is neither as truculent nor as ill-mannered as that of the less accepted Richler.

303. Cohen, Sarah Blacher. "Saul Bellow's Chicago." *Modern Fiction Studies* 24.1 (1978): 139-46.

Describes briefly the effects of Chicago on all who encountered it, then traces Bellow's very important stylistic and thematic use of it in his fiction.

304. Cohen, Sarah Blacher. "Sex: Saul Bellow's Hedonistic Joke." *Studies in American Fiction* 2 (1974): 223-29.

Details Bellow's treatment of sex as a laughable preoccupation in which the hero "experiences some difficulty in learning the rules and familiarizing himself with the other players' techniques." Sex in the Bellow novel is depicted primarily as a game. Usually the hero feels duped into thinking that through sex he has fused with another person.

305. Coren, Alan. "Displaced Persons." *Punch* 19 Oct. 1966: 603.

306. Cowley, Malcolm. "The Literary Situation, 1965." *University of Mississippi Studies in English* 6 (1965): 91-98.

While answering questions at a literary conference, Cowley comments that though Bellow lacks the brilliance of some of

the other writers of the period, he makes up for that with
his tremendous integrity. Cowley also comments that each
new book constitutes a fresh start.

307. Davis, Robert Gorham. "The American Individualist Tradition."
     *The Creative Present: Notes on Contemporary American
     Fiction.* Eds. Nona Balakian and Charles Simmons. Garden
     City, NY: Doubleday, 1963. 111-41.

     An early essay on the struggle for identity within the
     Bellow novel. Makes useful comparisons with Styron. A good
     overview of the novels with regard to the plights of the
     central characters.

308. Dickstein, Morris. "Cold War Blues: Notes on the Culture of
     the Fifties." *Partisan Review* 41.1 (1974): 30-53.

309. Dickstein, Morris. "For Art's Sake." *Partisan Review* 33.4
     (1966): 617-21.

310. Dommergues, Pierre. *L'Alienation dans le roman americain
     contemporain.* Vol. 1. Paris: Union Generale d'Editions, 1977.
     355-429. 2 vols. 1976-77.

311. Dougherty, David C. "Finding Before Seeking: Themes in *Hen-
     derson the Rain King* and *Humboldt's Gift.*" *Modern Fiction
     Studies* 25.1 (1979): 93-101.

     Bellow's characters frequently discover aphorisms which, if
     properly comprehended, help them to understand and shape
     their lives. Charlie Citrine cherishes a sentence from a book
     by Valery that Humboldt lent him: "*Trouve avant chercher*"
     ["Finding before seeking"], which says a great deal about
     Bellow's comic vision in general, as well as about this novel;
     it becomes the key to the structure of *HG*. Dougherty goes
     on to point out how Bellow's paradoxical comic vision is
     symbolized by this aphorism as Charlie learns to cease
     actively seeking for meaning in life and to reverse his
     expectations.

312. Ebon, Martin. "Saul Bellow: The Worldly Insight and Mystical Core of a Nobel Laureate." *New Realities* 1.1 (1977): 26-30.

    A brief and generalized article on the surface social structure and mystical core of Bellow's work. A useful thematic overview of the canon.

313. Edelman, Lily. "In Praise of Saul Bellow." Rev. of *Herzog, Mr. Sammler's Planet,* and *Great Jewish Short Stories." National Jewish Monthly* Apr. 1971: 47-48.

314. Eiland, Howard. "Bellow's Crankiness." *Chicago Review* 32.4 (1981): 92-107.

    Claims that Bellow is a particular kind of crank with an acute sense of appropriate boundaries. Likewise, Joseph is also cranky and given to strange states. This strangeness signals a deep religious impulse. In Bellow it is actually a Jewish-American version of modernist dis-ease. With Nietzsche, he shares an obsessive distrust of bourgeoise self-fashioning, the cult of therapy and an excessive need to guard his individuality. Bellow's crankiness, and that of his protagonists, is the tragi-comic crankiness of the modern temper, which is grounded in ambivalence. This allegiance is divided between the claims of consciousness and spontaneity. Examines each successive protagonist for evidence of his temperament. Concludes that if Bellow portrays himself as a crank it is because he feels the rectifying pull of "axial lines" in spite of the "ambiguous dominion of the heart."

315. Eisinger, Chester E. "Saul Bellow: Love and Identity." *Accent* 18.3 (1958): 179-203.

    Places Bellow within the historical context of post-war American society which is so inimical to the processes of the imagination. Then he proceeds to identify two major themes--love and identity--as Bellow's solution to either radical socialism or religious revival and conservatism. Asserts the essential Jewishness of Bellow's work and its debt to Yiddish folk literature and Hassidism as he develops the idea of joy central to the Bellow novel.

316. Eisinger, Chester E. "Saul Bellow: Man Alive, Sustained by Love." *Fiction of the Forties.* Chester E. Eisinger. Chicago: U of Chicago P, 1963. 341-62.

Claims that Bellow has provided a remarkable sense of his time in the novels, and that he is primarily concerned with the relationship of man to society. This is why Bellow sets himself and his protagonists up against the society around him. Explains Bellow's particular position with regard to fashionable alienation theory. Does not examine any one novel in depth.

317. Elmen, Paul. "Bellow's Gift." *Christian Century* 24 Nov. 1976: 1033-36.

A general tribute to Bellow, discussing his child-like sense of humor and play, his style, his philosophical interests his men and women, his acceptance of life and his latest novel, *HG.*

318. Fairman, Lynette A. "Finitude, Anxiety and Affirmation in Saul Bellow's Novels." *Saul Bellow Journal* 3.2 (1984): 40-46.

Discusses how from the beginning the critics have examined death in the Bellow novel as both symbol and theme. "Yet while many critics discuss the role of death in Bellow's novels, they do not fully analyze the anxiety the characters' experience as a result of their mortality."

319. Fiedler, Leslie A. "Literature and Lucre: A Meditation." *Genre* 13.1 (1980): 1-10.

320. Fiedler, Leslie A. "Saul Bellow." *Prairie Schooner* 31 (1957): 103-10. Rpt. in *On Contemporary Literature: An Anthology of Critical Essays on the Major Movements and Writers of Contemporary Literature.* Ed. Richard Kostelanetz. New York: Avon, 1964. 286-95; *Saul Bellow and the Critics.* Ed. Irving Malin. New York: New York UP, 1967. 1-24; *The Modern Critical Spectrum.* Eds. Gerald Jay Goldberg and Nancy Marme Goldberg. Englewood Cliffs, NJ: Prentice, 1962. 155-61.

Places Bellow as a young writer in the tradition of other

beginning writers. Also describes the dilemma of being the Jewish-American writer and his role in describing the problems of Jewish assimilation. Makes general comments on style and theme in the early novels and concludes that Bellow's art begins with the collapse of the proletarian novel of the 1930's.

321. Field, Leslie. "Saul Bellow: From Montreal to Jerusalem." *Studies in American Jewish Literature* [University Park, PA] 4.2 (1978): 51-59. Joint issue with *Yiddish* 3.3 (1978).

Field borrows Irving Howe's phrase "tradition as discontinuity" to describe the Jewishness of Bellow's novels. For Field *H* is the most Jewish of the novels, since it portrays Bellow's vision of "a world of Jews transplanted to North America." The article goes on to deal with TJB and concludes that perhaps Bellow "now joins Jewish-American writers Henry Roth, Herbert Gold, and others as born-again Jews."

322. Field, Leslie. "Saul Bellow and the Critics After the Nobel Award." *Modern Fiction Studies* 25.1 (1979): 3-13.

A literary historical treatment of the aftermath of the award of the Nobel Prize for Literature to Saul Bellow. Ends with a summary of the current scholarship and interest in Bellow.

323. Fineman, Irving. "The Image of the Jew in Fiction of the Future." *National Jewish Monthly* Dec. 1967: 48-51.

A general article dealing with the image of the American Jew in twentieth-century literature. Makes brief mention of Bellow within this context.

324. Finkelstein, Sidney. "Lost Social Convictions and Existentialism: Arthur Miller and Saul Bellow." *Existentialism and Alienation in American Literature.* Sidney Finkelstein. New York: International, 1965. 252-69.

Compares Miller and Bellow in terms of their fictional biographies and their brilliant witty dialogue. Discusses both writers in terms of the intellectual milieu of the 1950's and its preoccupation with existentialism. Talks of the "religious existentialism" of *H* and of the existentialist ideas found throughout the novels up to *H*.

325. Fishman, Ethan. "Saul Bellow's 'Likely Stories.'" *Journal of Politics* 45.3 (1983): 615-34.

326. Fleischmann, Wolfgang Bernard. "The Contemporary 'Jewish Novel' in America." *Jahrbuch fur Amerikastudien* 12 (1967): 159-66.

327. Fossum, Robert. "The Devil and Saul Bellow." *Comparative Literature Studies* 3.2 (1966): 197-206. Rpt. in *Mansions of the Spirit: Essays in Literature and Religion*. Ed. George A. Panichas. New York: Hawthorn, 1967. 345-55.

Though professing no allegiance to any theological system and filling his novels with largely non-religious Jews, Bellow, along with many contemporary American and European writers, is concerned with questions about the nature and state of the contemporary soul. Fossum goes on to articulate the contraries within the Bellow character which indicate the presence of both good and evil within man, and the ever-present Faustian tempter whose literary origins are Goethean.

328. Fossum, Robert. "Inflationary Trends in the Criticism of Fiction: Four Studies of Saul Bellow." *Studies in the Novel* 2.1 (1970): 99-104.

This article grants Bellow major status, yet Fossom doubts that his work "warrants the detailed explication given it" in four books on Bellow by Tony Tanner, Keith Opdahl, James J. Clayton and Irving Malin. Of the four he approves of only Tanner's work.

329. Frank, Reuben. "Saul Bellow: The Evolution of a Contemporary Novelist." *Western Review* 18.2 (1954): 101-12.

Characterizes Bellow's evolution as a contemporary writer in terms of his move from "tightness and sparsity to a free and rich form; attitudinally, from despair to a kind of reserved affirmation." Sees Bellow as a writer who is able to immerse himself as "the perceptions and consciousness of the first-generation American, suspended between the new American and old European cultures, and to speak out with a voice that is uniquely his."

330. Freedman, Ralph. "Saul Bellow: The Illusion of Environment." *Wisconsin Studies in Contemporary Literature* 1.1 (1960): 50-65. Rpt. in *Saul Bellow and the Critics*. Ed. Irving Malin. New York: New York UP, 1967. 51-68.

Relates Bellow's first two novels to the traditions of the social or naturalistic novel, and explains how, as a reaction against determinism, he experiences the world as private experience rendered as art. With the later novels, Bellow changes the earlier tradition. Society now reflects the hero's consciousness instead of being in opposition to him. The middle period novels take the process one step further by showing the hero and world related in a rather light dialectic. Both the hero and the world prove to be evanescent as well as stable. The novels of this period also create the victim character as an extension and a mockery of his environment. Examines these concepts primarily within the early novels.

331. Friedman, Alan Warren. "The Jew's Complaint in Recent American Fiction: Beyond Exodus and Still in the Wilderness." *Southern Review* 8.1 (1972): 41-59.

Friedman articulates at length the situation of the Jewish writer in mid-century American culture and ranges across the works of a number of American-Jewish writers in the process. His remarks on Bellow's *HRK* are of particular interest.

332. Fuchs, Daniel. "Bellow and Freud." *Studies in the Literary Imagination* 17.2 (1984): 59-80.

A landmark article which traces in immense detail the influences of Freud's thinking and world view upon Bellow's work. Provides an in-depth introduction to Freudian thought and develops the thesis that Bellow identifies Freud as the preeminent modern thinker. Demonstrates how Bellow's ultimate reflection of modernism is couched primarily in terms of his rejection of Freudian estimates and premises. A major article.

333. Fuchs, Daniel. "Saul Bellow and the Modern Tradition." *Contemporary Literature* 15.1 (1974): 67-89. Expanded version rpt. in *Saul Bellow: Vision and Revision.* Daniel Fuchs. Durham, NC: Duke UP, 1984. 3-27.

Calls Bellow a post-modernist par excellence. Shows how he throws over the Flaubertian and modernist pereoccupation wit style. Traces this through the works of Flaubert and Joyce. Illustrates Bellow's break with nihilist premises which also characterize much modern fiction, along with his questioning of modernist assumptions such as alienation, fragmentation, break with tradition, isolation, magnification of subjectivity and hatred of civilization. Treats each of the novels in terms of this thesis. A major article.

334. Fuchs, Daniel. "Saul Bellow and the Example of Dostoevsky." *The Stoic Strain in American Literature: Essays in Honor of Marston La France.* Ed. Duane J. MacMillan. Toronto: U of Toronto P, 1979. 157-76. Revised version rpt. in *Saul Bellow: Vision and Revision.* Durham, NC: Duke UP, 1984. 28-49; *Saul Bellow.* Ed. Harold Bloom. Modern Critical Views. New York: Chelsea, 1986. 211-33. Originally delivered as a lecture at the second annual meeting of the Austrian American Studies Association, Schloss Leopoldskron, Salzburg, Oct. 1955.

Denies that we can go on saying with Hemingway that all American literature comes from *Huckleberry Finn.* Much contemporary American literature comes from Flaubert and the Russians. Bellow is the leading exponent of the Russian way. Of particular note is the influence of Dostoevsky on Bellow. An erudite and major analysis.

335. Gallagher, Michael Paul. "Bellow's Clowns and Contemplatives." *Month* Apr. 1977: 131-34.

Argues that Bellow's clowns are "heroes of crowded consciousness, not intellectuals whom we are meant to take seriously as such." Describes them as caught up in the culture chatter that passes for knowledge. However, finding this is such a source of despair, they then seek for real knowledge.

336. Galloway, David D. "The Absurd Man as Picaro: The Novels of Saul Bellow." *Texas Studies in Literature and Language* 6.2

(1964): 226-54. Rpt. in *Absurd Hero in American Fiction: Updike, Styron, Bellow, Salinger.* David D. Galloway. Austin: U of Texas P, 1966. 82-139. Rev. ed. 1970.

A very detailed article based on the observation that modern writers after Camus have used the myth of the absurd man and produced a modern version of the picaresque novel. Applies this to Bellow's novels in a careful analysis. Concentrates largely on *AM.* Concludes that it is this application of the absurd and the picaresque that provides the distinguishing feature of hope in the Bellow novel. A major article.

337. Galloway, David D. "Clown and Saint: The Hero in Current American Fiction." *Critique* 7.3 (1965): 46-65.

Traces the development of the urban landscape and technology in the American consciousness as a backdrop for discussion of Bellow's urban landscapes. Emphasizes the challenge such a landscape presents for the twentieth-century city dweller. Two types emerge in the novel, representative of the human attempt to resist the dissipation inherent in such a life-style--the clown and the saint. Sees Augie March as a philosophical clown, along with Henderson. Sees them also as contemporary saints of sensibility. These saintly clowns wage the battle of the spirit in a world of curtailed expectation, "threading the increasingly narrow path around suicide and despair toward a refurbished vision of man."

338. Galloway, David D. "Culture-Making: The Recent Works of Saul Bellow." *Saul Bellow and His Work.* Ed. Edmond Schraepen. Brussels: Centrum voor Taal-en Literatuurwetenschap, Vrije Universiteit Brussel, 1978. 49-60. Proceedings of a symposium held at the Free University of Brussels (V.U.B.) on 10-11 Dec. 1977.

Argues that while Bellow has successfully domesticated the novel of ideas in the U.S., and countered the WASP irony of philosophy and science, European intellections, and othe materials with a God older than that worshipped by the pilgrim fathers, his variety is illusory. Bellow elaborates repeated characters, themes, parallels, motifs and expressions throughout the novels. Galloway then details the successive bankruptcy of Bellow's imagination from *MSP* onward. Finally, he accuses Bellow of constructing thin

plots, presenting ideas instead of literature, creating weak
characters, and of manifesting a marked disinterest in
formal experimentation.

339. Gard, Roger. "Saul Bellow." *Delta* [Cambridge, Eng.] 36 (Summer
     1965): 27-30.

340. Geismar, Maxwell. "The Jewish Heritage in Contemporary
     American Fiction." *Ramparts* 2.2 (1963): 5-13.

341. Geismar, Maxwell. "Saul Bellow: Novelist of the Intellectuals."
     American Moderns: From Rebellion to Conformity. Maxwell
     Geismar. New York: Hill and Wang, 1958. 210-24.

     Sees Bellow as a member of an intellectual and moral caste
     who has fought all his life to struggle out of that caste, to
     go beyond it, and to write fiction in spite of it. Sees within
     Bellow "a deep and primary core of Jewish feeling and of
     biblical righteousness" which defeats some of his efforts at
     neat intellectual synthesis. Treats the novels up to *SD* chrono-
     logically. Concludes by comparing Bellow to Crane, since he
     claims both were "consumed in the flames of [their] own
     oedipal and religious conflicts."

342. Gibson, Walker. "Free-Style: The Rhetoric of Unreliable Narra-
     tors." *Tough, Sweet and Stuffy: An Essay on Modern American
     Prose Styles.* Walker Gibson. Bloomington, IN: Indiana UP,
     1966. 59-63.

     A simple discussion of prose style in Bellow, but one of the
     only exclusive treatments of style in the secondary literature.
     Attempts to place Bellow historically. Concentrates mostly
     on *AM.*

343. Gindin, James. "The Fable Begins to Break Down." *Wisconsin
     Studies in Contemporary Literature* 8.1 (1967): 1-18.

     Traces the development of fabulation in mid-sixties British and
     American fiction. Places Bellow's letter writing device in *H*
     in the category of mythic exploration of human possibilities.
     Describes use of fable in *HRK* also. Brief exposition only.

344. Gindin, James. "Saul Bellow." *Harvest of a Quiet Eye: The Novel of Compassion.* James Gindin. Bloomington, IN: Indiana UP, 1971. 305-36.

> Provides a general overview of the novels up to *MSP*, discussing Bellow's protagonists in terms of WW II existentialism and the prevailing model of the a-hero or anti-hero. Concentrates largely on the remarkable degree of communication each of the protagonists achieves within the novels despite the alienated condition of each.

345. Girgus, Sam B. "After the Sixties: The Continuing Search." *The Law of the Heart: Individualism and the Modern Self in American Literature.* Sam B. Girgus. Austin: U of Texas P, 1979. 140-50.

> Discusses *MSP* as a book in which the protagonist protests perverted forms of individuality. Shows how this novel and the others offer a program for individualism that stands in strong contrast to the idea of "selfishness as a fierce moral idea."

346. Gitenstein, Barbara. "Saul Bellow and the Yiddish Literary Tradition." *Studies in American Jewish Literature* [University Park, PA] 5.2 (1979): 24-46. Joint issue with *Yiddish* 4.1 (1979).

> Argues that, along with the influence of French, Russian and English literary models, Bellow, by virtue of his upbringing, was influenced by Yiddish models. Gitenstein then proceeds to provide both a general introduction to the conventions of Yiddish literature and a series of brief applications to the Bellow canon. Among the conventions analyzed are Bellow's particular humor, the mock heroic elements, Jewish humanism, picaresque conventions, monologue, didacticism, authorial intrusion, realism, and numerous character types.

347. Gitenstein, Barbara. "Saul Bellow of the 1970's and the Contemporary Use of History in Jewish-American Literature." *Saul Bellow Journal* 1.2 (1982): 7-17.

> Gitenstein argues that in the 1970's a number of Jewish writers made the choice of history for the outline of art, and the choice of historical events to validate personal

values. Of these, Saul Bellow is the most successful in transforming the facts of history into the art of fiction. In a close study of his novels, the reader can see strong parallels between his "Enlightenment" views of history in art and nineteenth-century American ideals. Illustrates Bellow's thesis that art borrows from fact only what it needs. Gives a detailed account of the use of "facts" in *HG*. Concludes this thorough exegesis by suggesting that a major theme of the novel is that the individual poet must be in time, but should not be overwhelmed by fact and history. If he is, he will lose his ironic distance from the detail; he will be unable to feel dream-states. Jewish-American writers of the 1970's seem unable to overlook the impact of history on life and art; they try to explain the meaning of being in America in the second half of the twentieth-century through a factual base in history.

348. Golden, Daniel. "Mystical Musings and Comic Confrontations: The Fiction of Saul Bellow and Mordecai Richler." *Essays on Canadian Writing* 22 (1981): 62-85.

Given the closeness of their immigrant and orthodox roots, the two writers offer instructive contrasts in some of the aspirations and contrasts inherent in American and Canadian Jewish experience. Goes on to compare and contrast both writers in terms of their ethnic backgrounds, search for identity, allegiances, treatment of assimilation themes and comic gifts. Suggests that both writers document the larger plight of mankind and their respective cultures. Both share the ghetto landscape of memory. Both are fascinated with petty crooks, hustlers, and *luftmenschen*. Both write of legitimate and not-so-legitimate business. Bellow is more mystical and Richler more humorous in response to experience. Contains an excellent discussion of Bellow's utilization of the occult to mediate the failure of intellect and rationality.

349. Goldman, Arnold. "A Remnant to Escape: The American Writer and the Minority Group." *American Literature Since 1900*. Ed. Marcus Cunliffe. History of Literature in the English Languag 9. London: Barrie, 1975. 312-43.

350. Goldman, Liela H. "The Holocaust in the Novels of Saul Bellow." *Modern Language Studies* 16.1 (1986): 71-80.

Describes Bellow's statement on the subject of the Holocaust
in terms of his analysis of the misguided Romantic origins of
German culture, which in turn gave rise to the phenomenon
of Nazism. Goldman sees Nazism as an attack on Western
Humanism and characterizes Bellow's novelistic processes of
thought as consistently Jewish in their defense of humanistic
philosophy. Discusses miso-Germanism in terms of specific
Bellow characters throughout the novels and in terms of
Bellow's critique of German philosophers responsible for the
philosophical bases of German Romanticism.

351. Goldman, Liela H. "Saul Bellow and the Philosophy of Judaism."
Studies in the Literary Imagination 17.2 (1984): 81-95.

Briefly defines Judaism as an ethical, bible-centered monotheism which is fundamentally anthropocentric and which
provides reasons for man's existence based on assumptions
of human confidence and sufficiency. Within this context
Goldman develops the thesis that Bellow is first and foremost
Jewish in his philosophy, based as it is on a definable
ethical monotheism. Clearly, Bellow believes in a hierarchic
universe in which man is created in the image of God with
his place a little lower than the angels. The major single
article on this subject.

352. Goldsmith, Arnold L. "A 'Curse on Columbus': Twentieth Century
Jewish-American Fiction and the Theme of Disillusionment."
Studies in American Jewish Literature [University Park, PA]
5.2 (1979): 47-55. Joint issue with *Yiddish* 4.1 (1979).

353. Gollin, Rita K. "Understanding Fathers in American Jewish
Fiction." *Centennial Review* 18.3 (1974): 273-87.

Argues that even a weak Jewish father is capable of passing
on the understanding of compassion and comprehension of
human limits even when he has failed to master his traditional
role as Jewish father. Hence, the Jewish father "remains at
the moral center of Jewish fiction." Discusses Asa Leventhal
in *TV*. Asa must, like many Jewish males, "learn to be a
father unlike his own." Discusses also *H* and *MSP* in terms
of these types of fathers.

354. Gross, Theodore L. "Saul Bellow: The Victim and the Hero."
     The Heroic Ideal in American Literature. Theodore L. Gross.
     New York: Free Press, 1971. 243-61.

> In the context of a chapter entitled "The Quixotic Hero,"
> Gross suggests that unlike Hemingway and Fitzgerald, Bellow
> has involuntarily favored the more conforming or melioristic
> side of the question of idealism or nihilism. In Bellow's
> work the hero has become an Americanized fusion of Dos-
> toevsky's *Underground Man* and Kafka's *Joseph K.*, not so
> much a victim of external authority as of his own weaknesses,
> someone who has forced himself out of that society. Their
> condition is suffering toward love.

355. Grossman, Edward. "The Bitterness of Saul Bellow." *Midstream*
     16.7 (1970): 3-15.

> Comments that all of Bellow's protagonists suffer from more
> than their fair share of temperament. Mr. Sammler suffers
> from the same ailment, and, like others, refuses to throw
> over his illusions about goodness. What follows is a general
> appraisal of the novel focusing on a variety of elements.
> Condemns Bellow for his skepticism and concludes, "If the
> most respected and intelligent novelist of the Establishment
> has only this to say about us, why bother with other more
> profound and disturbing things he has to say about America."

356. Gunn, Drewey Wayne. *American and British Writers in Mexico,
     1556-1973.* Austin: U of Texas P, 1974. 204-08.

357. Guttmann, Allen. "Mr. Bellow's America." *The Jewish Writer in
     America: Assimilation and the Crisis of Identity.* Allen
     Guttmann. New York: Oxford UP, 1971. 178-22.

> Discusses each of the novels under the heading of its own
> title up to *MSP*. Concentrates on the twin ideas of Jewish
> assimilation and the quest for identity in each case, treating
> the protagonists as marginal men, as Jews and as typical
> urban Americans. A major chapter.

358. Guttmann, Allen. "Saul Bellow's Humane Comedy." *Comic Relief:
     Humor in Contemporary American Literature.* Ed. Sarah Blacher

Cohen. Urbana: U of Illinois P, 1978. 127-51.

Argues that Bellow's chief subject is the mind's comical
struggle with ideas. Begins with some brief references to
Bummidge in *LA*. In this major article on Bellow and the
comic artist, Guttmann reviews each of the novels in turn.
In the course of this exhaustive analysis he discusses sources,
influences, and style of humor. He also discusses ideas,
philosophy, characters, and the language of humor itself.
Guttmann's overriding thesis is the essential humanity of the
comic vision in Bellow. Concludes that the comic triumphs
of *HRK*, *H*, and *MSP* have not been equalled in the later
fiction.

359. Hall, James. "Portrait of the Artist as a Self-Creating, Self-
Vindicating, High Energy Man: Saul Bellow." *The Lunatic
Giant in the Drawing Room: The British and American Novel
Since 1930*. James Hall. Bloomington, IN: Indiana UP, 1968.
127-80.

Discusses the characters as "walking syntheses of modernism."
Hall claims they differ from other modern heroes in that they
consider themselves problem-solvers and refuse to remain
passive. Claims that they are high-energy men who contain
within themselves layers and layers of ideal human images
from the last seventy-five years. They are the heirs of
modernism and accidental revolutionaries. Hall is primarily
concerned with mapping the values of the Bellow protagonist
from this perspective.

360. Halperin, Irving. "Saul Bellow and the Moral Imagination."
Jewish Affairs 33.2 (1978): 33-36. Rpt. in *Judaism* 28.1 (1979):
23-30; *New England Review* 1 (1979): 475-88.

Contains an imaginary conversation between Mr. Sammler and
the author. The basic import of this is Halperin's delineation
of the non-Manichean dimensions of Bellow's sophisticated
moral imagination and affirmation of life.

361. Hansen-Love, Friedrich. "Die Peripetien Saul Bellows." *Merkur*
31.1 (1977): 66-76.

362. Harper, Gordon L. "Ideas and the Novel." *Dialogue* 2 (1969):
     54-64.

363. Harper, Howard M., Jr. "Saul Bellow--The Heart's Ultimate
     Need." *Desperate Faith: A Study of Bellow, Salinger, Mailer,
     Baldwin and Updike.* Howard M. Harper, Jr. Chapel Hill, NC:
     U of North Carolina P, 1967. 7-64.

     An early and important general discussion on the issues of
     faith and crisis in the Bellow novel. Outlines most of the
     critical issues that will come to dominate Bellow criticism,
     including those of yearning for order, awareness of entropic
     forces, the city, loss of identity, existential dangling, modern-
     ism, and commitment.

364. Harper, Howard M., Jr. "Trends in Recent American Fiction."
     Contemporary Literature 12.2 (1971): 204-29.

     Discusses a number of trends in post-war American fiction,
     including that of Saul Bellow. A major work in social and
     intellectual trends from modernism to post-modernism. Deals
     only briefly with Bellow's canon.

365. Hassan, Ihab H. "Saul Bellow: Five Faces of a Hero." *Critique*
     3.3 (1960): 28-36.

     Develops the thesis that Bellow's fiction keeps the everlasting
     Yes and the everlasting No in perpetual tension. Discusses
     Bellow's first five heroes from this perspective.

366. Hassan, Ihab H. "Saul Bellow: The Quest and Affirmation of
     Reality." *Radical Innocence: Studies in the Contemporary
     American Novel.* Ihab Hassan. Princeton, NJ: Princeton UP,
     1961. 290-324.

     Acclaims Bellow for being, both in a new and an old-fashioned
     sense, "a sustained fantasist of the real." Discusses the plight
     of the Bellow hero faced with the cosmos he can scarcely
     apprehend, and yet who maintains a powerful sense of life
     that encompasses the cosmic and the quotidian. An erudite and
     classic early essay on the issues of affirmation and the void
     in the Bellow novel.

367. Hassan, Ihab H. "Saul Bellow." *Antioch Review* 40.3 (1982): 266-73.

Praises Bellow for the universality of his work, traces his cultural origins and provides a general assessment of Bellow's thematic directions and overall achievement as a novelist.

368. Hassan, Ihab H. "The Way Down and Out." *Virginia Quarterly Review* 39.1 (1963): 81-93.

Reflects on the spiritual state of American fiction in general and the fiction of Saul Bellow in particular. Primarily laments the distorted images of man as grotesque. Points out the irony of contemporary fiction depicting the way "down" as the way "out" of spiritual malaise.

369. Heiney, Donald. "Bellow as European." *Proceedings of the Comparative Literature Symposium: Modern American Fiction: Insights and Foreign Lights*, Jan. 27-28, 1972. Eds. Wolodymyr T. Zyla and Wendall M. Aycock. Lubbock, TX: Texas Technical University, 1972. 77-88.

Admits the usefulness of seeing Bellow within an American literary context and even within a Jewish context. Asserts, however, that to see him within a European context is to see certain matters that have been overlooked in the previous approaches, namely the pastoral impulse and Rousseauistic traits (notions such as the noble savage, primitivism and innocence).

370. Hoffman, Frederick J. "The Fool of Experience: Saul Bellow's Fiction." *Contemporary American Novelists*. Ed. Harry T. Moore. Crosscurrents/Modern Critiques. Carbondale, IL: Southern Illinois UP, 1964. 80-94.

Talks about the ludicrous and the absurd in the experience of the Bellow hero. Traces this sense of the absurd to the Eastern European shtetl. Also deals with issues of affirmation and denial in the novels.

371. Hollahan, Eugene. "Bellow's Affirmation of Individual Value Via

Classical Plot Structure." *Saul Bellow Journal* 2.1 (1982): 23-31.

This article contains information concerning the frequency of the word "crisis" in the Bellow novel and its ramifications for understanding Bellow's themes. These ideas are treated in a much more lengthy article published in the following year in *Studies in the Novel* (see item 372).

372. Hollahan, Eugene. "'Crisis' in Bellow's Novels: Some Data and a Conjecture." *Studies in the Novel* 15.3 (1983): 249-64.

Provides an erudite etymology of the word "crisis." Then shows how often this word figured in the works of Smollett, Austen, Dickens, George Eliot, and, more recently, in the works of Robert Coover. In Bellow, as in these other writers, the word itself establishes a pattern. It has been a crucial part of his experimentation and development as an affirmative thinker in the novelistic form. Hollahan provides an extended and sophisticated definition of the word, as well as a frequency chart for the number of times the word appears in individual Bellow novels. Shows how Bellow uses the word in increasingly complex ways. Each novel is seen as being marked by a crisis or turning point that functions to elaborate a developmental concept regarding the value of the individual. Bellow's fusion of the great tradition with modern culture seems to center on the problem of crisis-consciousness and individual action. Hence, these crisis-centered plots may represent one of his most generous gifts to his beleaguered fellow men.

373. Hollahan, Eugene. "Design as Defense: Saul Bellow's Classical Plots as Defenses of the Beleaguered Modern Individual." *Design, Pattern, Style: Hallmarks of a Developing American Culture.* Ed. Don Harkness. Tampa, FL: American Studies Press, 1983. 44-45.

374. Hollahan, Eugene. "Editor's Comment." *Studies in the Literary Imagination* 17.2 (1984): 1-5.

Contains a very rational and erudite defense of studying literature from a philosophical perspective. Discusses the synthesis of thought and feeling in Wordsworth and goes on to discuss Bellow's relationship to that tradition. A very useful overview of Bellow's philosophical roots and the articles which follow in this special Bellow issue of *Studies in the Literary Imagination* entitled "Philosophical Dimensions of Saul Bellow's Fiction" (1984).

375. Howe, Irving. "Mass Society and Post-Modern Fiction." *Partisan Review* 26.3 (1959): 420-36. Rpt. in *A World More Attractive.* Irving Howe. New York: Horizon, 1963. 77-97.

Provides a definition of mass society and post-modern society by first outlining the concerns of Dostoevsky and then showing similarities and differences in the work of post-modern writers like Bellow. Modern writers, according to Howe, assumed the existence of values which could be tested in the novel by "dramatizing the relationships between mobile characters and fixed social groups." In the post-modern period mass society has obliterated these distinctions and, hence, presented the writer with a very different set of social assumptions. Deals with Bellow and several other post-modern writers.

376. Hux, Samuel. "Character and Form in Bellow." *Forum* [Houston] 12.1 (1974): 34-38.

Commends Bellow as being a writer truly in charge of his form, despite his apparently anarchic and anti-literary qualities. This expansiveness is one of Bellow's strengths. Goes on to describe formalistically the relationship between the theory of form and Bellow's particular style of characterization.

377. Ichikawa, Masumi. "A Bhuddistic Interpretation of Saul Bellow's Three Novels--*Dangling Man, The Victim* and *Seize the Day.*" *Chu-Shikoku Studies in American Literature* 19 (June 1983): 36-47. Cited in *MLA Bibliography*, 1983.

378. Jacobs, Rita D. "'Truths on the Side of Life': Saul Bellow, Nobel Prize 1976." *World Literature Today* 51 (1977): 194-97.

A generalized brief comment on the affirmations in the Bellow novels which justify his receiving the Nobel Prize. More

conversational than analytical. Contains some biographical
information.

379. James, E. Anthony. "The Hero and the Anti-Hero in Fiction."
     Four Quarters 23 (Autumn 1973): 3-23.

380. Johnson, Gregory Allen. "Spatial Dialogue in Bellow's Fiction."
     Mosaic 16.3 (1983): 117-25.

     Johnson asserts that verbal exchange is not the only means
     of communication in the Bellow novel, and that engagement
     is regulated by the laws of social space. These laws hold
     that a writer's characters are related metonymically--that is,
     by contiguity. The article explores this principle of communi-
     cation through several key scenes and novels. Bellow's
     fiction is distinct in the emphasis he places on spatial
     dialogue. Related to his general concern with man as a
     sign-making being is his awareness that non-verbal exchange
     is frequently a simpler, sounder and truer form of dialogue
     than speech.

381. Josipovici, Gabriel. "Freedom and Wit: The Jewish Writer and
     Modern Art." *European Judaism* 3.1 (1968): 41-50.

     Pursues the relationship between Jewishness, modernism,
     romanticism, and Christianity. Erudite and philosophical in
     orientation. Minimal analysis of individual novels.

382. Josipovici, Gabriel. "Saul Bellow." *The Lessons of Modernism and
     Other Essays*. Gabriel Josipovici. Totowa, NJ: Rowman, 1977.
     64-84. Previously published as the introduction to *Portable
     Saul Bellow*. New York: Viking, 1974. vii-xxiv.

     Provides an overview of all of the novels from the point of
     view of tone and voice. That, says the author, is characterized
     by "utmost formality" and "utmost desperation." Argues that
     each novel is a development of the very first novel, *DM*, and
     that each hero dangles in a slightly different way.

383. Kannan, Lakshmi. "The Confessional Strain in Saul Bellow's

Fiction." *Journal of the Department of English* [Calcutta] 15.1 (1979-80): 86-92.

Commends Bellow for being able to create and sustain the urgency of personal, individual, private voice in each of his protagonists. Briefly traces the history of the confessional mode of literary discourse from St. Augustine forward. Also relates this mode to modern theories of knowledge such as those of F. H. Bradley and William James. Describes its advantages with regard to irony. Proceeds chronologically through each of these novels.

384. Kannan, Lakshmi. "The 'Infected' Area in Saul Bellow's Fiction." *Literary Half-Yearly* 18.2 (1978): 103-19.

Points up the neglect by formalist criticism of the subjective or "infected" area of Bellow's fiction. Proceeds to discuss the advantages of subjectivism to the novelist and critic.

385. Kannan, Lakshmi. "That Small Voice in Bellow's Fiction." *Visvabharati Quarterly* [India] 42 (1977): 191-206.

Discusses Bellow's tendency to uphold the value of the individual against the superstructure of mass society. Discusses subjectivism as the small voice which speaks through the novels.

386. Karl, Frederick R. "Bellow's Comic 'Last Men'." *Thalia* 1.2 (1978): 19-26. Cited in *MLA Bibliography*, 1978.

Describes the Bellow novel as one in which surface (irony, wit and comedy) and subsurface ("endless tunnels of torment and pain in the Kafkaesque mode") are constantly in tension. Discusses the thesis generally and then deals with *H*, *MSP*, and *HG*.

387. Karl, Frederick R. "Picaresque and the American Experience." *Yale Review* 57.2 (1968): 196-212.

Begins with a review of James' influence on the structure of the novel, proceeds to a historical survey of the European picaresque form and then relates both traditions to the

unique circumstances of the American tradition. Demonstrates
how the tradition of the American anti-heroic picaro
develops and briefly deals with the Bellow picaro within this
framework.

388. Kazin, Alfred. "Absurdity as a Contemporary Style." *Mediterra-
     nean* 1.3 (1971): 39-46. Revised version rpt. as "The Absurd
     as a Contemporary Style: Ellison to Pynchon" in *Bright Book
     of Life: American Novelists and Storytellers from Hemingway
     to Mailer.* Ed. Alfred Kazin. Boston: Little, Brown, 1973.
     243-81.

389. Kazin, Alfred. "Bellow's Purgatory." *New York Review of Books*
     28 Mar. 1968: 32-36.

390. Kazin, Alfred. "The Earthly City of the Jews: Bellow to Singer."
     *Bright Book of Life: American Novelists and Storytellers from
     Hemingway to Mailer.* Alfred Kazin. Boston: Little, Brown,
     1973. 125-62.

391. Kazin, Alfred. "Mr. Bellow's Planet." *New Republic* 6 Nov. 1976:
     6-8.

392. Kazin, Alfred. "The World of Saul Bellow." *Contemporaries.*
     Alfred Kazin. Boston: Little, Brown, 1962. 217-23.

     A brief introduction to the Bellow novel.

393. Klein, Jeffrey. "Armies of the Planet: A Comparative Analysis of
     Norman Mailer's and Saul Bellow's Political Visions."
     Soundings: An Interdisciplinary Journal 58.1 (1975): 69-83.

     Believes that both Bellow and Mailer recognized by the late
     1960's that the most serious threat to America was not the
     Vietcong or the counter-culture and Black power movements,
     but the failure of the traditional WASP culture. Analyzes *MS*
     and other novels from this perspective.

394. Klein, Marcus. "A Discipline of Nobility: Saul Bellow's Fiction." *Kenyon Review* 24.2 (1962): 203-26. Rpt. as "Saul Bellow: A Discipline of Nobility." *After Alienation: American Novels in Mid-Century.* Marcus Klein. New York: World, 1964. 33-70; Freeport, NY: Books for Libraries, 1970; Chicago: Chicago UP, 1978.

Sees Bellow's fiction as moving, along with much other fiction of the 1950's and 1960's, from alienation to accommodation. Bellow's work, however, is more imaginative and severe. Each hero must meet "with a strong sense of self, the sacrifice of self demanded by social circumstance." Discusses in detail the demanding world of the protagonists in each of the novels.

395. Klug, M. A. "Saul Bellow: The Hero in the Middle." *Dalhousie Review* 56.3 (1976): 462-78.

From the beginning of his career, "Bellow has consciously tried to avoid what he sees as extremes of the modern American tradition and at the same time to work those extremes as the central conflict within his own work." Locates the Bellow hero squarely between the romantic tradition of triumph and the naturalistic tradition of inevitable defeat.

396. Knopp, Josephine Zadovsky. "Jewish America: Saul Bellow." *The Trial of Judaism in Contemporary Jewish Writing.* Josephine Zadovsky Knopp. Urbana, IL: U of Illinois P, 1975. 126-56.

Argues that the fictional world of Saul Bellow has often been discussed from "the point of view of its relationship to the works of Roth and Malamud," but despite some obvious similarities in their treatment of moral tensions inherent in Jewish life in America, that there are many valid comparisons to be made between the religious Hassidic mysticism of Elie Wiesel and the secular mysticism of Bellow. Discusses Leventhal's victimization, Herzog's roots in the European shtetl, Sammler's newfound God-conscious pieties, Elya's Jewishness, and the importance of Meister Eckhardt to Mr. Sammler. Concludes that Bellow seems to be suggesting that Jewish historical consciousness provides a "potent counter to doctrines of despair."

397. Kondo, Kyoko. "Pursuit of One Theme: Saul Bellow's Early Novels, *Dangling Man, The Victim* and *Seize the Day*." *Sophia English Studies* [Japan] 3 (1978): 86-98. Cited in *MLA Bibliography*, 1981.

398. Kort, Wesley A. "Simplicity and Complexity in Saul Bellow's Fiction." *Moral Fiber: Character and Belief in Recent American Fiction*. Philadelphia: Fortress, 1982. 74-83.

399. Krupnick, Mark. "He Never Learned to Swim." *New Review* 2.22 (1976): 33-39.

   While the bulk of this article concerns the literary career of Philip Rahv and the publication *Modern Occasions*, it also contains an entertaining and accurate account of Bellow's literary criticism which appeared in the journal. Krupnick places Bellow's jeremiad on modern media intellectuals in a very useful historical and cultural framework.

400. Kulshrestha, Chirantan. "The Bellow Gyroscope: Letters to Richard G. Stern." *Saul Bellow Journal* 2.1 (1982): 36-43.

   Bellow's letters to Richard Stern provide a penetrating glimpse of his creative anxieties, his creative problem-solving in writing, and his growing belief in the affirmative power of art. In addition, they record the progress of a warm, self-revealing relationship on Bellow's part. These letters span the crucial period following the publication of *SD* and "bristle with aspirations, uncertainties, and contemplated strategies." Here Bellow tests many of his embryonic theories of the role of the artist, using Stern as sounding board. The letters relating to the period surrounding the writing of *HRK* show his deepening awareness as an artist. They are also frank and full of unselfconscious personal information. In addition, they contain many of Bellow's responses to Stern's own novels.

401. Kulshrestha, Chirantan. "The Making of Saul Bellow's Fiction: Notes from the Underground." *American Studies International* 19.2 (1981): 48-56.

A brief article reporting Kulshrestha's findings in the Bellow files at the Department of Special Collections at the University of Chicago's Joseph Regenstein Library.

402. Kumar, P. Shiv. "From Kavanah to Mitzvah: A Perspective on *Herzog* and *Mr. Sammler's Planet.*" *Indian Journal of American Studies* 10.2 (1980): 30-39.

Herzog lives by a code he calls his "law of the heart," whereas Mr. Sammler lives in search of the higher terms of his contracts. *H* is the last of a line of novels searching for the basic law, while *MSP* is the beginning of a new kind of search for "higher activity."

403. Kumar, P. Shiv. "Saul Bellow and the Hebraic Prophetic Tradition." *Journal of English Studies* [India] 11.2 (1980): 756-65.

Rather loosely defines the Hebraic prophetic tradition in terms of prophecy, emphasis on moral perfectability of man, rejection of ritual, primacy of morality over cultic practices of popular religion, indifference toward theological speculation, the achievement of oneness and of belonging to the humanity of his existence, and the coming Messianic age. Proceeds to discuss Bellow's views on the relation of art and artist in society to this Hebraic sense of life. Discusses also Bellow's optimism, his belief in the universe as planned and ordered, and his belief in humankind as indicative of the influence of the Hebraic prophetic tradition.

404. Kyria, Pierre. "Le Monde Americain." *Revue de Paris* Mar. 1967: 120-25.

405. Labarthe, Elyette. "L'Apocalypse selon Saul Bellow." *Le Facteur religieux en Amerique du nord.* Ed. Jean Beranger. Bordeaux: Maison des Sciences de l'Homme d'Aquitaine, Univ. de Bordeaux III, 1981. No. 2, *Apocalypse et autres travaux*: 121-42.

406. Labarthe, Elyette. "Le Facteur religieux chez un ecrivain juif contemporain: Saul Bellow." *Le Facteur religieux en Amerique*

du nord. Ed. Jean Beranger. Talence: Centre d'Etudes
Canadiennes en Sciences Sociales, Univ. de Bordeaux III,
1981. Vol. 2, *Les Etats-Unis:* 33-57.

407. Leaf, Mark. "The Novels of Saul Bellow." *Kolokon* 2 (Spring
1967): 13-23. Cited in *British Humanities Index,* 1967.

Provides a general overview of theme, form and style in the
Bellow novel from the perspective of the English critic.

408. Lehan, Richard. "Existentialism in Recent American Fiction:
The Demonic Quest." *Texas Studies in Literature and Languag*
1 (1959): 181-202.

After a somewhat generalized discussion of the mutual
influence of the French and American modern novel, the
discussion turns to the critical problem of the influence of
French existentialism on Bellow's early novels. A fairly
general treatment.

409. Lehan, Richard. "Into the Ruins: Saul Bellow and Walker Percy."
*A Dangerous Crossing: French Literary Existentialism and the
Modern American Novel.* Richard Lehan. Carbondale, IL:
Southern Illinois UP, 1973. 107-45.

Concentrates on the dialectic between the romantic impulse
and the modern apocalypse. Discusses the plight of the Bello
protagonist in terms of his French and European counterpar
Locates Bellow squarely within the traditions of French
literary existentialism. A major essay.

410. Lemaster, J. R. "Saul Bellow: On Looking for a Way through the
Cracks." *American Bypaths: Essays in Honor of E. Hudson
Long.* Eds. Robert G. Collmer and Jack W. Herring. Waco, TX
Markham Press Fund of Baylor UP, 1980. 109-44.

Suggests that Nathan A. Scott is right in seeing Bellow as a
radically religious novelist concerned about the importance
covenants made with a God who has long since died. Examir
the endings of the novels to see how Bellow works out the
death and contract questions. Sees evidence of Zen and San-
skrit ideas, as well as notions from Plotinus and Philo.

Concludes that Bellow's novels are interesting because of their theoretical, religious and theological concerns, not just for their social realism.

411. Levenson, J. C. "Bellow's Dangling Men." *Critique* 3.3 (1960): 3-14. Rpt. in *Saul Bellow and the Critics.* Ed. Irving Malin. New York: New York UP, 1967. 39-50.

Discusses the phenomenon of the sociologically marginal or "dangling man" in American literature from James Fenimore Cooper forward. Sees these earlier prototypes invigorating Bellow's characters with their energy and exuberance, plus their determination to wrest from the American experience their freedom. Traces also the Russian influences on the shapes of these Bellow heroes, as well as the Jewish influences. Deals with each of the novels up to *HRK.*

412. Lombardo, Agostino. "La narrativa di Saul Bellow." [Saul Bellow's Fiction]." *Studi Americani* 11 (1965): 309-44. Cited in *MLA Bibliography,* 1967.

The Bellow novel is a means to face life and the crowds. Writing is having faith in both art and man. Bellow portrays the modern city and the stress city life brings to men. Describes Joseph's attempt in *DM* to become free. Compares Bellow with other contemporary authors, including Singer. Shows how every character portrait adds to the setting and discusses Bellow's Jewish element, the search for language: daily, popular language, jargon, with Yiddish terms. Discusses how in the Bellow novel history initiates man to life. Sees the main characters as instruments to represent society.

413. Lombardo, Agostino. *Realismo e Simbolismo: Saggi di letteratura americana contemporanea.* Biblioteca di Studi Americani 3. Rome: Edizioni di Storia e Letteratura, 1957.

414. Lutwack, Leonard. "Bellow's Odysseys." *Heroic Fiction: The Epic Tradition and American Novels of the Twentieth Century.* Leonard Lutwack. Carbondale, IL: Southern Illinois UP, 1971. 88-121.

Discusses the journey metaphor and the use of the myth of

Odysseus in the Bellow novel. Provides a detailed exegesis of
Herzog as Odyssean wanderer. Comments at length on the
mock epic elements in the novels and other attributes of
heroic literature. Concludes the discussion with an analysis
of *MSP.*

415. Lycette, Ronald L. "Saul Bellow and the American Naturalists."
Discourse 13.4 (1970): 435-49.

Argues that because Bellow is a social novelist "He occupies
a place in an American tradition of naturalism that extends,
by some arguments, as far back as Melville." Yet, Lycette sees
Bellow as representing "an evolution beyond naturalism becau
his characters refuse to accept defeat." Compares Bellow with
naturalists who precede him, and who are contemporaneous
with him. Emphasizes Bellow's stress on the melting pot, the
deterministic necessities of it, and on his appraisal of what
it means "to be less than human." Concludes with the
observation that the element of optimism makes Bellow
different from other naturalists.

416. Lyons, Bonnie. "Bellowmalamudroth and the American Jewish
Genre--Alive and Well." *Studies in American Jewish Literature*
[University Park, PA] 5.2 (1979): 8-10. Joint issue with *Yiddis.*
4.1 (1979).

Examines whether or not there was ever a recognizable schoc
of Jewish-American fiction and whether such a genre can be
seen coming to an end. Concludes that American-Jewish ficti
is surviving largely because of the postwar writers, including
Bellow.

417. Lyons, Bonnie. "From *Dangling Man* to 'Colonies of the Spirit.'"
Studies in American Jewish Literature [University Park, PA]
4.2 (1978): 45-50. Joint issue with *Yiddish* 3.3 (1978).

Attempts a reconsideration of Bellow's novels through an
examination of *DM.* Although this is Bellow's first novel, it
nevertheless exhibits his "inherited intellectual and emotiona
starting point" and his "dialectical roots." Such beginnings
include: the divided self, existential freedom, Dostoevskian
alienation, accommodation, contemporary conditions, childho

remembrances of poverty, and assertions of the basic
goodness of life.

418. Malin, Irving. "Saul Bellow." *London Magazine* Jan. 1965: 43-54.

Provides a general introduction for the British reader of
Bellow's first six novels under the headings: 1) Madness versus
Sanity and 2) Prophecy versus Preaching.

419. Malin, Irving. "Seven Images." *Saul Bellow and the Critics*. Ed.
Irving Malin. New York: New York UP, 1967. 142-76.

Argues that Bellow most effectively conveys his metaphysics
through patterns of images which recur throughout the novels.
Traces these image patterns carefully through all the novels
to date and relates them to the ideas they are meant to
underscore. This is a major key to the understanding of any
Bellow novel and the most thorough of all the studies of
Bellow imagery. The seven images are not only documented
and related to theme, but are seen interlocking and rein-
forcing each other to produce the effect of unity and
intensified meaning in the novels.

420. Mandra, Mihail. "Saul Bellow's Novel in the Context of European
Thought: A Greek World." *Synthesis* 7 (1980): 191-205.

Bellow succeeds in working out a special kind of novel Mandra
calls "anthropologie." Bellow strikes a paradoxical note in the
whole history of American fiction because of this European
grounding. His novels belong to the state subsequent to the
great classics, coming as they do after the 1940's. The focus
is on ideas. "He is closer to the classical traditions of the
American and European novel because he rejects the
socio-philosophical theories and the American psychosis
dominated by cycnical holocaust theories. He works in the
same ardently humanistic plane, vigorously combining Benjamin
Franklin's moral balance with Hemingway's virile sense of
life." An erudite study of Bellow's relation to Western
intellectual and literary history.

421. Manske, Eva. "Das Menschenbild im Prosaschaffen Saul Bellows
Anspruch und Wirklichkeit." *Zeitschrift fur Anglistik und*

Amerikanistik [East Berlin] 21 (1973): 270-88, 360-83. Cited in *MLA Bibliography*, 1973.

422. Marcus, Steven. "Reading the Illegible: Some Modern Represen-
     tations of Urban Experience." *Visions of the Modern City:
     Essays in History, Art and Literature.* Eds. William Sharpe and
     Leonard Wallock. Proceedings of the Heyman Center for the
     Humanities. New York: Columbia U Heyman Center for the
     Humanities, 1983. 228-43. Rpt. in *Southern Review* [Baton
     Rouge] 22.3 (1986): 443-64. Cited in *MLA Bibliography*, 1983;
     Arts and Humanities Citation Index, May-Aug. 1986.

423. Mariani, Gigliola Sacerdoti. "Saul Bellow tra politica e lettera-
     tura" [Saul Bellow between Politics and Literature]. *Nuova
     Antologia* [Rome] 532 (1977): 281-89.

     Describes the importance of the scholars' political and social
     obligation and the Jews' precarious state in history. Bellow
     describes the brevity of human life and social commitment. F
     records faithfully the voices of his times and Mid-East
     problems which have been centered on Jerusalem since the
     beginning of its history.

424. Markus, Manfred. "Bellow's Vermachtnis: Zur Rezeption eines
     Nobelpreistragers in der Bundesrepublik Deutschland."
     Zeitschrift fur Kulturaustausch 28 (1978): 101-09.

425. Mathy, Francis. "Zetsubo no kanata ni." *Sophia* [Tokyo] 19
     (1970): 356-77. Cited in *MLA Bibliography*, 1971.

426. Maw, Joe. "Method in his Madness: Bellow Develops the Theme
     of Insanity." *Saul Bellow Journal* 3.2 (1984): 1-12.

     Discusses the references to madness made by numerous Bello
     protagonists. Focuses on the chronological progression of the
     commentary and on Bellow's answers to the questions sur-
     rounding why contemporary craziness exists and what can b
     done about it.

427. May, Keith M. *Out of the Maelstrom: Psychology and the Novel in the Twentieth Century.* London: Paul Elek, 1977. 94-97.

> Provides a brief treatment of Bellow's existentialism, the issue of freedom, and the treatment of the phenomenal world in Bellow novels.

428. McConnell, Frank D. "Saul Bellow and the Terms of our Contract." *Four Postwar American Novelists: Bellow, Mailer, Barth, and Pynchon.* Frank McConnell. Chicago: U of Chicago P, 1977. 1-57. Rpt. in *Saul Bellow.* Ed. Harold Bloom. Modern Critical Views. New York: Chelsea, 1986. 101-14.

> Attempts to place Bellow historically within a confusing postwar world where both realism and experimentalism have determined literary reputations. Bellow has benefited from the one fashion and suffered because of the other. Also discusses the central issues surrounding Jewish novelists and novels with reference to Bellow's historical position. Finally locates Bellow as an ideological novelist. A major article.

429. McCormick, John. "Historical Event in the Prose Fiction of Henry de Montherlant and Saul Bellow." *Eigo Seinen* 125.3 (1979): 118-21.

> Sees Bellow and de Montherlant as "ordering history in ways that are purely individual, yet in ways that reflect an awareness of history that must be distinguished from apprehensions of the past, of the great writers of the nineteenth-century and many writers of the twentieth-century who remain close to the nineteenth-century tradition."

430. McDowell, Edwin. "About Books and Authors." *New York Times Book Reviews* 21 Feb. 1982: 38.

431. McSweeney, Kerry. "Saul Bellow and the Life to Come." *Critical Quarterly* 18.1 (1976): 67-72.

> Sees in Bellow's novels the same kind of belief in the immortality of souls and the spirits of the dead seen in Yeats' "A Vision" and Wordsworth's "Ode: Intimations of Immortality." Provides a brief treatment of the theme.

432. Melani, Sandro. "Bellow in corso." [Bellow in Progress]." *Ponte*
     [Florence] 33 (1977): 979-82.

433. Mendelson, M. O. "Social Criticism in the Works of Bellow,
     Updike, and Cheever." *Soviet Criticism of American Literature
     in the Sixties: An Anthology.* Ed. and trans. Carl R. Proffer.
     Ann Arbor, MI: Ardis, 1972. 63-70. Part of a longer article
     published in *Problems of Twentieth-Century American
     Literature.* Moscow, 1970.

434. Mesher, David R. "Saul Bellow: Confessions of a Jewish Odium
     Eater." *Delta* 19 (Oct. 1984): 67-91.

     This article ranges across a variety of topics including
     whether or not there is such a thing as Jewish-American
     literature, Bellow's treatment of Blacks, stereotypes of
     various kinds, Bellow's revision of romanticism, women
     characters, his studied indifference to Jewish issues and his
     deliberate attempts to distance himself from ethnic stereo-
     typing.

435. Moro, Kochi. "Monolog and Dialog: The Distance Between J.
     Joyce and S. Bellow." *Josai Jinbun Kenkyu. Studies in the
     Humanities.* Sakado, Iruma-Gun, Saitama, Japan: Josai
     University Keizai-Gaku-Kai, 1973. Cited in *MLA Bibliography*
     1973.

436. Morrow, Patrick. "Threat and Accommodation: The Novels of
     Saul Bellow." *Midwest Quarterly* 8.4 (1967): 389-411.

     Places Bellow within a context of both pessimistic writers
     and optimistic writers, and identifies him as breaking the
     Hemingway death code, the cult of the neurotic and the
     black humor of the ironists. Depicts Bellow heroes as
     finding accommodation more "valuable than rebellion."
     Provides a useful overview of the canon to this point.

437. Mudrick, Marvin. "Malamud, Bellow, and Roth." *On Culture and
     Literature.* Marvin Mudrick. New York: Horizon, 1970.
     200-33.

Considers Bellow and Malamud Jewish provincials who are
unable to meet the standards Faulkner has set, and who
create the fictional American Jew when the subject of the
literary Jew in American literature was already slipping out
of sight. Primarily concerned with the Jewishness of the
novels.

438. Mukerji, Nirmal. "The Bellow Hero." *Indian Journal of English
Studies* 9 (1968): 74-86.

439. Mukerji, Nirmal. "Bellow's Measure of Man." *Indian Studies in
American Fiction.* Dharwar, India: Karnatak University; Delhi:
Macmillan India, 1974. 286-95.

Argues that at the center of Bellow's world lies a desperate
search for the answer to the question of what it means to be
truly human. Examines this in *AM*, *TV*, and *H*. Sees freedom
of choice to be Bellow's answer to the question.

440. Narasaki, Hiroshi. "Saul Bellow and the Early 1940's: A Critical
Heritage." *American Literature in the 1950's: Annual Report
1976.* Tokyo: Tokyo Chapter of the American Literature
Society of Japan, 1977. 41-49.

Outlines the prevailing modes of fiction of the decade, then
discusses Bellow in relation to them. Concentrates mostly on
the metaphor of dangling.

441. Nevius, Blake. "Saul Bellow and the Theater of the Soul."
Neuphilologische Mitteilungen [Helsinki] 73 (1972): 248-60.
Cited in *MLA Bibliography*, 1972.

442. Newman, Judie. "Bellow's Sixth Sense: The Sense of History."
Canadian Review of American Studies 13.1 (1982): 39-51.

Identifies Bellow's historical sense as a kind of Nietzschean
sixth sense "pervading the philosophy, history and culture of
the modern era." Discusses how at the International Symposium on Saul Bellow, Malcolm Bradbury alone set aside the
"transcendental" sense discussed by most other participants
and argued that "Bellow's novels encounter chaos and contingency of the historical world remaining within the historical

and experiential continuum." Newman argues that Bellow's work "presents an increasingly overt tension between the timeless and the time-bound, with a consequent modification of his forms from the spatially ordered forms of *DM* and *TV* to 'loose baggy monsters' which express the contingency of the historical process." Newman starts with "The Mexican General" and moves forward chronologically in illustrating her thesis.

443. Nilsen, Helge Normann. "Bellow and Transcendentalism: From *The Victim* to *Herzog*." *Dutch Quarterly Review of Anglo-American Letters* 14.2 (1984): 125-39.

Traces elements of transcendentalism throughout all the novels up to and including *H*. Comments at length on the use of the language of transcendentalism and mysticism, in addition to overt reference to existentialist thinkers and tenets.

444. Nilsen, Helge Normann. "Helt eller klovn? Omkring noen uloste konflikter i Saul Bellows forfatterskap" [Hero or Clown? On Certain Unresolved Conflicts in Saul Bellow's Work]. *Edda* (1980): 93-102. Cited in *MLA Bibliography*, 1980.

445. Nilsen, Helge Normann. "Saul Bellow and Wilhelm Reich." *American Studies in Scandinavia* 10 (1978): 81-91.

This article attempts to show Bellow's complex attitude toward Reichianism in *SD* and *HRK*. Rather than espousing the philosophy wholeheartedly, as previous critics have suggested (Nilsen's view), Nilsen claims that Bellow treats Reichian idea ironically, comically and ambivalently.

446. Nilsen, Helge Normann. "Trends in Jewish-American Prose: A Short Historical Survey." *English Studies* 64.6 (1983): 507-17.

447. Noble, David W. "The Present: Norman Mailer, James Baldwin, Saul Bellow." *The Eternal Adam and the New World Garden: The Central Myth in the American Novel Since 1830*. David W. Noble. New York: Grosset, 1968. 195-223.

448. Normand, J. "L'Homme Mystifie: Les Heros de Bellow, Albee, Styron et Mailer." *Etudes Anglaises* 22.4 (1969): 370-85.

449. Oates, Joyce Carol. "Imaginary Cities: America." *Literature and the Urban Experience: Essays on the City and Literature*. Eds. Michael C. Jaye and Ann Chalmers Watts. New Brunswick, NJ: Rutgers UP, 1981. 11-33.

    Claims that for Bellow the city is depicted as "an archetype of amoral dynamism." It is also a place of congestion and drama. Oates argues that the cityscapes in *AM* are to be compared only with Joyce's Dublin cityscapes. Goes on to discuss a variety of novels and stories from this perspective. Concludes that the Bellow hero is always able to transcend the limitations imposed on him by the city.

450. O'Connell, Shaun. "Bellow: Logic's Limits." *Massachusetts Review* 10 (Winter 1969): 182-87.

    Briefly discusses the issue of Bellow's "obsession" with "knowing" and the limits of mere logic. Sees Bellow dramatizing the theme of logic's limits in a series of "beautiful stories portraying people who think themselves in the damndest fixes, neither able to control life with their ideas nor protect themselves from life with their rationalizations."

451. Opdahl, Keith M. "The Discussion: Refining the Issues." *Studies in American Jewish Literature* [University Park, PA] 5.2 (1979): 15. Joint issue with *Yiddish* 4.1 (1979).

452. Opdahl, Keith M. "God's Braille: Concrete Detail in Saul Bellow's Fiction." *Studies in American Jewish Literature* [University Park, PA] 4.2 (1978): 60-71. Joint issue with *Yiddish* 3.3 (1978).

    Opdahl praises Bellow's style for its remarkable concrete detail which adds meaning and signification to the realism of the text. He describes the style at its best as simple, direct, lacking ornamentation, transparent and supple. The article goes on to describe the process by which Opdahl believes Bellow has achieved this technique.

453. Opdahl, Keith M. "The Mental Comedies of Saul Bellow." *From Hester Street to Hollywood: The Jewish-American Stage and Screen.* Ed. Sarah Blacher Cohen. Bloomington, IN: Indiana UP, 1983. 183-96.

This is probably the definitive article thus far on Bellow as playwright. Describes thoroughly the Jewish influence in the Bellow plays.

454. Opdahl, Keith M. "Saul Bellow and the Function of Representational Feeling." *Delta* 19 (Oct. 1984): 31-45.

Praises Bellow for achieving a rare vitality of style and for taking mimesis a layer or two deeper than it has gone before. This he achieves by fitting the sequence and content of his words to the process of the imagination. The article goes on to describe what the process is and how feeling is not conveyed as a mind-movie but much more subtly. Opdahl attempts to explain precisely how Bellow does this through style, thus arriving at an effect he calls "representational feeling."

455. Opdahl, Keith M. "Stillness in the Midst of Chaos: Plot in the Novels of Saul Bellow." *Modern Fiction Studies* 25.1 (1979): 15-28.

Bellow flirts with loose, episodic plots in order to be interesting. But Bellow is, in fact, absorbed with plot. His plots maintain a rational order, as do those of the nineteenth-century realists. Analyzes what obstacles to plot-making Bellow must overcome. Describes what elements of style, theme or vision cause him difficulty and why.

456. Opdahl, Keith M. "Strange Things, Savage Things: Saul Bellow's Hidden Theme." *Iowa Review* 10.4 (1979): 1-15.

"Sex [and sensuality] is everywhere and permeates Bellow's imaginative world with an overwhelming presence and yet is seldom remarked by the protagonist." Sees the characters as victims of the forces that lie behind sexuality, "so that the anger of their women is nothing compared to the threat that lies just beyond the vision--the threat of an immense and angry force to which sexuality belongs." Gives the canon a structuralist reading from this perspective. Broadens out into a discussion of how the sensual is what bridges the gap in Bellow fiction between social and metaphysical awareness.

457. Opdahl, Keith M. "True Impressions: Saul Bellow's Realistic Style." *Saul Bellow and His Work.* Ed. Edmond Schraepen. Brussels: Centrum voor Taal-en Literatuurwetenschap, Vrije Universiteit Brussel, 1978. 61-71. Proceedings of a symposium held at the Free University of Brussels (V.U.B.), 10-11 Dec. 1977.

Gives a formalistic explication of Bellow's use of concrete detail and several other aspects of style.

458. Oppel, Horst. *Die Suche nach Gott in der Amerikanischen Literatur der Gegenwart [The Search for God in Modern American Literature].* Abhandlung der Geistes und Sozial-wissenschaftlichen Klasse, 1972, 8. Mainz: Akademie der Wissenschaften und der Literatur; Weisbaden: In Kommission bei. F. Steiner, 1972. Cited in *Year's Works in English Studies,* 1972.

459. Pal, K. S. "Saul Bellow: Motion Stillness." *The Literary Endeavor: A Quarterly Journal Devoted to English Studies* 4.1-2 (1982): 58-63. Cited in *MLA Bibliography,* 1983.

This paper deals with the motifs and themes of motion and stillness in the Bellow canon. Describes some characters as embracing one quality, other characters its opposite and Mr. Sammler as being a mystical still point of resolution between the two opposing principles. Motion is posited against still-ness as a fictional strategy also. Though as an artist Bellow maintains a consistent tension between stillness and motion, "focus remains on the ideal of stillness which signifies a way of life dependent upon peace, joy and solitude."

460. Pavilioniene, Ausrine. "Herojaus auka ankstyvojoje Solo Belou kuryboje." *Literatura* 24.3 (1982): 20-30. Cited in *MLA Bibliography,* 1982.

461. Pearce, Richard. "The Ambigious Assault of Henderson and Herzog." *Saul Bellow: A Collection of Critical Essays.* Ed.

Earl Rovit. Twentieth Century Views. Englewood Cliffs, NJ:
Prentice, 1975. 72-80.

Henderson's aggressive response to the world, like Ahab's, is
an assault on reality. But it is an ambigious assault, for,
unlike Ahab's, it contains an element of tenderness as well
as a Whitmanesque embrace. Sees Henderson as a physical
giant and Herzog as a mental giant. Through letters Herzog
assaults reality, as Henderson seized the wooden goddess.
Both attempts, however, are deeply fraught with ambiguity.
Concludes that while H leaves a feeling of inertia and
entropy, HRK leaves a feeling that change has occurred.

462. Pearce, Richard. "The Walker: Modern American Hero." *Massa-
      chussets Review* 5 (1964): 761-64.

463. Petillon, Pierre-Yves. "De La 'Culture' en Amerique." *Critique*
      [Paris] 33 (1977): 27-46.

464. Petillon, Pierre-Yves. "Les Derniers Jours: Signaux de vie."
      Critique [Paris] 38. (1982): 983-98.

465. Petillon, Pierre-Yves. *La Grand route: Espace et ecriture en
      Amerique.* Fiction & Cie. Paris: Seuil, 1979. 60-65, 76-82,
      114-18, 126-33.

466. Pinsker, Sanford. "Meditations Interruptus: Saul Bellow's
      Ambivalent Novel of Ideas." *Studies in American Jewish
      Literature* [University Park, PA] 4.2 (1978): 22-32. Joint issue
      with *Yiddish* 3.3 (1978).

The alternations in Bellow's early works between "claustrophobic intensity and imaginative space, between exercises
in moral seriousness and wildly comic celebrations" actually
form a synthesis in Bellow's later work. In these later works
"Saul Bellow cannot avoid imparting his own considerable
intelligence to the novels he writes, but neither can he avoid
adding those strains which make him our richest chronicler
of modern life's continuing comedy."

467. Pinsker, Sanford. "The Psychological Schlemiel of Saul Bellow." *The Schlemiel as Metaphor: Studies in the Yiddish and American Jewish Novel.* Crosscurrents/Modern Critiques. Carbondale, IL: Southern Illinois UP; London: Feffer, 1971. 125-57.

Provides a definition of the archetypal *schlemiel* and proceeds to describe its psychological dimensions within the Bellow novel.

468. Pinsker, Sanford. "Saul Bellow and the Special Comedy of Urban Life." *Ontario Review* 8 (1978): 82-94. Cited in *MLA Bibliography*, 1978.

Discusses Bellow as "the most articulate geographer of the urban condition, charting its assets and liabilities against the cunning that is history and those continuing needs which comprise the human spirit." Attempts to account for Bellow's attachment to and fictional use of Chicago as home and fictional metaphor.

469. Pinsker, Sanford. "Saul Bellow Going Everywhere: History, American Letters and the Transcendental Itch." *Saul Bellow Journal* 3.2 (1984): 47-52.

Explores briefly the mystical tendencies of the Bellow hero, tendencies which take him "deeper than his affinities with the Chicago Naturalists in particular, and American Realists in general." Bellow heroes inevitably plumb deeper than real facts and encounter realms of mystical experience.

470. Pinsker, Sanford. "Saul Bellow, Soren Kierkegaard and the Question of Boredom." *Centennial Review* 24.1 (1980): 118-25.

Argues convincingly that Charlie Citrine's thesis and Bellow's throughout the novels is Kierkegaard's theory on the relationship between existential boredom and universal psychic pain. The Kierkegaaridan influence on Bellow results in his way of "simultaneously indulging in an orgy of ideas and maintaining a necessary, ironic balance, of inviting serious critical attention and keeping a firm grip of the critic's leg." Both Bellow and Kierkegaard make extremely witty remarks about

the subject of boredom. Traces several other parallels
between the two writers.

471. Pinsker, Sanford. "The *'Schlemiel'* in Yiddish and American
   Literature." *Chicago Jewish Forum* 25.3 (1967): 191-95.

472. Pinsker, Sanford. "Sustaining Community of 'Reality Instructors':
   The City in Saul Bellow's Later Fiction." *Studies in American
   Jewish Literature* 3.1 (1977): 25-30.

   Cites Bellow as America's most articulate "geographer of the
   urban landscape, charting its assets and liabilities against
   the cunning that is history and those continuing needs which
   comprise the human spirit." It is the ever-present city that
   creates the demand for explanations in the Bellow thinker,
   and it is the city which provides the ever-present community
   of "reality instructors."

473. Podhoretz, Norman. "The Adventures of Saul Bellow." *Doings
   and Undoings: The Fifties and After in American Writing.*
   Norman Podhoretz. New York: Farrar, 1964. 205-27.

   Calls Bellow the greatest virtuoso of language since Joyce.
   However, insists that Bellow's fame derives from what he
   had to say about the exhausted traditions of the *avant-
   garde* movement which preceded him. The discussion proceeds
   discursively and hits upon many of the oft-repeated critical
   commonplaces.

474. Porter, M. Gilbert. "Hitch Your Agony to a Star: Bellow's
   Transcendental Vision." *Saul Bellow and His Work.* Ed. Edmond
   Schraepen. Brussels: Centrum voor Taal-en Literatuurweten-
   schap, Vrije Universiteit Brussel, 1978. 73-88. Proceedings of
   a symposium held at the Free University of Brussels
   (V.U.B.), 10-11 Dec. 1977.

   Acknowledges Bellow's debt to Platonic and German idealism,
   the classical epic, Hassidic wisdom literature, Freudian
   psychology, Russian realism, Yiddish humor and English
   romanticism. Then he proceeds to discuss Bellow's major
   debt to the American transcendentalists under such headings
   as guilt, nature, democracy, death, immortality, and art.

475. Porter, M. Gilbert. "Is the Going Up Worth the Coming Down?
     Transcendental Dualism in Saul Bellow's Fiction." *Studies in
     the Literary Imagination* 17.2 (1984): 19-37.

   Sees Bellow's novels as representing a paradigm of long-
   standing tensions in American literature between pessimism
   and optimism, determinism and self-determination, victimization and possibility. All of Bellow's thinkers suffer from
   ontological dualities. Such ambivalence represents not only
   the dualism of Bellow's American literary ancestors, but also
   "the comic and tragic masks of human experience."

476. Possler, Katherine E. "The Significance of Structure in *Dangling
     Man* and *Humboldt's Gift*." *Studies in American Jewish
     Literature* 3.1 (1977): 20-24.

   Draws comparisons between the two works in terms of
   seasonal structure, diary form, use of traditional Jewish
   holidays, common themes, and similarities in plot and
   character.

477. Prabhakar, T., and P. Palanivel. "In Defense of Humanity: Saul
     Bellow's Novels." *Journal of English Studies* [India] 12.1 (1980):
     820-27.

   Discusses the canon generally pointing up Bellow's romantic
   and optimistic tendencies, along with his attack on modernist
   nihilism. Examines the novels from a traditional humanistic
   perspective.

478. Pritchett, V. S. "Saul Bellow: Jumbos." *The Tale Bearers: Essays
     on English, American, and Other Writers.* V. S. Pritchett.
     London: Chatto, 1980. 146-55.

   Discusses Bellow's power to draw intellectual response but
   complains that he disperses himself too much in the larger
   works. Prefers Bellow's short fiction. Comments on the
   perpetual sense of comedy in the novels and the outsized
   heroes. Concludes with commentary on Bellow's inability to
   "talk" a character into life through dialogue.

479. Radeljkovic, Zvonimir. "Bellow's Search for Meaning." *Yugoslav Perspectives on American Literatue: An Anthology.* Ed. James L. Thorson. Trans. Pavlinka Georgiev. Ann Arbor, MI: Ardis, 1980. 181-84.

      A general survey of Bellow's fiction and themes. Identifies Bellow as spurning discussion of social defeats and victories and as concentrating instead on human individuality in relation to society.

480. Rans, Geoffrey. "The Novels of Saul Bellow." *Review of English Literature* 4.4 (1963): 18-30.

      A generalized, chronological reading of the novels through to *HRK.*

481. Raymer, John. "A Changing Sense of Chicago in the Works of Saul Bellow and Nelson Algren." *Old Northwest* 4.4 (1978): 371-83.

482. Rodrigues, Eusebio L. "Beyond All Philosophies." *Studies in the Literary Imagination* 17.2 (1984): 97-110.

      The Bellow hero inevitably reaches beyond all the formulations of Western philosophy for a dynamic vision of love and brotherhood, characterized by the search for psychic unity and a "truly human condition." Passing beyond the formulations of other thinkers, the Bellow protagonist finally accepts the mystery of life.

483. Rosenberg, Ruth. "Contemporising Kabbalah: Saul Bellow Confirms Cosmic Connection." *Journal of Reform Judaism* 27 (Spring 1980): 40-54.

      Bellow celebrates his medievalism and provides a renewed Kabbalistic mythological world view in order to restore to the Jew a sense of the transcendent sacredness of life. Examines the concept of *Ibbur* (impregnation of another soul into a man) developed in the thirteenth century, and the related concept of restitution. Examines *HG* as establishing the conditions for the initiation and termination of *Ibbur.* Discusses also concepts such as the counterpart soul and the inner voice, and the phenomenon of the *Maggid* or itinerant preacher who, impregnated with the voice of an angel, can speak inspired utterances. Many of these medieval Jewish mystical concepts are applied to *HG* and more particularly, to Charlie Citrine.

484. Rosenfeld, Alvin H. "Saul Bellow, On the Soul." *Midstream* 23.10 (1977): 47-59.

Discusses the broad issue of truth and the matters of the religious sensibility within the Bellow canon. Bellow disguises them beneath a "spoofing humor" and pursues them more vigorously with each new novel. A general essay rather than an in-depth analysis.

485. Ross, Theodore J. "Notes on Saul Bellow." *Chicago Jewish Forum* 18 (1959): 21-27. Cited in *MLA Bibliography*, 1959.

Accuses Bellow of attempting to Christianize the Jewish experience in his novels for the sake of transmuting that unique context into "something vaguely acceptable to everybody under the sun."

486. Rossani, Wolfgang. "Il Nobel a Bellow" [The Nobel Prize to Saul Bellow]." *Osservatore Politico Letterario* 22.11 (1976): 85-88.

487. Roston, Murray. "The Flight of Jonah: A Study of Roth, Bellow and Malamud." *Asian Response to American Literature.* Ed. C. D. Narasimhaiah. New York: Barnes, 1972. 304-12.

Talks generally about the Israeli student of literature looking with interest at American literature dealing with Jewish alienation and assimilation. Discusses Herzog and several other Bellow protagonists from this perspective.

488. Roth, Henry. "Segments." *Studies in American Jewish Literature* [University Park, PA] 5.1 (1979): 58-62.

489. Roth, Philip. "Imagining Jews." *New York Review of Books* 3
     Oct. 1974: 22-28. Rpt. in *Reading Myself and Others.* Ed.
     Philip Roth. New York: Farrar, 1975. 215-46.

490. Rothermel, Wolfgang P. "Saul Bellow." *Amerikanische Literatur
     der Gegenwart.* Ed. Martin Christadler. Stuttgart: Kroner, 1973.
     69-104.

     The first Bellow survey in German, intended as an introduc-
     tion to a general readership. Working simultaneously on two
     levels, the chronological and systematic, Rothermel illustrates
     the development, refinement and variations of Bellow's themes,
     specifying as more prominent Bellow's commitment to the
     intellectual in an anti-intellectual (urban) world and his
     position among modern Jewish-American writers. This essay
     also touches upon the largely autobiographical nature of
     Bellow's novels, and comments on the seeming discrepancies
     between his fictional and non-fictional writings, but refrains
     from trying to explain these.

491. Rovit, Earl. "Jewish Humor and American Life." *American
     Scholar* 36.2 (1967): 237-45.

492. Rovit, Earl. "Saul Bellow and Norman Mailer: The Secret
     Sharers." *Saul Bellow: A Collection of Critical Essays.* Ed.
     Earl Rovit. Twentieth Century Views. Englewood Cliffs, NJ:
     Prentice, 1975. 161-70.

     Claims that the 1960's in American literature has been
     dominated by two radically differing counterclaims in the
     works of both Bellow and Mailer. Notes first some areas of
     confluence between the two writers, and then proceeds to
     discuss the radical differences. Compares the two writers in
     terms of their treatments of such issues as: Jewishness,
     women, politics, time, history, evil, and the value and
     function of art.

493. Rovit, Earl. "Saul Bellow and the Concept of the Survivor." *Saul
     Bellow and His Work.* Ed. Edmond Schraepen. Brussels: Cen-
     truum voor Taal-en Literatuurwetenschap, Vrije Universiteit
     Brussel, 1978. 89-101. Proceedings of a symposium held at
     the Free University of Brussels (V.U.B.), 10-11 Dec. 1977.

Discusses Hemingway's "negative fatherhood" to Bellow in his projection of an artist as one who could survive only in death. Points out the combination of Christian sacrifice and Faustian enterprise in the protagonists of both authors. Argues that Bellow is reluctant to accept either model, however. Many of his protagonists learn the ineffectuality of both modes and finally avoid either model by engaging in incessant motion. Accepting their limitations, they determine to "act well." Like the wandering Jew archetype, the Bellow hero is doomed to eternal loneliness and eternal movement emblematic of man's "naked consciousness." Death is neither mastered nor accepted. It simply becomes a destination.

494. Rubin, Louis D. "Southerners and Jews." *Southern Review* ns 2.3 (1966): 697-713.

Compares the Southern literary "Renascence" with a "Jewish Literary Jubilee." Discusses these movements using novels by William Humphrey, Flannery O'Connor, Saul Bellow and Edward Lewis Wallant. Focuses most on *H.*

495. Rupp, Richard H. "Saul Bellow: Belonging to the World in General." *Celebration in Postwar American Fiction: 1945-1967.* Richard H. Rupp. Coral Gables, FL: U of Miami P, 1970. 189-208.

Concentrates mainly on the affirmations found in the Bellow novel, their humanity and their endlessly varied reflections of a distinctly American reality. Concludes that for Bellow, "engagement is intermittent, expressed largely in secular celebrations. The quality of life and its very reality rest upon the quality of those celebrations."

496. Saposnik, Irving S. "Bellow, Malamud, Roth . . . . and Styron? or One Jewish Writer's Response." *Judaism* 123 (1982): 322-32.

Talks of these three writers in terms of the degree to which their protagonists seem to have stopped fleeing the world of their fathers and accepted the world they live in.

497. Saposnik, Irving S. "Yasha Mazur and Harry Houdini: The Old Magic and the New." *Studies in American Jewish Literature* 1 (1981): 52-60.

498. Sarma, G. V. L. N. "Saul Bellow and the Indian Intellectual." *Journal of English Studies* [India] 12.1 (1980): 828-32.

Discusses in brief outline the basic Jewish values in the novels and how these correlate with such basic tenets of Indian life as *Gemiluth Chasadim*, or "a making good to fellow men for the glory of God."

499. Sarotte, George-Michel. "Le temperament feminin-masochiste de certains personnages juifs." *comme un frere, comme un amant: l'homesexuality masculine dans le roman et la theatre americains de Herman Melville a James Baldwin*. Paris: Flammarion, 1976. 245-53.

500. Savanio, Piero. "Il Romanzo di Saul Bellow." *Studi Americani* 2 (1956): 261-84. Cited in *MLA Bibliography, 1957*.

501. Scheer-Schaezler, Brigitte. "Die Farbe als dichterisches Gestalt-ungsmittel in den Romanen Saul Bellows." *Sprachkunst* 2 (1971): 243-64. Cited in *Annual Bibliography of English Language and Literature*, 1971.

502. Scheer-Schaezler, Brigitte. "Epistemology as Narrative Device in the Work of Saul Bellow." *Saul Bellow and His Work*. Ed. Edmond Schraepen. Brussels: Centrum voor Taal-en Litera-tuurwetenschap, Vrije Universiteit Brussel, 1978. 103- 18. Proceedings of a symposium held at the Free University of Brussels (V.U.B.) on 10-11 Dec. 1977.

Accuses critics of lacking a vocabulary of praise for a writer like Bellow. Argues that his writing is a process of discovery which refuses to supply pat solutions. Knowing, not knowledge, is the goal and must be pursued by intuition, not rationality. The struggle is against sleep. After self-searching and self-teaching comes conforming to new insights about inner knowledge. Hence, the endings of the novels are not weak. Rather, the novelistic structures reflect a process of inquiry which proceeds by association of ideas instead of logic. Bellow is primarily interested in insight as a function of intelligence and the relationship between the imagination and knowledge, hence the nature and function of Bellow's metaphors.

503. Scheer-Schaezler, Brigitte. "Saul Bellow's Humor and Saul Bellow's Critical Reception." *Delta* 19 (Oct. 1984): 47-65.

Considers Bellow as a serious writer in the Arnoldian sense, and as a humorist. Shows how his early critical reception ignored this humorous aspect of the novels, which she goes to some lengths to define. Discusses *HG* and *MSP* in terms of their humor and the critical reception they got.

504. Scheffler, Judith. "Two-Dimensional Dynamo: The Female Character in Saul Bellow's Novels." *Wascana Review* 16.2 (1981): 3-19.

Sees a "passive, introspective protagonist" surrounded by female "eccentrics" who, though essential to the development of plot and theme, and even the characterization of the protagonist, seldom "draw breath of their own in the novels."

505. Schraepen, Edmond. "The Rhetoric of Saul Bellow's Novels." *Rhetoric et Comunication: Actes du Congres de Rouen, 1976.* Societe des Anglicistes de l'Enseignement Superieur. Etudes Anglaises 75. Paris: Didier, 1979.

506. Schroeter, James. "Saul Bellow and Individualism." *Etudes de Lettres* ser. 4. 1.1 (1978): 3-28.

507. Schulz, Max F. "Saul Bellow and the Burden of Selfhood." *Radical Sophistication: Studies in Contemporary Jewish-American Novelists.* Max F. Schulz. Athens, OH: Ohio U P, 1969. 110-53.

Demonstrates the anti-positivist thrust of Bellow's fiction and elaborates on the issue of freedom from divisions within and without faced by the protagonists. Relates Bellow's thought to that of Blake with respect to mistrust of reason and intellect. Emphasizes how the Bellow hero opts constantly for human experience rather than intellectual abstractions. Notes the numerous bondage images throughout the novels. A generally admiring essay which concludes approvingly that "Bellow would have us realize that order does not issue necessarily out of conformity, that human well-being does not depend upon totalitarian methods, that virtue does not come in ready-made packages."

508. Scott, Nathan A., Jr. "Bellow's Vision of the 'Axial Lines.'" *Three American Moralists: Mailer, Bellow, Trilling.* Nathan A. Scott, Jr. Notre Dame: IN: U of Notre Dame P, 1973. 101-49.

An expanded version of the essay "Sola Gratia--The Principle of Bellow's Fiction," published in his book *Craters of the Spirit: Studies in the Modern Novel* (1968). Concentrates on the issues of morality, grace and transcendence in the novels. A major essay.

509. Scott, Nathan A., Jr. "Sola Gratia--The Principle of Bellow's Fiction." *Adversity and Grace: Studies in Recent American Literature.* Nathan A. Scott, Jr. Chicago: U of Chicago P, 1968. 27-57. Rpt. in *Craters of the Spirit: Studies in the Modern Novel.* Nathan A. Scott, Jr. Washington, DC: Corpus, 1968. 253-65.

Denounces those who, after witnessing the great outpouring of novelistic talent in the 20's and 30's, would declare the novel in the postwar era dead. Cites Bellow, among others, as evidence that it is not. Condemns Geismar for reducing Bellow to a mere social historian and Klein for his circular definition that Bellow characters are "reducible to a single problem: to meet with a strong sense of self the sacrifice of self demanded by social circumstance." Scott proceeds to show how the Bellow hero transcends the pressures of environment and engages with the larger issues at the heart of phenomenology. A major essay.

510. Shaw, Peter. "The Tough Guy Intellectual." *Critical Quarterly* 8.1 (1966): 13-28.

Traces the cult of the tough guy intellectual under various and sundry American presidencies. Cites Bellow's break with the Hemingway tough guy cult and his tendencies toward accommodation rather than nihilism. Provides a brief overview of the canon as he develops this thesis.

511. Shechner, Mark. "Down in the Mouth with Saul Bellow." *American Review* 23 (1975): 40-77. Cited in *American Literary Scholarship*, 1975.

Discusses the effects of Wilhelm Reich on Bellow.

512. Shechner, Mark. "Saul Bellow and Ghetto Cosmopolitanism." *Studies in American Jewish Literature* [University Park, PA] 4.2 (1978): 33-44. Joint issue with *Yiddish* 3.3 (1978).

Bellow, Roth and Malamud all share in common an awareness of their ghetto and shtetl roots. Bellow, its most prominent spokesman, exhibits this in typically Jewish humor, which contrasts the vulgarity of the "Yid" inside the sophisticated American urban Jewish intellectual. According to Schechner, this is best summarized by the "sudden shifting of planes up or down, the undercutting of intellectual pretension by bodily needs or deep-seated ghetto habits, . . . or the strained efforts to achieve a minor transcendence amid the depressingly, scatological, ordinary."

513. Shibuya, Yuzaburo. "Chicago: Hanzai to Shigokoro." *Eigo Seinen* 128.4 (1982): 209-10.

514. Shibuya, Yuzaburo. "Machine, Business, Lawyers, Gangsters: Bellow no Chicago." *Eigo Seinen* 129 (1983): 64-65. Cited in *MLA Bibliography*, 1983.

515. Shibuya, Yuzaburo. "Saul Bellow Ron--Moralist to shite no Sokumen wo Chushin ni." *Eigo Seinen* 118 (1972): 254-56. Cited in *MLA Bibliography*, 1972.

A generalized comment on the moralistic aspects of Bellow.

516. Shibuya, Yuzaburo. "Saul Bellow: Politics and the Sense of Reality." *The Traditional and the Anti-Traditional: Studies in*

Contemporary American Literature. Ed. Kenzaburo Ohashi.
Tokyo: Tokyo Chapter of the American Literature Society of
Japan, 1980. 43-56.

Reviews Bellow's early associations with Trotskyism in the
1920's. Summarizes the evolution of Bellow's political
thinking through a semi-chronological examination of the
novels and short stories from the viewpoint of Trotskyism
and totalitarianism. Points up Bellow's conversion away from
Utopian political dreams to a liberal revision. Shows his
abandonment of ideas concerning collectivist salvation. His
early political radicalism becomes a mixed form of contemplation, antagonism, spiritualism and secularism in the sixties
and seventies.

517. Shulman, Robert. "The Style of Bellow's Comedy." *PMLA* 83.1
(1968): 109-17.

Describes Bellow's particular comic style as descending
through such writers as Twain, the Chicago naturalists,
Yiddish humor, the English picaresque and the European
existentialists. Sees all of these as most fully developed in
Moby Dick. Traces the lines of descent through *Moby Dick*
on down into the Bellow novels.

518. Siegel, Ben. "Saul Bellow and the University as Villain."
Missouri Review 6.2 (1983): 167-88. Cited in *MLA Bibliography,*
1983.

A major article drawing extensively upon Bellow's essays,
interviews and novels for evidence of Bellow's life-long
antipathy for academia. Establishes nevertheless, how Bellow
like many other American novelists and poets, remains rooted
in academia "while making it a frequent target."

519. Singh, Yashoda. "Saul Bellow and the Modern American City."
Osmania Journal of English Studies [India] 17 (1981): 39-47.

Points out previous critical neglect of Bellovian technique
and use of language to define his vision of the city. Shows
Bellow's disgust with "wasteland" visions of modern civilization, yet demonstrates his full awareness of its ugliness.
Discusses how much Bellow enjoys its protean vitality and

restlessness, despite the ugliness. Compares Bellow's descriptions of the city to Balzac's and Dickens. Like them, Bellow
uses verbal art to transmute the brutal qualities of the city.
Demonstrates his thesis through close textual analysis of the
passages from *DM*, *AM*, and *HG*. Shows how the intensity of
the language arises from the abundance of surface detail,
catalogues, color, and sound words, as well as the distinctive language of the various narrators. Hence, the city
emerges as iridescent, vitally alive, and a "seething primeval
sea which is shot with beauty."

520. Sire, James W. "The Human Understanding of Saul Bellow."
Christianity Today 21 Jan. 1977: 20, 22.

521. Siskin, E. E. "Saul Bellow in Search of Himself." *Journal of
Reform Judaism* 25 (Spring 1978): 89-93. Cited in *Index to
Jewish Periodicals*, Jan.-June 1978.

522. Solotaroff, Theodore. "Philip Roth and the Jewish Moralists."
Chicago Review 13.4 (1959): 87-99. Cited in *Abstracts of
English Studies*, 1961.

Compares Roth's style with that of Bellow and other Jewish
writers.

523. Steinke, Russell. "The Monologic Temper of Bellow's Fiction."
Junction [Brooklyn College] 1.3 (1973): 178-84.

524. Stevenson, David L. "The Activists." *Daedalus* 92.2 (1963):
238-49.

Stevenson sees postwar fiction as primarily occupied with
the "active self-consciousness of characters full of high
energy who are intellectual immigrants from the norms of
domestic morality and ambition in a close money-making society." The central characters are all "ontologists" or "avid
investigators into the essential qualities of the events and
the human relationships that chance their way. All remain
intrepid opportunists of the self." Sees Bellow's novels in
this context.

525. Stock, Irvin. "The Novels of Saul Bellow." *Southern Review* 3.1
     (1967): 13-42. Rpt. in *Fiction as Wisdom: From Goethe to
     Bellow.* Irvin Stock. University Park, PA: Pennsylvania
     State UP, 1980. 190-224.

     A critical tribute to Saul Bellow which focuses on Blakean
     and Wordworthean affirmations in the Bellow novel. Discursi
     and thorough.

526. Sullivan, Victoria. "The Battle of the Sexes in Three Bellow
     Novels." *Saul Bellow: A Collection of Critical Essays.* Ed.
     Earl Rovit. Twentieth Century Views. Englewood Cliffs, NJ:
     Prentice, 1975. 101-14.

     Argues that Bellow is not a sexist if one considers his
     unflattering portraits of men. "The women in his novels are
     like the men, a sad, crazy, mixed-up lot. They tend to fall
     into two basic categories: the victims and the victimizers,
     the latter tending to be more colorful. If they appear less
     three-dimensional than the men, and if they are certainly
     less sensitive than Doris Lessing's heroines, this is the
     natural consequence of novels in which the protagonist tends
     to be a middle-aged Jewish male with a world view to match
     his ethnic bias." Concludes that Bellow's great talent is in
     chronicling the painful consequences of human behavior,
     ethnic identity, gender relations and cultural frustration,
     male as well as female.

527. Symons, Julian. "Bellow Before Herzog." *Critical Occasions.*
     London: Hamilton, 1966. 112-18.

     Provides a general overview of the early novels, placing
     Bellow squarely within the "great tradition" of the Anglo-
     American novel. Commends Bellow for his extraordinary
     skill, "demotic" language and seriousness.

528. Takizawa, Juzo. "Schopenhauer and Nietzsche in Bellow's Work."
     American Literature in the 1950's: Annual Report 1976.
     Tokyo: Tokyo Chapter of the American Literature Society of
     Japan, 1977. 50-59.

     Discusses the importance of the *weltanshauung* of these two
     writers in studying Bellow's fiction, and of the influence of

Schopenhauer and Nietzsche in Bellow's works. Scholarly but not exhaustive.

529. Tanner, Tony. Afterword. *Saul Bellow and His Work.* Ed. Edmond Schraepen. Brussels: Centrum voor Taal-en Literatuurwetenschap, Vrije Universiteit Brussel, 1978. 131-38. Proceedings of a symposium held at the Free University of Brussels (V.U.B.), 10-11 Dec. 1977.

Provides a summary statement of the proceedings of a conference held in 1977 at the Free University of Brussels. The general opinions stated in this essay appear in much amplified form in Tanner's 1979 book on Bellow.

530. Tanner, Tony. "The American Novelist as Entropologist." *London Magazine* ns 10.7 (1970): 5-18.

531. Tanner, Tony. *City of Words: American Fiction 1850-1970.* New York: Harper, 1971. 64-84, 295-321.

532. Tanner, Tony. "Saul Bellow: The Flight from Monologue." *Encounter* [London] 24.2 (1965): 58-65, 67-70. Rpt. in *Herzog: Text and Criticism.* Ed. Irving Howe. New York: Viking, 1976. 445-65.

Traces the phenomenon of monologue in the Bellow novels through a chronological treatment of each protagonist. Concludes that in the ending lies the evidence that each of these characters finally flees from self and monologue into community and communion.

533. Teodorescu, Anda. "Saul Bellow: An Ironical Humanist." *Cahiers Roumains d'Etudes Litteraires* 4 (1979): 107-12.

Bellow heroes are disillusioned failures significant primarily because of the wide range of feelings they are capable of. They are introspective versions of the code hero with whom they share loneliness, uncertainty, striving for moral dignity, a sense of irony and an understanding of the futility of their efforts. Bellow's humanism implies freedom through an act of comprehension. Therefore, the protagonists can be great without having to be heroic. After examining each novel, Teodorescu concludes that Bellow's is an ironical optimism, "a ambiguous solution involving art and nature, man and the universe."

534. Tijeras, Eduardo. "Saul Bellow." *Cuadernos Hispanoamericanos* [Madrid] 317 (1976): 425-28. Cited in *MLA Bibliography*, 1977.

535. Trachtenberg, Stanley. "Saul Bellow's *Luftmenschen*: The Compromise with Reality." *Critique* 9.3 (1967): 37-61.

Describes in detail the characteristics of the Bellow hero that qualify him for the title *Luftmensch*. Treats each of the novels to date and concludes that it is the conflict with reality and uncertainty that determines the final compromise with reality achieved by the *luftmenschen* in the novels that provides them with their distinctive character. Illustrates how very useful a model this is for conveying a contemporary vision of the indeterminacy of the self and the outlines of existence in twentieth-century America. A major article.

536. Trachtenberg, Stanley. "Saul Bellow and the Veil of Maya." *Studies in the Literary Imagination* 17.2 (1984): 39-57.

Establishes Schopenhauer's original use of this term and traces its philosophical use and adaptation in *H* and other works. Concludes that "Struggling to maintain it [freedom of will] among the illusory veils of intellect, imagination, as well as those distractions of society and powers of nature, Bellow, throughout his fiction, remains pessimistic about what seems certain to be a losing battle."

537. Tripathy, Biyot Kesh. "A Door in the Sky: Terminal Configurations." *Osiris N.: The Victim and the American Novel.* Amsterdam: Gruner, 1985. 227-56.

538. Ustvedt, Yngvar. "Saul Bellow--en amerikansk natidsdikter." *Samtiden* 80 (1971): 273-82. Cited in *MLA Bibliography*, 1971.

539. Varela, Lourdes Y. "Man, Society and Literature." *Literature and Society: Cross-Cultural Perspectives.* Ed. Roger J. Bresnahan. [n.p.]: U. S. Information Service, 1977. 84-94. Eleventh American Studies Seminar held Oct. 1976, Los Banos, Philippines.

540. Venkatramaiah, S. "Saul Bellow and His Novels." *Triveni: A Journal of the Indian Renaissance* 51.4 (1983): 65-70. Cited in *Abstracts of English Studies.* 1986.

541. Vinoda. "The Comic Mode in Saul Bellow's Fiction." *Journal of English Studies* [India] 10.2 (1979): 662-67.

    Describes Bellow's comic modes as being implicit in his vision of life as well as in the techniques used to project that vision. Provides descriptions of comedy and character in the novels and goes on to a discussion of language and other techniques.

542. Vinoda. "The Dialectic of Sex in Bellow's Fiction." *Indian Journal of American Studies* 12 (1982): 81-87.

    Sees one of the Bellow novels' major failings as its inability to make the "imaginative leap into the consciousness of its female characters." Examines the struggles of the Jewish male protagonist with regard to women by elucidating cultural assumptions implicit in the Eastern European shtetl. The partially assimilated Bellow protagonist finds domestic women dull and intellectual women not domestic enough. Between these two categories are sensual women whose task it is to minister to the male protagonist's sexual needs. Vinoda concludes: "The novels furnish substantial evidence to conclude that the Bellow protagonist, being a second generation Jew of the East European extraction, looks upon the American mores in much the same way as does a stranger. . . . Bellow's 'dissent' from 'modernism' could also be seen from his opposition to the emancipated female ethic."

543. Vinoda. "Saul Bellow and Gustave Flaubert." *Saul Bellow Newsletter* 1.1 (1981): 1-5.

    Discusses Bellow's initial adherence to a subsequent break with Flaubert's aesthetics. Vinoda argues that this is due to

Bellow's Jewish moral passion and humanistic faith in conflict
with a prevailing literary modernism. Traces Bellow's statements against the Flaubertian standard throughout his fiction,
essays, interviews and addresses, as he has attempted to
restore dignity and moral authority to literature. Summarizes
Flaubert's aesthetic creed and its relation to the debate on
deconstructionist criticism. Details Bellow's specific objec-
tions to the Flaubertian aesthetic, his definition of the role
of the writer as latter-day prophet, teacher, or clergyman.
Demonstrates Bellow's dissent from both European deconstruc-
tionists and American post-modernists.

544. Vinoda. "The Theme of Death in the Novels of Saul Bellow."
     Journal of English Studies [India] 12.1 (1980): 812-19.

Discusses the death theme from the perspective of protagonists who are continually aware of their earthbound
experience and progressively humbled by it. Argues that, for
the Bellow hero, only the presence of death will restore the
sense of life. Points up some similarities between Bellow and
Tolstoy in this regard.

545. Walden, Daniel. "Bellow, Malamud and Roth: Part of the
     Continuum." *Studies in American Jewish Literature* [University
     Park, PA] 5.2 (1979): 5-7. Joint issue with *Yiddish* 4.1 (1979).

Defends the tradition of Jewish-American literature.
Provides a brief historical survey of the genre and suggests
that Bellow and Malamud might be the mid-point of the
continuum rather than the end of it.

546. Walden, Daniel. "The Resonance of Twoness: The Urban Vision
     of Saul Bellow." *Studies in American Jewish Literature*
     [University Park, PA] 4.2 (1978): 9-21. Joint issue with
     Yiddish 3.3 (1978).

In this essay Walden examines Saul Bellow's solution to the
twin problems of the alienation of the artist from popular
American culture and his avoidance of the "art" novel which
is equally removed from reality, sterile and negative. Bellow's
specific dilemma is that in urban society "too much autonomy
and too much individualism involve loss of world, but too
little leads to loss of self."

547. Walden, Daniel. "Urbanism and the Artist: Saul Bellow and the Age of Technology." *Saul Bellow Journal* 2.2 (1983): 1-14.

> This article begins with the assertion that for many years Bellow has been evolving a rationale for the struggle between old art and new technology, and for the issue of urbanism and art. Explores the entire issue of technology and its impact not only upon the artist, but also upon the protagonist-intellectuals of Bellow's novels. Correlates the relevant statements from Bellow's essays with references to individual works of fiction. Concludes that, in spite of the claims of technology and art, they are "saviors." Art, according to Bellow, attempts to find in the universe that which is enduring, fundamental and essential. The center has not been preempted by technology or urbanism. (See 548 for similar treatment of these ideas.)

548. Walden, Daniel. "Urbanism, Technology and the Ghetto in the Novels of Abraham Cahan, Henry Roth and Saul Bellow." *American Jewish History* 73.3 (1984): 296-306.

> Similar to his "Urbanism and the Artist: Saul Bellow and the Age of Technology" (see item 547).

549. Waterman, Andrew. "Saul Bellow's Ineffectual Angels." *On the Novel: A Present for Walter Allen on His 60th Birthday from His Friends and Colleagues.* Ed. B. S. Benedikz. London: Dent, 1971. 218-39.

> Discusses, with relation to several of the novels, how Bellow resolves the issue of meliorism through art. Concludes that only in *MSP* does Bellow provide an example of the really good man, but that goodness is ineffectual in this character as in all the others.

550. Weinberg, Helen. "Kafka and Bellow: Comparisons and Further Definitions." *The New Novel in America: The Kafkan Mode in Contemporary Fiction.* Ithaca, NY: Cornell UP, 1970. 29-107.

> Traces evidences of direct and indirect influences of Kafka upon Bellow. Also traces the possible influence of Buber's thinking, via Kafka, upon the development of the post-victim era hero. Examines all of the novels up to *H* from this

perspective, making comparisons and drawing connections
between Bellow and Kafka in terms of Bellow's heroes. A
major essay.

551. Weinstein, Mark. "Bellow's Imagination-Instructors." *Saul Bellow
Journal* 2.1 (1982): 19-22.

The most prominent instructors in the novels--Tamkin, Dahf
and Humboldt--are Blakeans who emphasize seeing because
they believe that imaginative vision creates reality. Movement comes from the inside out, but the protagonists never
fully trust these imagination-instructors because, though
they feel their visions, they cannot dismiss external reality.
However, these imagination-instructors do provide a balance
considering the number of them around. They do address de
emotional and imaginative needs, and assert the nobility of
the individual and the possibility of change. The Bellovian
protagonist learns that real life is a relationship between
here and now.

552. Widmer, Kingsley. "Poetic Naturalism in the Contemporary
Novel." *Partisan Review* 26 (1959): 467-72.

553. Wieting, Molly Stark. "The Function of the Trickster in Saul
Bellow's Novels." *Saul Bellow Journal* 3.2 (1984): 23-31.

Discusses the dual nature of the helper-trickster reality
instructor in the Bellow novel. Concentrates primarily on
Dahfu and Tamkin in developing this thesis. Concludes that
each generation must discover and reinterpret the trickster
anew, as Bellow has done for this generation.

554. Wieting, Molly Stark. "The Symbolic Function of the Pastoral in
Saul Bellow's Novels." *Southern Quarterly* 16 (1978): 359-74.

Argues that while most critics focus on the Jewish, urban
milieu of the Bellow novel, they have missed a correspondin
pastoral element, "an excursion, either physical or mental,
to an environment that is free from the clutter and chaos
of the protagonists' urban existence. They create a pervasive
pattern that forms a cohesive motif in Bellow's fiction." Thi
pastoral motif signals the possibility of spiritual renewal.

555. Wisse, Ruth R. "The Schlemiel as Liberal Humanist." *The
     Schlemiel as Modern Hero.* Ruth R. Wisse. Chicago: U of
     Chicago P, 1971. 91-107. [Paperback ed. 1980.] Rpt. in *Saul
     Bellow: A Collection of Critical Essays.* Ed. Earl Rovit.
     Twentieth Century Views. Englewood Cliffs, NJ: Prentice,
     1975. 90-100.

     Discusses the Bellow hero as a representative modern
     schlemiel. Deals primarily with *H.* Discusses a variety of
     aspects including humor, fate, the Jewish son, the family
     psychodynamics, his complacency, and witness of horrors.

556. Zietlow, E. R. "Saul Bellow: The Theater of the Soul." *Ariel* 4.4
     (1973): 44-59.

     Zietlow describes how "The theater of the soul represents
     Bellow's elaboration of the idea of a power within us and
     its relationship to daily life." Argues that Bellow goes from
     a concern in the early novels with the impact of the objective
     world of the individual to a concern in the later novels to
     the "theater of the soul," or becoming versus being.

557. Aithal, S. Krishnamoorthy. "American Ethnic Fiction in the
  Universal Human Context." *American Studies International* 21.5
  (1983): 61-66.

558. Alam, Fakrul. "A Possible Source of Augie's Axial Lines." *Notes
  on Contemporary Literature* 10.2 (1980): 6-7.

    Traces the concept of the "axial lines" reference to Karl
    Jaspers' essay "The Axial Age of Human History," published
    in 1948 in *Commentary*, a journal to which Bellow occa-
    sionally contributed.

559. Aldridge, John W. "The Society of Three Novels." *In Search of
  Heresy: American Literature in an Age of Conformity*. John
  W. Aldridge. New York: McGraw-Hill, 1956. 126-48. Rpt. as
  "The Society of Augie March" in *The Devil in the Fire:
  Retrospective Essays on American Literature and Culture,
  1951-1971*. John W. Aldridge. New York: Harper Magazine
  Press, 1972. 224-30.

    Sees *AM* as a spiritual picaresque--a later form of the
    bildungsroman. Here the hero is consciousness rather than
    swashbuckling rogue, and as such is required to develop,
    deepen, strike through its first illusion to the truth, which,
    at the end of the road, it discovers to be its fate. But this
    novel begins with the aphorism that "Man's character is his
    fate" and ends with the aphorism transposed "man's fate is
    his character." The learning is in the transposition.

560. Alter, Robert. "Heirs of the Tradition." *Rogue's Progress:
  Studies in the Picaresque Novel*. Robert Alter. Harvard
  Studies in Comparative Literature 26. Cambridge, MA:
  Harvard UP, 1964. 106-32.

119

Bellow adapts the picaresque form into the novelistic idiom
of the mid-twentieth-century. Augie is a typical picaroon in
his insatiable quest for experience and limitless curiosity.
Alter calls the Whitmanesque catalogue sentences crammed
with vitality and his vision of the world "multiverse." By
refusing to fall prey to the systematizers, Augie has appeal
for the modern audience. Like the typical picaroon he is
appealing to both men and women. Ultimately he is an
atypical picaroon because Bellow is using also the *bildungsroman* model of search for self-identity. Unlike the picaroon,
Augie never seeks experience for its own sake.

561. Bergler, Edmund. "Writers of Half-Talent." *American Imago* 14.2
     (1957): 155-64.

     Claims that Bellow is a writer of half talent, neither truly
     creative nor a hack. Writers in this sub-group describe
     persons and situations vividly. Because the characters they
     depict are seemingly alive, they hold the reader's interest,
     but something is still missing. The missing link consists of
     frantic avoidance of the most decisive human motivation:
     unconscious psychic masochism. As a result the writer piles
     up a plethora of "interesting" situations; he overstresses sex;
     he substitutes external events for internal vicissitudes. In
     short, his characters are static rather than dynamic. Eluci-
     dates *AM* from this perspective.

562. Berryman, John. "A Note on Augie." *The Freedom of the Poet.*
     New York: Farrar, 1940. 222-24.

     Places *AM* in the Dreiserian naturalistic tradition.

563. Bromwich, David. "Some American Masks." *Dissent* 20 (Winter
     1973): 35-45.

     Bromwich claims that *AM* comes close to being a great
     novel, a rallying cry and a great portent. Augie, as a drifter,
     becomes dark angel of our representative mass fictions, and
     yet Bellow relies too heavily on the reader to infer his
     qualities. Adds strength to the traditions of the realistic
     novel.

564. Chapman, Sara S. "Melville and Bellow in the Real World: *Pierre* and *Augie March.*" *West Virginia University Bulletin. Philological Papers* 18 (1971): 51-57.

> *AM* is a modern romantic novel about a typically nineteenth-century explorer-discoverer somewhat removed from the civil state, who bears many resemblances to Melville's Pierre. Pierre may be seen as a tragic prototype for the less unfortunate Augie. Both are sensitive young men through whom the respective authors attempt to reveal "what is." Both have a vision of heroism and participate in youthful tragedy. Chapman details a convincing number of parallels in the two heroes, the philosophical issues discussed and in the major themes.

565. Crozier, Robert D. "Theme in Augie March." *Critique* 7.3 (1965): 18-32.

> With Salinger, Bellow is the forerunner of a more maturely intellectual and spiritual America. The theme complex in *AM* is a pentagonal pattern concentrating on character--fate, power, money, love, and urbanization. Underlying these are thoughts about masculine and feminine personality, history, nature, society, and civilization. All of these are dealt with in a complex relation to the action of the novel and produce splendid unity.

566. Decap, Roger. "Picaresque et Nouveau Roman: *The Adventures of Augie March.*" *Caliban* 22 (1983): 69-81.

> Provides a generalized discussion of previous critical opinions on Bellow and an equally generalized series of speculative comments on distinctive features of *AM*, including the element of the picaresque.

567. Frohock, W. M. "Saul Bellow and his Penitent Picaro." *Southwest Review* 53 (Winter 1968): 36-44.

> What distinguishes this book from the older picaresque novels is its moral awareness. This is the source of its human richness. In contrast with the older picaros, Augie has interest in and affection for those around him. The fundamental tone of the novel is "matter of factness" rather than

joviality. Unlike the conventional picaro, Augie lacks humor
and does not live peacefully within his own skin. *AM* is
really a confessional novel that uses the picaresque form.
Augie, unlike Holden Caulfield and the Invisible Man, is the
prisoner, not of innocence, but of "un-innocence."

568. Fuchs, Daniel. "*The Adventures of Augie March*: The Making of
     a Novel." *Americana-Austriaca: Beitrage zur Amerikakunde.*
     Ed. Klaus Lanzinger. Vol. 5. Vienna: Universitats-Verlags-
     buchandlung, 1980. 27-50.

     Discusses what has been enlarged upon in the notebooks or
     discarded for a clear perception of Bellow's intention in the
     actual novel. A fine comparison by one of the few critics to
     deal with Bellow's original manuscripts. Likens Augie to
     Whitman in his evasion of self-definitions. Points out that
     Augie, while possessing the will to moral certitude, more
     often embraces love as his chief function. Both in its
     inception and in its final form the novel manifests an
     unresolved tension between love and use. Linguistically *AM*
     points to activity, event, and history. The novel is best
     understood as a writer's expression of a particular historical
     moment, the revisionist liberal early 1950's. As *ingenue* Augie
     expectations exceed his consumations. Critics have exaggerate
     the optimism of the book. Bellow was one of the first to
     register the loss of the power of positive thinking.

569. Gerbaud, Colette. "Aventure(s) et Sacre dans *Les Aventures
     d'Augie March*." *Aspects du Sacre dans la Litterature
     Anglo-Americaine.* Reims: Publications du Centre de Recherch
     sur l'Imaginaire dans les Litteratures de Langue Anglaise,
     1979. 107-29.

570. Gerson, Steven M. "The New American Adam in *The Adventures
     of Augie March*." *Modern Fiction Studies* 25.1 (1979): 117-28.

     Augie is similar to the nineteenth-century Adams evident in
     Cooper, Emerson, Thoreau, and Whitman. However, events in
     the last half of the novel leave him pessimistic, defeated,
     and broken--traits that are anathema to early American
     Adamism. Yet he does envision paradise as the fulfillment of
     the American dream and paradise as escape from modern
     dilemmas. This Adam differs from R. W. B. Lewis's model

because his consciousness has been shaped by twentieth
century horrors. Augie is actually Bellow's deliberate
transformation of an early American Adam into a modern one.

571. Goldberg, Gerald Jay. "Life's Customer, Augie March." *Critique*
3.3 (1960): 15-27.

Bellow's form is right for his content, but his content is not
always right for his form. Augie is not a substantial fictional
creation. There is too much emphasis on milieu and no
dynamic focal point. Bellow's dual purposes create confusion.
He is torn between nostalgic re-creation of an old world he
has known and writing a cohesive novel. Details the points
of similarity between *Tom Jones* and *AM*. Finally points up
the differences between Fielding's comic epic and Bellow's
comic romance.

572. Guerard, Albert J. "Saul Bellow and the Activists: On *The
Adventures of Augie March.*" *Southern Review* 3 (1967): 582-96.
German translation ["Saul Bellow und die Aktivisten: Uber *The
Adventures of Augie March*") appeared in *Der Amerikanische
Roman im 19. und 20. Jahrhundert.* Trans. Anton Kaes. Ed.
Edgar Lohner. Berlin: Schmidt, 1974. 353-65.

Locates Bellow among activist writers (belief in energy and
vitality) such as Roth, Gold, Percy, Engel, Baldwin, Algren,
Donleavy, Kerouac, Kesey, Pynchon and Wright Morris. *AM*
is the seminal work behind these more recent contributions.
Attributes much of the activist energy in *AM* to its rhetorical
novelty. Relates this to technical issues arising from the use
of the picaresque form and point of view problems. Accuses
Bellow of lacking an accurate ear and of periodic rhetorical
self-indulgence.

573. Jones, David R. "The Disappointments of Maturity: Bellow's *The
Adventures of Augie March.*" *The Fifties: Fiction, Poetry and
Drama.* Ed. Warren French. Deland, FL: Everett/Edwards, 1970.
83-92.

Discusses the conditions in Paris under which the novel was
written and its relationship to the early unpublished manuscript entitled "The Crab and the Butterfly." Jones goes on
to criticize the novel for its reckless strategy of flinging a

hero out across the surface of a very large work, at which point he tends to lose the focus of his material. Questions also the nature of the hero with his circular motions and demented jabbering in the face of alternating demands. Comments also on the pitch of the prose. Finally, man and his city have become superficies to the novel's many successes and to its potential.

574. Levine, Paul. "Saul Bellow: The Affirmation of the Philosophical Fool." *Perspective* 10.4 (1959): 163-76.

575. Lewis, R. W. B. "Recent Fiction: *Picaro* and Pilgrim." *A Time of Harvest: American Literature 1910-1960.* Ed. Robert E. Spiller. American Century Series 50. New York: Hill and Wang, 1962. 144-53.

Sees Bellow as typical of post-war novelists in the sprawling picaresque nature of his fiction. Argues that he represents a cunning fusion of Anglo-American literary traditions with Yiddish tradition. Augie retains pride and isolation in his refusal to be recruited by a world not worthy of him. He is willing to take on with marvelously inadequate equipment as much of the world as is available to him without fully submitting to its determinism. He struggles tirelessly and at times absurdly to realize the full potential of his Adamic predecessor. Bellow engenders a hopeful and vulnerable sense of life in this novel.

576. Lindberg, Gary. "Playing for Real." *The Confidence Man in American Literature.* Gary Lindberg. New York: Oxford UP, 1982. 231-58.

Discusses how in contemporary literature the confidence man is treated increasingly straightforwardly. Conning becomes admirable. Discusses *AM* in this context. Augie comprises two traditions of American con men--"the omnivorous jack-of-all-trades and the rogue-survivor." Augie's shapeshifting becomes a mode of being as well as a means of survival.

577. Meyers, Jeffrey. "Brueghel and Augie March." *American Literature* 49.1 (1977): 113-19.

Breughel's painting "The Misanthrope" (1568) forms a symbolic center of meaning in the complex and variegated book and expresses some of its dominant themes: the earthly pilgrimage, the relation of character and fate, pessimism about human misery, the conflict between acceptance and rejection of the world, and idealistic longing for rustic simplicity. Finally, Breughel's painting portrays three distinct ways of dealing with the hostile world: joining its corruption, making a partial renunciation, and retreating to the bucolic ideal. Augie ponders all three. However, he resists the pessimism of Breughel's "Misanthrope."

578. Nakajima, Kenji. "Freedom in *The Adventures of Augie March.*" *Kyushu American Literature* 23 (May 1982): 11-24.

Argues that as the book opens, Augie is an open personality subject to change. As he changes, he finally seeks freedom from people and from love. He ends as a solipsistic egoist.

579. Newman, Judie. "Saul Bellow and Ortega y Gasset: Fictions of Nature, History and Art in *The Adventures of Augie March.*" *Durham University Journal* 77.1 (1984): 61-70. (ns 46.1).

Contends that *AM* reveals a close familiarity with Ortega's philosophy that dictates both the intellectual argument of the book and the major incidents in its plot. Newman argues that indeed the novel advances a literary manifesto that relies to a large extent on a systematic rejection of Ortega's ideas centering on an examination of the dictum that "Man has no nature, what he has is history."

580. Overbeck, Pat Trefzger. "The Women in *Augie March.*" *Texas Studies in Literature and Language* 10.4 (1968): 471-84.

Overbeck contends that it is the unlettered Rebecca and the women who supplant her in Augie's life who ground him emotionally and objectify his apocalpytic vision of his independent fate. This configuration of women gives the novel its fulcrum and structural support. Overbeck then traces the successive encounters with these women and shows how Augie as narrator distorts and stereotypes them into either virago or victim. Overbeck concludes that in Stella March Augie has finally acquired an understanding of women that

is atypical of the contemporary male as he observes how
similar to him she really is.

581. Parkinson de Saz, Sara M. "*The Adventures of Augie March*, de
     Saul Bellow: Norteamerica: Fermento de Picaros?." *La
     picaresca: Origenes, textos y estructuras. Actas del I
     Congreso Internacional sobre la Picaresca organizado por el
     Patronato "Arcipreste de Hita."* Madrid: Fundacion Universi-
     taria Espanola, 1979. 1177-83.

     Provides a detailed review of *AM*. Relates the novel to the
     old Spanish picaresque tradition as well as to the contem-
     porary North American novelistic tradition.

582. Petillon, Pierre-Yves. "Picaro en democratie [Picaro in Demo-
     cracy]." *Caliban* 20 (1983): 61-67.

583. Pizer, Donald. "Saul Bellow: *The Adventures of Augie March*."
     *Twentieth-Century American Literary Naturalism: An
     Interpretation*. Donald Pizer. Crosscurrents/Modern Critique/
     New Series. Carbondale, IL: Southern Illinois UP, 1982.
     133-149.

     Discusses *AM* as a novel about all the forces that compel,
     condition, and shape mankind, including such things as
     decay, death, and the shaping power of other human wills.
     Calls the book a naturalistic novel of ideas.

584. Popkin, Henry. "American Comedy." *Kenyon Review* 16 (1954):
     329-34.

     AM presents a richly comic pattern of aspiration and disaster
     all cast in unmistakable tones of hyperbole. Augie is con-
     stantly reminding the reader that he is not Timur, Tallyrand,
     Christ, Cecil Rhodes, or any other hero. Yet he dreams of
     greatness, commanding personalities, secret sources of
     power, and women with style. His adventures are faltering
     steps toward these ideals. Augie finally discovers that his
     dreams of glory have outrun his achievements. This novel is
     at its strongest when it is representing Augie's distinctive
     amalgam of aspiration, disaster, and optimism.

585. Riggan, William. "The *Picaro*." *Picaros, Madmen, Naifs, and Clowns: The Unreliable First-Person Narrator*. Norman, OK: U of Oklahoma P, 1981. 38-78.

    Sees A*M* directly in the picaresque tradition, unlike most modern works with their "consciously reflective and existential" concerns.

586. Rodrigues, Eusebio L. "Augie March's Mexican Adventures." *Indian Journal of American Studies* 8.2 (1978): 39-43.

    Rodrigues claims that the strange world of Thea and Mexico owes its existence to the real-life adventures of Daniel and Jule Mannix, two famous hunters in Taxco, Mexico. Bellow visited this couple in Mexico in 1940 while they were on their honeymoon. They had trained a bald eagle called Aguila which they used to capture dragon iguanas. When this episode was published by *Harper's Bazaar*, Mannix wanted to sue Bellow and was persuaded not to. Rodrigues goes on to detail Bellow's debt for landscape and other detail to this trip and geographic area. He also details what Bellow borrowed from the Mannix's articles on training the eagle and concludes that Bellow's imaginative use of the material more than adequately transforms it for the purposes of fiction.

587. Rosu, Anca. "The Picaresque Technique in Saul Bellow's *Adventures of Augie March*." *Analele Universitatii Bucuresti* 22 (1973): 191-97.

    Describes how Bellow has adapted the method of the picaresque novel of previous centuries because it provides him with the autobiographical mode he wants, along with the appearance of simplicity, candor and ingenuousness necessary for depicting an alternate kind of hero from the typically distorted intellectual characteristic of the twentieth-century novel.

588. Sherman, Bernard. "*The Adventures of Augie March*." *The Invention of the Jew: Jewish-American Education Novels (1916-1964)*. Bernard Sherman. New York: Barnes; London: Yoseloff, 1969. 132-45.

Provides a general discussion of *AM* as an example of the *bildungsroman* in the tradition of the Jewish-American novel. Touches on several novels and miscellaneous topics.

589. Silol, Robert. "*Augie March* ou les balancements delicats d'un moi a la recherche de soi." *Delta* 19 (1984): 93-107.

Discusses *AM* as a debate on liberty; describes the duality which organizes the book; finally sees it as a "serious interrogation--a quest."

590. Tackach, James M. "Saul Bellow's Dingbat Einhorn, Nails Nagel and the American Dream." *Saul Bellow Journal* 2.2 (1983): 55-58.

AM is a parody of the American rags-to-riches story based on the myth that hard work, purity and virtue will bring success to even the most downtrodden. Bellow destroys that Horatio Alger myth in the episode on Einhorn and Nails Nagel.

591. Trilling, Lionel. Introduction. *The Adventures of Augie March*. New York: Modern Library, 1965.

592. Warren, Robert Penn. "The Man with No Commitments." *New Republic* 2 Nov. 1953: 22-23. Rpt. in *Saul Bellow*. Ed. Harold Bloom. Modern Critical Views. New York: Chelsea, 1986. 9-12.

Sees *AM* as Bellow's most important novel to date. Identifies Augie as a "latter-day example of the Emersonian ideal Yankee who could do a little of this and a little of that." Criticizes Augie for having no commitments and for being a static character.

593. Way, Brian. "Character and Society in *The Adventures of Augie March*." *Bulletin of the British Association for American Studies* ns June 1964: 36-44. Cited in *Abstracts of English Studies*, 1966.

Reviews

594. Amis, Kingsley. *Spectator* 21 May 1954: 626.

595. "Broadening the Mind." *Times Literary Supplement* 4 June 1954: 357.

596. Cassidy, T. E. "From Chicago." *Commonweal* 2 Oct. 1953: 636.

597. Connole, John M. *"The Adventures of Augie March."* *America* 31 Oct. 1953: 133-34.

598. Crane, Milton. "Sprawling, Episodic Tale of a Chicagoan." *Chicago Sunday Tribune Magazine of Books* 20 Sept. 1953: 4.

599. Davis, Robert Gorham. "Augie Just Wouldn't Settle Down." *New York Times Book Review* 20 Sept. 1953: 1, 36.

600. Finn, James. *Chicago Review* 8.2 (1954): 104-11.

601. Geismar, Maxwell. "The Crazy Mask of Literature." *Nation* 14 Nov. 1953: 404.

602. Harwell, Meade. "Picaro from Chicago." *Southwest Review* 39 (1954): 273-76.

603. Hicks, Granville. "Two New Novels of Life's Mystery by Wright Morris and Saul Bellow." *New Leader* 21 Sept. 1953: 23-24.

604. Kristol, Irving. "American Ghosts." *Encounter* July 1954: 73-75.

605. Mizener, Arthur. "Portrait of an American, Chicago Born." *New York Herald Tribune Book Review* 20 Sept. 1953: 2.

606. Pickrel, Paul. "Outstanding Novels." *Yale Review* 43.1 (1953): x.

607. Podhoretz, Norman. "The Language of Life." *Commentary* Oct. 1953: 378-82.

608. Prescott, Orville. "Books of the Times." *New York Times* 18 Sept. 1953: 21.

609. Priestley, J. B. "A Novel on the Heroic Scale." *Sunday Times* 9 May 1954: 5.

610. Pritchett, V. S. "That Time and That Wilderness." *New Statesman* 28 Sept. 1962: 405-6.

611. Rolo, Charles J. "A Rolling Stone." *Atlantic* Oct. 1953: 86-87.

612. Rosenberg, Dorothy. "Augie March Travels from Chicago to Paris--Looking for Himself." *San Francisco Sunday Chronicle* 25 Oct. 1953: 18.

613. "Rough Life." *Newsweek* 21 Sept. 1953: 102-103.

614. Schorer, Mark. "A Book of Yes and No." *Hudson Review* 7.1 (1954): 136-41.

615. Schwartz, Delmore. "Adventure in America." *Partisan Review* 21.1 (1954): 112-15.

616. Webster, Howey Curtis. "Quest Through the Modern World." *Saturday Review* 19 Sept. 1953: 13-14.

617. West, Anthony. "A Crash of Symbols." *New Yorker* 26 Sept. 1953: 140, 142, 145.

618. West, Ray B., Jr. *Shenandoah* 5.1 (1953): 85-90.

619. "What Makes Augie Run." *Time* 21 Sept. 1953: 114, 117.

620. Wilson, Angus. "Out of the Ordinary." *Observer* [London] 9
    May 1954: 9.

Dangling Man

621. Aharoni, Ada. "The Search for Freedom in *Dangling Man.*" *Saul Bellow Journal* 3.1 (1983): 47-52.

Aharoni sees the novel as a discussion of the twin questions "How much freedom do we really have?" and "What should we do with it?" Discusses the deteriorating effects of freedom on Joseph and his ultimate ability to understand not only his own freedom but that of others.

622. Anderson, David D. "The Room, the City and the War: Saul Bellow's *Dangling Man.*" *Midwestern Miscellany* 11 (1983): 49-58.

Anderson discusses the room, the city and the war, as the three dimensions of Joseph's experience that provide both the background and metaphor for what is at once freedom from an identity and enslavement by the search for it.

623. Baim, Joseph. "Escape from Intellection: Saul Bellow's *Dangling Man.*" *University Review* [Kansas City] 37 (Autumn 1970): 28-34.

Baim sees Bellow as neither an intellectual nor a Jewish humanistic writer, but a mystical one. He constantly encourages his heroes to escape history and "break the spirit's sleep" by refusing to see the self as merely the product of its own historical past. In *DM* the hero finally rejects intellect and static definitions of the past as sole definitions of self. Joseph see-saws between reason and nihilism and finally experiences illumination through an intuitive experience that only comes when intellectual responses become impossible.

624. Brans, Jo. "The Dialectic of Hero and Anti-Hero in *Rameau's Nephew* and *Dangling Man.*" *Studies in the Novel* 16.4 (1984): 435-47.

Discusses how in the earlier European tradition hero and anti-hero reflected two diametrically opposed stances toward reality while engaging in some dialectics and exchange of attitudes. Relates the modern hero to this tradition and argues that these semi-polar attitudes are often found within the same character in modern fiction. Goes on to compare both of these trends in *DM* through an illustration of the similarities between *DM* and Diderot's *Rameau's Nephew*.

625. David, Gerd. "Leiden im Exil: Saul Bellow's *Dangling Man.*" *Literatur in Wissenschaft und Unterricht* 9 (1976): 231-43.

626. Donoghue, Denis. "Commitment and the *Dangling Man.*" *Studies: an Irish Quarterly Review of Letters, Philosophy and Science* 53 (1964): 174-87. Expanded version rpt. in *The Ordinary Universe: Soundings in Modern Literature.* Ed. Denis Donoghue. New York: Macmillan, 1968. 194-220.

Donoghue argues that the Dangling Man is not an outsider or stranger, but a man in an interim situation in which action is merely motion drained of meaning. Such a man is a worthier image of our condition than the outsider because he is an exceptional man able to throw light upon our interim condition precisely because he develops a spirit of opposition in face of false simplifications, thus realizing his total responsibility in a palpable world. The quest is the search for the strength to overcome the fear of choice and avoid public institutions whose claims are hostile to the imagination and to individual autonomy.

627. Glenday, Michael K. "'The Consummating Glimpse': *Dangling Man*'s Treacherous Reality." *Modern Fiction Studies* 25.1 (1979): 139-48.

Bellow's novels deny the post-modernist strain of aversion to representational modes of narrative and self-reflexibility. Yet Bellow does explore new mental versions of reality as he attempts to relocate modern man. While not a realist in the

Dreiserian sense, he is as subversive as any post-modern
writer, and before his time. He is an explorer in the field of
human reality. In *DM* Bellow shows Joseph recoiling from
the idea of an objective reality subscribed to by collective
assent.

628. Kaler, Anne K. "Use of the Journal/Diary Form in the Development of the Odyssean Myth in *Dangling Man.*" *Saul Bellow
Journal* 5.1 (1986): 16-23.

Argues that modern man has no exterior voice such as a
gleeman or scop. The modern anti-hero has only his own
voice, which is not intended for public oral presentation but
for private reading. This ancient and yet modern voice has
been achieved through the journal voice in *DM* and functions
to underscore his sung epic as he develops a modern version
of the Odyssean myth in the novel.

629. Kulshrestha, Chirantan. "Affirmation in Saul Bellow's *Dangling
Man.*" *Indian Journal of American Studies* 5 (1975): 21-36.

Argues that *DM* has been undervalued. Discusses in depth the
artistic implications of the journal form. The seemingly
fragmented diary-form is the product of an artistry conscious
of its aims, according to Kulshrestha, who goes on to point
up the aesthetic and point-of-view ironies possible through
such sophisticated and deliberate use of the form. Provides
some alternate conclusions on the nature of Joseph's quest
and discovery.

630. Lehan, Richard. "Existentialism in Recent American Fiction: The
Demonic Quest." *Texas Studies in Literature and Language*
1.2 (1959): 181-202. Rpt. in *Recent American Fiction: Some
Critical Views.* Ed. Joseph J. Waldmeir. Boston: Houghton,
1963. 63-83.

Outlines the affinity of spirit that exists between the French
existentialists and the contemporary American novelist whose
hero is engaged in the same existential quest for identity.
Compares *DM* with Sartre's *Nausea* and Camus's *The Stranger.*
Joseph is compared to Roquentin and Meursault. Lehan
develops an elaborate and scholarly discussion on the
existentialist issues of freedom and death both central to *DM*.

631. Lyons, Bonnie. "From *Dangling Man* to 'Colonies of the Spirit'."
     Studies in American Jewish Literature 4.2 (1978): 45-50.
     Joint issue with *Yiddish* 3.3 (1978).

     Provides a re-evaluation of *DM*, recapitulating many earlier
     observations concerning sources and influences on the novel.
     Argues that *DM* is not simply an updating of Dostoevsky,
     nor merely an illumination of the American 1940s moral
     dilemma. It is an elaborate working out of the many stages,
     kinds and degrees of alienation. All minor characters repre-
     sent unacceptable alternatives to alienation. All of the positive
     themes of the later novels are prefigured in this novel.

632. Mellard, James. "*Dangling Man*: Saul Bellow's Lyrical Experiment."
     Ball State University Forum 15.2 (1974): 67-74.

     Asserts that previous criticism fails to confront the serious
     formal experimentation that takes place in *DM*. It is best
     understood through the concept of "lyrical fiction." Such a
     point of view resolves the problem of the author-narrator
     relationship because the lyrical point of the journal mode
     becomes at once author, hero and audience. External actions,
     characters and settings are simply absorbed into the lyrical
     pattern. The rhythms of the plot are governed by the logic
     of lyric association, even when the associations become
     disjunctive. Mellard's tracing of various associative patterns
     of imagery is enlightening and sophisticated.

633. Petillon, Pierre-Yves. "*Un Homme en Suspens*." *Critique* [Paris]
     427 (1982): 983-98.

634. Pinsker, Sanford. "*Rameau's Nephew* and Saul Bellow's *Dangling
     Man*." *Notes on Modern American Literature* 4 (1980):Item22.

     Notes in considerable detail the similarities between Joseph
     and Rameau's nephew. Illustrates how Diderot's *Rameau's
     Nephew* may have provided structural and philosophical
     models for the development of *DM*.

635. Rao, R. M. V. R. "Chaos of the Self: An Approach to Saul
     Bellow's *Dangling Man*." *Osmania Journal of English Studies*
     [India] 8.2 (1971): 89-103.

636. Saposnik, Irving S. "*Dangling Man*: A Partisan Review." *Centennial Review* 26.4 (1982): 388-95.

While *DM* is in many ways noticeably European in style, its ending is definitely that of the contemporary American novel. The novel depicts the paradigm of Joseph's generation's conflict between 1930's ideology and 1940's pragmatism as a metaphor for radical displacement. Saposnik attempts to portray the intellectual world of which Bellow was an active participant during the period dealt with in the novel.

637. Schwartz, Delmore. "A Man in his Time." Rev. of *Dangling Man.*" *Partisan Review* 11.3 (1944): 348-50.

Commends Bellow for being the first to seize and record the experience of the WW II generation who have witnessed the depression and the New Deal following it. There is much that is familiar and recognizable in the settings, relationships, non-essential marriage and family life. Yet Joseph's uniqueness lies in his refusal to yield to the organized lack of imagination that has produced the life of the times. Criticizes the book for using the journal form and missing many dramatic possibilities that would relieve the linearity of the plot.

638. Wilson, Edmund. "Doubts and Dreams: *Dangling Man* Under a Glass Bell." *New Yorker* 1 Apr. 1944: 78, 81, 82.

Sees *DM* as an excellent account of the non-combatant in wartime, and a remarkably honest piece of testimony on the psychology of a whole generation. Compares the novel to many others of its type that feature disillusioned communists and dangling heroes. Depicts the refusal of the hero to defend the status quo, his insistence on meeting the challenge of fascism and his frustrated artistic and intellectual impulses.

Reviews

639. "At the End of the Rope." *Times Literary Supplement* 11 Jan. 1947: 21.

640. Chamberlain, John. "Books of the Times." *New York Times* 25 Mar. 1944: 13.

641. De Vries, Peter. "Portrait in Depth of Youth Suspended Between Worlds." *Chicago Sun Book Week* 9 Apr. 1944: 3.

642. Fearing, Kenneth. "Man Versus Man." *New York Times Book Review* 26 Mar. 1944: 5, 15.

643. Hale, Lionel. "In Mid-Air." *Observer* 12 Jan. 1947: 3.

644. Heppenstall, Rayner. "New Novels." *New Statesman and Nation* ns 28 Dec. 1946: 488-89.

645. "Introspective Stinker." *Time* 8 May 1944: 104.

646. *Kirkus* 1 Feb. 1944: 48.

647. Kristol, Irving. *Politics* June 1944: 156.

648. Mayberry, George. "Reading and Writing." *New Republic* 3 Apr. 1944: 473.

649. O'Brien, Kate. "Fiction." *Spectator* 3 Jan. 1947: 26.

650. Rothman, Nathan. "Introducing an Important New Writer." *Saturday Review of Literature* 15 Apr. 1944: 27.

651. Schorer, Mark. "Fictions Not Wholly Achieved." *Kenyon Review* 6.3 (1944): 459-61.

652. Le Sidaner, Jean-Marie. "Saul Bellow: Un Homme en Suspens." *Europe--Revue Litteraire Mensuelle* 631 (1981): 236.

653. Trilling, Diana. "Fiction in Review." *Nation* 15 Apr. 1944: 454-55.

654. Anderson, David D. "The Dean's Chicago." *Midamerica* 12 (1985): 136-47.

655. Atlas, James. "Interpreting the World." Rev. of *Dean's December*. *Atlantic* Feb. 1982: 78-82.

Sees Corde as a highly strung thinking man, like his predecessors. Of messianic temperament, he insists his testament can make a difference. However, Corde is no more than another reformed liberal who eventually retreats to his high-rise apartment overlooking Lake Michigan. Atlas complains that the prose is less powerful, the characters less than believable, and the dialogue wooden compared to earlier novels. He also accuses Bellow of open hostility to some of his characters. The generally hectic style and the demotic voice are labored and monotonous. Finally, he accuses Bellow of haste in chronicling the latest events in his personal life at the expense of art.

656. Beatty, Jack. "A Novel of East and West." Rev. of *The Dean's December*. *New Republic* 3 Feb. 1982: 38-40.

According to Beatty, this novel shows a loss of plastic representation and sensuous immediacy. Sheer thought displaces powerfully realized images, scenes, and characters. Mostly it lacks the intensity of former novels. Worse, the intellectual obsessions are not dramatized. Corde is a thin invention. However, the vision of the novel is indisputable, mirrored as it is in the austere, clipped tone and broken prose of the novel.

657. Betsky, Seymour. "In Defense of Literature: Saul Bellow's *The Dean's December*." *Universities Quarterly: Culture, Education*

and Society 39.1 (1984-85): 59-84.

Discusses this novel in light of Bellow's statements from all
previous novels, essays and reviews on the subject of what
constitutes a good novel. Sees this as one of Bellow's most
powerful novels. Examines characters, themes, and language

658. Bragg, Melvyn. "Eastward Ho!" Rev. of *The Dean's December*.
     Punch 31 Mar. 1982: 536.

Bragg assesses *DD* not as vintage Bellow but as new ground
This novel is Dostoevskian in its social criticism and displa
some Thoreauvian tendencies. Bragg objects to the concept
of Corde as a Huguenot when he feels more like an Americ
Jewish intellectual. Complains that the organization of the
novel into flashbacks and winding documentary does not w

659. Chavkin, Allan. "The Feminism of *The Dean's December*."
     Studies in American Jewish Literature 3 (1983): 113-27.

Suggests that critics of *DD* have ignored the feminist
consciousness that informs the work, and that the book
attempts to atone for previous prejudices. Distorted views
because of a disturbed first person narrator do not appear
in *DD*. Bellow's feminism is a product of a radical politica
vision that defies traditional labeling, and is neither libera
nor conservative. Corde and Bellow refuse to be tagged wi
labels that would vastly underestimate the severity of
contemporary problems and limit human freedom--i.e., the
"slum of the innermost being." While working out the them
concerning the inequality between the races, he also subtly
delineates subsidiary and complementary problems, such as
the inequality between the sexes.

660. Chavkin, Allan. "Recovering 'The World That Is Buried under
     the Debris of False Description.'" *Saul Bellow Journal* 1.2
     (1982): 47-57.

661. Chupin, Helen. "Bellow's Changing Attitude to Couples: *The
     Dean's December*." *Etudes Anglaises* 36.4 (1983): 455-60.

Reviews the theme of love and Bellow's attitudes toward

female characters and marriage in earlier novels. Sees *DD* as a surprising departure from the failure of the relationships in the earlier novels. Concentrates primarily on Minna as an independent professional woman. Remarks also on the community of women in the novel. Concludes that Bellow now believes in the possibility of love and harmony between marriage partners.

662. Clemons, Walter. "A Tale of Two Cities." Rev. of *The Dean's December*. *Newsweek* 18 Jan. 1982: 86.

Clemons claims that *DD* is Bellow's dourest and most dispirited book since *MSP*. It contains his most meagerly fleshed hero. However, the novel becomes absorbing as a novelistic essay. Though the book is uneven, the prose is an instrument of exact pitch and wide-ranging expressiveness.

663. Cohen, Joseph. "Saul Bellow's Heroes in an Unheroic Age." *Saul Bellow Journal* 3.1 (1983): 53-58.

Sees *DD* as a watershed work. The Dean, seemingly devoid of heroic propensities, may turn out to be his best balanced hero, which is to say, his most human and, therefore, most appealing character. The Dean does not indulge in excesses bordering on lunacy. He does manage to cope with women. Neither is he as narcissistic. Flattering portraits of women have replaced misogyny. Likewise, his treatment of urban Blacks has been adjusted. Turning further away from Jewish values, Bellow makes this new hero an Irish Huguenot.

664. Cohen, Matt. "A Tale of Two Cities." Rev. of *The Dean's December*. *Books in Canada* 12 May 1982: 12, 14.

Praises Bellow generally and provides an admiring overview of the chief characters, themes, and plot events in the novel. Though not Bellow's best book, its strength lies in Bellow's capacity for maintaining contradictions, its superb prose, and its sheer ambition. Briefly discusses structural flaws.

665. Colbert, Robert E. "Saul Bellow's King of Confidence." *Yiddish* 4.4 (1982): 41-47.

666. Croghan, L. A. "WLB Book Reviews." Rev. of *The Dean's December*. *Wilson Library Bulletin* Feb. 1982: 466-67.
     Corde is appealing to readers of Bellow because of his inten
     concentration on mortality and morality, his melancholy and
     his ability to engross. Sees Corde as a hero who has made
     and unmade himself, and who is about to make himself aga
     like one reborn.

667. Cronin, Gloria L. "Through a Glass Brightly: Dean Corde's
     Escape from History in *The Dean's December*." *Saul Bellow
     Journal* 5.1 (1986): 24-33.

     Corde is seen here as Bellow's tool for resolving the
     longstanding philosophical dichotemy in Western Civilizatio
     between empirical and mystical modes of knowing. Corde
     becomes the pioneer who eschews the visions of society
     conferred by ordinary consciousness and who seeks to
     penetrate the *fantasmo imperium* where real facts are hidde
     from human perception. Beyond that, he is also the fictiona
     means by which Bellow and the reader may escape reductiv
     and nihilistic fabric of twentieth-century history to a
     corrected vision of that transcendental harmony both withi
     the individual and throughout the larger creation, a harmor
     which is discernible only to the person of corrected
     perceptual and emotional vision.

668. Dudar, Helen. "The Graying of Saul Bellow." *Saturday Review*
     Jan. 1982: 17-20.

     Dudor characterizes *DD* as a strange, bleak autumnal work,
     somewhat less than artistic. Its an uneven book that veers
     from drear to dazzle. The Dean is a vague image and his
     wife an embarrassed shadow. The Rumanian sequences sho
     Bellow's fatigue and there is altogether too much pallor of
     style. Tired tone and patchy structure betray his haste in
     writing. Only the Chicago passages leap to life.

669. Enright, D. J. "Saul Bellow's New Novel: Good Exists and
     Cannot Wholly be Credited to Favourable Weather." *Listener*
     1 Apr. 1982: 20.

     DD is really two novels. Though it suffers from a slightly
     over-insistent style and a double telling, it is an impressive

novel which, if it does not solve problems, at least accounts for them.

670. Evanier, David. "Bare Bones." Rev. of *The Dean's December*. *National Review* 2 Apr. 1982: 364-66.

This is the novel as essay, stripped of whimsy, decoration of character and fanciful prose. It is Bellow's worst novel because it is full of musty ideas, stilted language, mere cerebration, and vaporous characters. The Chicago scenes never transcend journalese. Its plot creaks in an inexplicably wrong tone. Concludes that *DD* contains Bellow's worst traits.

671. Fishman, Ethan. "Saul Bellow's 'Likely Stories.'" *Journal of Politics* 45.3 (1983): 615-34.

Discusses Bellow generally as a political novelist and *DD* as a particular evocation of Platonic thought. Claims that both Plato's *Republic* and *DD* represent attempts at justice in individual and political terms. To arrive at this definition, both authors find it necessary to explore other integrally related concepts within a classical philosophical framework. Discusses concepts such as salvation, transcendence, transitoriness, moral accountability and death.

672. Flower, Dean. "Fiction Chronicle." Rev. of *The Dean's December*. *Hudson Review* 35.2 (1982): 281-86.

Only Bellow and James could use such a withdrawn protagonist who feeds almost exclusively on his own thoughts. Too much weighty philosophizing. Yet Corde's thoughts do have a palpable immediacy and the prose has convincing shifts in tone, abruptness, big ideas, humor and self-doubt.

673. Goldman, Liela H. "*The Dean's December*: A Companion Piece to *Mr. Sammler's Planet*." *Saul Bellow Journal* 5.2 (1986): 36-45.

Discusses the extent to which *DD* bears an affinity to *MSP*. Compares the two works in terms of global political concerns, the deaths of key characters, repressive urban environments, moral/ethical alienation, the sacredness that lies at the core of life, the value of the individual, mood, tone, and style.

674. Halio, Jay L. "Contemplation, Fiction, and the Writer's
     Sensibility." *Southern Review* [Baton Rouge] 19.1 (1983):
     203-18.

675. Hall, Joe. "*The Dean's December*: A Separate Account of a
     Separate Account." *Saul Bellow Journal* 5.2 (1986): 22-31.

   Provides a defense and explanation of Bellow's experimentat
   with the seemingly plotless novel of reflection and philosoph
   ical thought. Describes Corde as a "satisfying artistic
   embodiment of the narrator's puzzling over his sense of
   ethical outrage; he finds his sources for judgment in the
   classical ethical tradition of Western Civilization, but he
   finds at the same time that this tradition and the account
   of the world which sustained it are dying."

676. Harmon, William. Rev. of *The Dean's December. Southern
     Humanities Review* 17.3 (1983): 280-81.

   Sees *DD* as a distillation of all Bellow's weaknesses and
   strengths. Admires the synthesis of previous intellectual
   concerns, and faults the novel for its point of view problems
   and for its stylistic shortcomings. Labels the ending
   sentimental. Also sees *DD* as an open-minded novel in which
   Corde draws us into his own sensibility and, consequently,
   we feel more through Corde than we could without him.
   Hence, this novel fulfills Joyce Cary's dictum that the
   function of the novel is to "make the world contemplate
   itself, not only as rational being, but as experience of
   value, as a complete thing."

677. Hunt, George W. "The Breadth and Breath of Life." Rev. of *The
     Dean's December. America* 20 Feb. 1982: 136, 137.

   Reveals Bellow's mastery of tonal shifts, variations in sentence structure, clarity of perception, lucidity of language a
   mastery of eccentric verbal styles. Also sees much of the
   old lively sassiness, ironic intelligence, self-deprecation and
   sheer verbal fun. Its strength is the flexibility of the
   narrative voice. Its weakness comes after the first one
   hundred pages where the voice fails to resonate and where
   the set pieces and crypto-monologues begin. This is Bellow

the professor-elf intruding like an essayist. However, these
are only small slips in an otherwise steady novel.

678. Johnson, Diane. "Point of Departure." Rev. of *The Dean's
December*. *New York Review of Books* 4 Mar. 1982: 6, 8.
Rpt. as "Saul Bellow as Reformer." *Terrorists and Novelists*.
Diane Johnson. New York: Knopf, 1982. 134-40.

Johnson accuses Bellow of approving of Corde too much and
of taking too little time to make him convincing. Really two
novels and each fades when focussed upon. The other
characters are faded and anonymous. Corde is not convincing
as a WASP. Essentially Bellow has written a book about how
and why nobody will read his book.

679. Johnson, Greg. "A Winter's Tale." Rev. of *The Dean's December*.
Southwest Review 67.3 (1982): 342-45.

Johnson claims that this novel is deliberately intended as a
"Winter's Tale." It represents an admirable risk by a writer
who, rather than repeat himself, offers us a somber, unassum-
ing, quietly lyrical evocation of intellectual disappointment.
The tone is appropriately elegiac rather than celebratory.
Renders movingly the natural and spiritual bleakness of
Bucharest and the unshakeable relationship between Corde
and his wife. Even the minor characters are drawn with a
convincing compassion. The book contains an abundance of
imaginative energy and freshly perceived life. Less entertaining than earlier novels but not less admirable.

680. Jones, Lewis. "Soul-searching." Rev. of *The Dean's December*.
Spectator 10 Apr. 1982: 21-22.

Jones sees *DD* comparing the hard nihilism of the Soviet bloc
and the soft nihilism of America. Corde, like Solzhenitsyn,
seeks to find meaning in suffering. Bellow's ideas are fully
rendered emotionally and his characters are created with
vigor and tenderness. The novel gives the impression of
having been written in haste and urgency. However, it
achieves overall mastery of form and, at times, sublime
intensity.

681. Kapp, Isa. "Bellow's New Reading." *New Leader* 8 Feb. 1982:
     14-16.

> *DD* is seen here as tantalizing, wryly self-critical and
> austerely demanding. Particularly in the Bucharest scenes,
> he disciplines himself into short, plain serviceable sentences
> in order to convey the necessary winteriness of tone. In
> other places we see the old rambunctious brilliance, crowds
> of images and clashing thoughts. Much sermonizing but also
> many engaging scenes and considerable charm. Several
> affectionate portraits of women distinguish this novel from
> the others. *DD* is part of the ongoing drama of Bellow self-
> correction.

682. Kennedy, William. "If Saul Bellow Doesn't Have a True Word to
     Say he Keeps his Mouth Shut." *Esquire* Feb. 1982: 49-54.

> A valuable reported Bellow interview about the social
> critique in *DD*. It also contains Bellow's critical assessments
> on John Cheever, Wright Morris, J. F. Powers, Bernard
> Malamud, Norman Mailer, I. B. Singer, Nadezhda Mandelstam
> Solzhenitsyn, Rebecca West, D. H. Lawrence, Samuel Beckett,
> and others.

683. Kenner, Hugh. "From Lower Bellowvia: Leopold Bloom with a
     Ph.D." *Harper's* Feb. 1982: 62-65.

> Kenner assesses this novel as part of the Nobel-certified
> "Novel as First-Draft Dissertation: A rumination on the
> sorry state of the world" genre. The characters are dead
> men and women. The ideas here are rehashes of the ideas of
> *MSP* and have not gained trenchancy with time. The opening
> of the novel is rich in possibility. No writer has more
> authority with the feel of place. However, ultimately the
> book fails for lack of a comic epiphany.

684. Klausler, Alfred P. Rev. of *The Dean's December*. *Christian
     Century* 31 Mar. 1982: 384-85.

> *DD* is one of Bellow's most distinguished novels. Contains
> elegiac descriptions, decent human beings, and scenes of
> passion and fury, as well as superb prose and characteristic
> irony.

685. Lively, Penelope. "Backwards and Forwards--Recent Fiction."
     Rev. of *The Dean's December*. *Encounter* June-July 1982:
     86-88.

          Praises the skill with which Bellow has slotted whole belts
          of time into the span of a few weeks. Such a novel makes
          nonsense of the supposition that the novel is a linear form.
          Praises the high craft of the flashback technique used in
          the novel. The very structure of the novel underscores the
          central theme of appearance and illusion. The novel is a
          vehicle for ideas but the ideas are seductively packaged.
          Settings are sharply defined and the language of Corde's
          polemics is equally intense. However, the novel has its
          longeurs and narrative disjointedness. Since there are not
          many fictional chroniclers of ideas in America, Bellow should
          be praised for this rich and provocative book.

686. MacFarlane, David. "A View of One's Own." Rev. of *The
     Dean's December*. *Macleans* 15 Feb. 1982: 54.

          DD is a refined example of Bellow's skill in the comic novel.
          Secondary characters, however, remain faceless and some
          incidents are less than believable. These are mere cavils
          though because of the undeviating manner in which Corde
          pursues his own thoughts and experiences.

687. Maloff, Saul. "Minding the World: Our Principal Novelist of
     Nutty Ideas." *Commonweal* 21 May 1982: 301-04.

          Provides a plot summary of *DD* and some impressions on a
          variety of comparative aspects of this novel and earlier works.

688. Montrose, David. "Conventional Wisdom." *New Statesman* 28
     May 1982: 20-21, 22.

689. Nagy, Peter. "*The Dean's December*." *New Hungarian Quarterly*
     94 (1984): 167-69.

690. Newman, Judie. "Bellow and Nihilism: *The Dean's December*."
     Studies in the Literary Imagination 17.2 (1984): 111-22.

Bellow's central idea, nihilism, is precisely integrated into
the action and structure of the novel. Corde's relationship
to Nietzsche's ideas is carefully explored as Nietzsche's ide
are categorized and ascribed to sets of characters within
the novel. Newman also explores the myth of Eros and Psy
in this same context and that of the community of support
women he finds in Bucharest under the matriarchy that
Valeria has established. Valeria is seen as the chthonian ea
mother who has projected her daughter, Minna, out into cc
mic space toward freedom. Hence, Corde is seen as a Psyc
who is distanced from the role of Eros monster by the pre
parallelism of the Chicago plot. Newman also demonstrates
the extent to which the book becomes a dramatization of
Bellow's analysis of the ills of American culture. Sees Lest
as akin to the younger Corde in his denial of the forces of
Eros. Traces the development of the Corde-Minna relation
in its renewed capacity to restore them both to their highe
and more integrated selves. Unlike previous novels, truth
and wisdom in this novel originate in the female. Corde's
tentative affirmation in the novel results from a renewed
perception of a starry archetype of the heavens arching
both over and within him.

691. Pinsker, Sanford. "A Kaddish for Valeria Raresh: Dean Alber
     Corde's Long Dark Month of the Soul." *Studies in America*
     Jewish Literature 3 (1983): 128-37.

     DD is seen here as another in a long series of death-bed
     meditations. A gray, drab Bucharest, a dying mother-in-la
     the season of death, a potentially sensational murder trial
     and Albert Corde's long dark night of the soul all conspire
     to give the novel its elegiac tone--its sense of an extended
     kaddish. The kaddish, however, may ultimately be for the
     world and ourselves.

692. Roberts, David. "Bellow's Month." Rev. of *The Dean's Decembe*
     Horizon Jan.-Feb. 1982: 22.

     Comments on the similarities of the prose spoken by Cord
     and that spoken by Nabakov's Professor Pnin. At first the
     reader is left to the utter jumble of associations in Corde'
     mind, and then suddenly the book comes together. The no
     is finally full of grand issues which cohere convincingly.

This is one of Bellow's most uncharacteristic novels in that its "undersea" shapes can easily be ignored.

693. Roudane, Matthew C. "A Cri De Coer: The Inner Reality of Saul Bellow's *The Dean's December*." *Studies in the Humanities* 11.2 (1984): 5-17.

For Roudane this novel reveals a successful fusion in the Coleridgean sense of idea and image. The novel forms a coherent whole through the objectification of Corde's inner reality, which mirrors our contemporary world far too accurately. The fact that the novel takes its form from the inner meditative processes of Corde's mind as he records the "slum of the psyche" should successfully counter arguments about its inertia. Characters are often arranged in groups and pairs as antagonists and sympathizers. However, morally central to the novel is Corde's relationship to Valeria because of the palpable love between them. The mature Corde is finally able to accept the giveness of the world and to celebrate its particulars. He experiences first a renewed spiritual bonding with his wife first, and then a transcendental existential freedom through the telescope on Mount Palomar. True to the derivations of his title "Dean," he becomes a kind of "poetic astrologer" who is balanced by the hard science of his wife.

694. Schwartz, Joseph. "Good Guys with no Labels." Rev. of *The Dean's December*. *Chronicles of Culture* 6.5 (1982): 8-11.

Sees the novel as a twentieth-century version of *A Tale of Two Cities* that is concerned only with the worst of times. Bellow sees himself as the corrective to Dickens' "the best of times." Sees Corde as Darnay, Minna as Lucy and Valeria as Dr. Manette. The most serious flaw in the novel is the incompleteness of Corde's ideas. This is Bellow's angriest book. Sees Bellow's ultimate target as Modernism. Concludes that as a devastating critique of haute couture, Bellow's message is urgent and necessary.

695. Spivey, Ted R. "Death, Love, and the Rebirth of Language in Saul Bellow's Fiction." *Saul Bellow Journal* 4.1 (1985): 5-18.

Sees Bellow as typical of Modernist literature in his

treatment of death and love but claims that Bellow is
undertaking a treatise on the subject of language renewal i
connection with these themes.

696. Sullivan, Walter. "Terrors Old and New: Bellow's Rumania and
Three Views of the Holocaust." *Sewanee Review* 90.3 (1982):
484-92.

Concentrates on the depiction of humane people harassed
by an inhumane bureaucracy. Though Corde's world does n
offer solutions, it does offer choices--and among them the
choice to live. Praises Bellow's ear for dialogue, his skill at
characterization, and his ability to maintain the velocity of
the narrative while constantly inserting lengthy intellectua!
asides.

697. Tipton, David. "Image Man." Rev. of *The Dean's December*.
London Magazine Apr.-May 1982: 131-33.

Claims that this novel deals more quietly and realistically *
social issues than his earlier works. Praises the cast of
memorable characters and the general complexity, ambiguit
and paradox achieved by the novel. Though it offers no
solutions, the novel is impressive and its flavor lingers long
after one has finished reading it.

698. Towers, Robert. "A Novel of Politics, Wit and Sorrow." Rev. of
The Dean's December." *New York Times Book Review* 10 Jan.
1982: 1, 22.

The comic spirit is different in this book. Ironic bemuseme
has given sway to open protest and revulsion. Bellow still
has dazzling powers of animation. Yet the same old problen
of narrative momentum is especially acute in *DD*. Switchin;
back and forth from Chicago and Bucharest results in nerv
flickering energy lighting up the two poles between which
the modern world oscillates. Concludes that Bellow is still
the best writer we have sentence by sentence and page by
page.

699. Updike, John. "Toppling Towers Seen by a Whirling Soul." Rev.
of *The Dean's December*. *New Yorker* 22 Feb. 1982: 120-28.

Commends the book for its "wit, vividness, tenderness, brave
thought, earthy mysticism, and a most generous, searching
humorous humanity. . . ." He complains, however, about the
strongly autobiographical element. This is a beautifully
written, interesting and unparaphraseable article.

700. Weinstein, Ann. "*The Dean's December*: Bellow's Plea for the
Humanities." *Saul Bellow Journal* 2.2 (1983): 30-41.

In this novel Bellow once again asks the question "How can
cities, culture, humanity, be saved from disappearing?"
Weinstein accuses critics of failing to concentrate on the
validity of Bellow's solution to the dilemma of culture
instead of seeking in his latest novel signs of the decay of
yet another Nobel Prize winner. Concentrates primarily on
Bellow's critique of culture and history.

701. Weinstein, Mark. "Communication in *The Dean's December*."
Saul Bellow Journal 5.1 (1986): 63-74.

Sees the main subject of *DD* as that of communication on a
variety of levels--personal, political, philosophical and
societal. Especially elaborated is the subject of communication
in both an open and a closed society. Argues that *DD* is a
tightly organized novel when viewed from this perspective.

702. Wilson, Jonathan. "Bellow's Dangling Dean." *Literary Review*
26.1 (1982): 165-75.

Suggests that the bleakness of the novel stems from Bellow's
having lost interest in making fiction. Sees Corde as
insufficiently distinguished from previous Bellow heroes.
Though it begins well, the novel fails to develop a wide
range of themes. Corde, like the dangling man, feels not
quite there, and neither is there a cast of inspirational
minor characters. This is one more solipsistic drama like the
previous two novels, and lacks enough concreteness to balance
the ideational weight increasingly borne by the central hero.
Besides, Corde fails to arouse the reader's interest. The only
character who interests Bellow is Bellow himself. The
weltanschauung of this novel is so familiar to the Bellow
reader he cannot help but have the feeling of *deja vu*.

703. Wisse, Ruth. "Saul Bellow's Winter of Discontent." *Commentary* Apr. 1982: 71-73.

> *DD* describes two cities, each of which is in the worst of times. Its strength is Bellow's ability to compass the philosophical speculations on these times and the precise pattern of tapes across the face of a stroke victim (Valeria hooked to a machine, plus everything in between. To the normal abundance of the Bellow novel is added a political study in contrasts between communism and democracy. The coldest of Bellow's novels, *DD* is intentionally disturbing. However, Bellow himself shows too clearly through the thin disguise of Corde and the claims made for the impact of th *Harper*'s articles seem unrealistic and exaggerated.

704. Wolcott, James. "Dissecting our Decline." Rev. of *The Dean's December. Esquire* Mar. 1982: 134, 36.

> Structurally the novel is a lumpy carryall, with reveries, flashbacks, flashbacks within flashbacks, and chunks of Corde's controversial *Harper*'s articles about Chicago bulgir like wads of clothing stuffed into a hastily packed valise. This is the most studiously dishevelled novel to date. The whole thing is controlled well by Bellow's lordly tone that turns playful, ironic, teasing, despairing and snappish by turns. Corde is a dullish prop and Minna is unmemorable. Bellow is too prone to buttonholing the reader and holding court. This book does not have the ease, splendor, and shapeliness of a great novel.

Reviews

705. "Avec Saul Bellow le franc-tireur." *Quinzaine Litteraire* 380 (1982): 11-12.

706. Christensen, John. *Best Sellers* Apr. 1982: 4.

707. Darras, Jacques. "Librairie du mois." *Esprit* Aug.- Sept. 1983: 170-71.

708. Inou, Kenji. "Shosetsuka kara Keiseika e." *Eigo Seinen* 128.4 (1982): 211-12.

709. Iwamoto, Gen. "Monogatari wa Dare no Te ni." *Eigo Seinen* 128.4 (1982): 213-14.

710. Jacobs, Rita D. "Fiction." *World Literature Today* 57.1 (1983): 107.

711. Jones, Lewis. "Soul-searching." *Spectator* 10 Apr. 1982: 21-22.

712. Josipovici, Gabriel. "A Foot in the Stockyard and an Eye on the Stars." *Times Literary Supplement* 2 Apr. 1982: 371.

713. *Kirkus* 1 Dec. 1981: Pt. II, 1472-73.

714. Maloff, Saul. "Critics' Christmas Choices: Saul Maloff." *Commonweal* 3 Dec. 1982: 664-666.

715. Miller, Stephen. *American Spectator* Apr. 1982: 33-36.

716. Oi, Koji. "America Sakka no Identity o Motomete." *Eigo Seinen* 128.4 (1982): 215-16.

717. Peck, Abe. "Bellow Is Back." *Progressive* Apr. 1982: 57-59.

718. Pollit, Katha. "Bellow Blows Hot and Cold." *Mother Jones* Feb.-Mar. 1982: 66-67.

719. Raban, Jonathan. "The Stargazer and His Sermon." *Sunday Times* 28 Mar. 1982: 14+.

720. Rushdie, Salman. "The Big Match." *New Statesman* 2 Apr. 1982: 22.

721. Scheffler, Judith A. "Reviews: *The Dean's December.*" *USA Today* May 1982: 64, 66.

722. Sheppard, R. Z. "Truth and Consequences." *Time* 18 Jan. 1982: 77, 80.

723. Stade, George. "I, Me, Mine." *Nation* 30 Jan. 1982: 117-18.

724. Stromberg, Ragnar. "Bellow's vagsakra stationsvagh mellan Bukarest och Chicago." *Bonniers Litterara Magasin* 51.6 (198 426-28.

725. Thomas, D. M. "Saul Bellow's Darkening Vision." *Washington Post Book World* 10 Jan. 1982: 1-2.

726. Wilson, William S. "Saul Bellow in Agreement." *American Book Review* May 1982: 6.

727. Abeltina, Renate. "Existentialism in Saul Bellow's Novel
     Henderson the Rain King." *Wissenschaftliche Zeitschrift der
     Wilhelm-Pieck-Universitat Rostok Gesellschafts Reihe* 33.7
     (1984): 32-36. Cited in *MLA Bibliography*, 1985.

728. Alter, Robert. "Jewish Humor and the Domestication of Myth."
     *Defenses of the Imagination: Jewish Writers and Modern
     Historical Crisis.* Robert Alter. Philadelphia: Jewish Publication
     Society of America, 1977. 155-67. Rpt. from *Harvard English
     Studies* 3 (1972).

     Describes the distinctive survival humor of the Eastern
     European shtetl and its stereotypes. Claims that literary
     modernism has created novels full of the collective disorders
     of our day and developed a sense of crisis. Bellow, espe-
     cially in *HRK*, domesticated for American literature some of
     the comic stances, stereotypes, and myths of Yiddish litera-
     ture. His chief act of domestication of Yiddish myth is the
     use of humor to both rob self-pity from and enhance the real
     existential dilemma of the protagonist through the comic
     bumbling quest depicted in *HRK*.

729. Arnavon, Cyrille. "Le Roman Africain de Saul Bellow: *Henderson
     the Rain King.*" *Etudes Anglaises* 14.1 (1961): 25-35.

730. Axelrod, Stephen Gould. "The Jewishness of Bellow's Henderson."
     American Literature 47.3 (1975): 439-43.

     Sees Henderson as the archetypal gentile American and heir
     to centuries of Christian and New World Culture. Yet Axelrod
     also sees him as implicitly Jewish in terms of physical attri-
     butes and a host of other symbolic overtones, one of which

is Henderson's self-casting as outsider among outsiders.

731. Baim, Joseph, and David P. Demarest, Jr. "*Henderson the Rain
     King*: A Major Theme and a Technical Problem." *A Modern
     Miscellany.* Carnegie Series in English 11. Pittsburgh:
     Carnegie-Mellon U, 1970. 53-63.

     Baim acknowledges that while Bellow's humanistic ideas have
     been traced to both Jewish and existentialist sources with
     regard to defining the problem of identity, they can also be
     defined mystically, spontaneously and intuitively. Demarest
     adds that "although *HRK* has some splendid comic moments,
     it is nonetheless not a thoroughly satisfying novel because
     of an ambiguity about the character of Henderson himself.
     How should the reader take Henderson--as a rounded charac-
     ter he can emphathize with, or as a two-dimensional comic
     fall guy? My feeling is Bellow tries to have it both ways and
     does not quite succeed in pulling it off."

732. Billy, Ted. "The Road of Excess: Saul Bellow's *Henderson the
     Rain King*." *Saul Bellow Journal* 3.1 (1983): 8-17.

     The dynamic cosmic vitalism of Blake informs the action of
     HRK, along with its imagery and characterization. Henderson
     carries Blake, in his pocket and the central metaphor for his
     spiritual quest stems from Blake's "The Mental Traveller."
     This poem provides the mythic foundation for Henderson's
     belief that "truth comes in blows." The article traces in
     detail direct allusions to Blake's poetry and concludes that
     this novel is the most explicit exposition of Blake's dialec-
     tic since Joyce Cary's *The Horse's Mouth.*

733. Brophy, Robert J. "Biblical Parallels in Bellow's *Henderson the
     Rain King*." *Christianity and Literature* 23.4 (1974): 27-30.

     Discusses Henderson as one who makes the inner safari and
     as one who has been built as a composite of such biblical
     figures as Adam, Cain, Ishmael, Jacob, Joseph, Moses, David,
     Daniel, and a host of others.

734. Butler, Robert James. "The American Quest for Pure Movement in Bellow's *Henderson the Rain King*." *Journal of Narrative Technique* 14.1 (1984): 44-59.

According to Butler, *HRK* is a vital example of a hero quest which seeks pure motion, not a particular point of arrival. It shows an undirected journey for the purpose of becoming rather than for a radical state of completed being, epitomizing the American search for radical forms of freedom, independence and possibility. This is confirmed not only by Henderson's actual journey, but the radically open ending which mitigates against certainty and probability. Henderson remains compelling evidence of the durability and vitality of the basic American values embodied in our picaresque tradition. Though free, the journey is purposeful and positive, not a "sick and hasty" ride through oblivion.

735. Campbell, Jeff H. "Bellow's Intimations of Immortality: *Henderson the Rain King*." *Studies in the Novel* 1.3 (1969): 323-33.

Bellow's central metaphor is drawn from the allusion to Wordsworth's "Intimations" Ode with which he closes the book. Henderson is seen as a modern Everyman who knows all the modern answers to estrangement and alienation and is unsatisfied with them. He turns back behind contemporary cliches to sources such as Homer, the Bible, Sophocles, Keats, Shelly, Tennyson, and Wordsworth, all of whom assume a greater significance when weighed against the implicit but unmistakable burlesque allusions to modern figures such as Henry Adams, Theodore Dreiser, William Faulkner, Ernest Hemingway, Albert Camus, and William Golding. The bulk of the story reflects his Wordsworthian insights.

736. Cecil, L. Moffitt. "Bellow's Henderson as American Imago of the 1950's." *Research Studies* 40.4 (1972): 296-300.

HRK, like the older modernist literature, maintains a vision of the absurdities and life-denying tendencies that are part of modern civilization, but departs from modernist literature in suggesting that alienation is, or should be, only a transitional condition for the more sensitive, alive protagonist. Henderson is a counter-image--an affirmative one. He appears as an awakening giant, on the verge of a new consciousness, representing the hopes and determinations of those who still

share the American dream and see the USA as the leaven
which will bring freedom and love to the world.

737. Chase, Richard. "The Adventures of Saul Bellow: Progress of a
Novelist." *Commentary* 27.4 (1959): 323-30. Rpt. in *Saul
Bellow and the Critics*. Ed. Irving Malin. New York: New
York, UP, 1967. 25-38; *Saul Bellow*. Ed. Harold Bloom. Modern
Critical Views. New York: Chelsea, 1986. 13-24.

A general discussion of a variety of aspects of the novel.
Primarily a first response review article. Many fruitful ideas
mentioned but not developed. Finds it not as satisfactory as
SD or *AM*.

738. Colbert, Robert E. "Saul Bellow's King of Confidence." *Yiddish*
4.4 (1982): 41-47.

Close scrutiny of the extent to which *HRK* is a parody of
Conrad's *Heart of Darkness* enables the reader to understand
the character of King Dahfu. This running Conradian parody
is one of the chief devices Bellow uses to maintain a necessary aesthetic distance from the dangerously fascinating,
but ultimately problematical, figure of the African monarch.

739. Cronin, Gloria L. "*Henderson the Rain King*: A Parodic Expose
of the Modern Novel." *Arizona Quarterly* 39.3 (1983): 266-76.

While steering a moderate course between the excesses of
disappointed idealism and nihilistic rage characteristic of
most modern literature, Bellow uses the antiseptic and corrective device of parody to hold up for our scrutiny the
false intellectual assumptions behind the modernist ideologies
of death, absurdity, mass society, estrangement, and stoicism.
At the same time, he has turned upside down the reasoning
of the wasteland ideologists, the Lawrentian primitivists, the
Freudian psychoanalysts, the Camus stoics, and the logical
positivists through the elaborate parody that forms the basis
of *HRK*.

740. Detweiler, Robert. "Patterns of Rebirth in *Henderson the Rain
King*." *Modern Fiction Studies* 12.4 (1966-1967): 405-14.

This novel focuses consistently and from many angles upon the single concept of rebirth. To do this, Bellow uses four devices: 1) a fundamental animal imagery that reveals the hero's gradual transformation from a lower into a higher creature, a kind of analogical chain of being progression from a pig-like to a lion-like nature, 2) Freudian and Jungian symbols of rebirth, 3) variations on the hero myth and the myth of the dying king, 4) an irony that saves each of the previous devices from the triteness of cliche and directs the ultimate meaning toward the paradox of redemption which rebirth signifies.

741. Edwards, Duane. "The Quest for Reality in *Henderson the Rain King*." *Dalhousie Review* 53 (1973): 246-55.

A hero in modern dress, Henderson, like grail-seekers before him, discovers that reality is not something which, once glimpsed, stands before one as clear and stationary as a statue. Continual effort, energy, will, discipline, and replenishment are required to keep it in sight. He learns also that "man must not demand a heaven of earth."

742. Goldfinch, Michael. "A Journey to the Interior." *English Studies* 43.5 (1962): 439-43.

Discusses briefly the symbolic and mythic content of *HRK* as journey fiction. Places Bellow as a typically American writer because of his focus on antiquity, spirituality and rediscovered roots.

743. Guttman, Allen. "Bellow's Henderson." *Critique* 7.3 (1965): 33-42. Rpt. in *The Jewish Writer in America: Assimilation and the Crisis of Identity*. Ed. Allen Guttman. New York: Oxford UP, 1971. 201-10.

Comments that fabulous Henderson begins where Jay Gatsby would have ended if he could have had all that the green light across the water symbolized. Sees Henderson as the "ironic hero of an age of affluence." Also sees the transcendental roots of Henderson's quest.

744. Hainer, Ralph C. "The Octopus in *Henderson the Rain King.*" *Dalhousie Review* 55 (1975): 712-19.

Discusses the death symbolism inherent in the brief initial reference to the octopus. Repeated references become an index to Henderson's ability to face death and his spiritual regeneration.

745. Hale, Thomas A. "Africa and the West: Close Encounters of a Literary Kind." *Comparative Literature Studies* 20.3 (1983): 261-75.

Discusses images of Africa in confrontation with the West found in Western literatures. Treats *HRK* in the context of a discussion of the white man's search for salvation in Africa. Discusses also some possible African counterparts for Bellow.

746. Hasenclever, Walter. "Grosse Menschen und Kleine Wirklichkeit: Erlebnisse eines Regenkonigs." *Monat* Feb. 1961: 71-75.

747. Hays, Peter L. *The Limping Hero: Grotesques in Literature.* Peter Hays. New York: New York UP, 1971. 55-59.

Bellow, in this novel, uses the stuff of myth half in joke and half in earnest. *HRK* can be seen as a quasi-parody of all fertility myths. The novel testifies that man can undergo degradation, a spiritual death, as a rite of passage to a life that is better, fuller, and more meaningful.

748. Heinsheimer, Hans. "Zeroing In." *Opera News* (16 Apr. 1977): 12-15.

An informative account of Leon Kirchner's depiction of the character of Henderson and the structure of the opera *Lily,* based on Bellow's novel. Useful for historical background on how the opera came into being.

749. Holm, Astrid. "Existentialism and Saul Bellow's *Henderson the*

Rain King." *American Studies in Scandinavia* 10.2 (1978):
93-109.

Holm, while acknowledging Bellow's debt to American romanticism, concentrates exclusively on the influence of the
French existentialists on his work. Of primary concern is
the influence of Jean-Paul Sartre. Holm concludes by theo-
rizing that Bellow "seems eventually to be able to reconcile
the two seemingly irreconcileable philosophical movements--
Transcendentalism and Existentialism."

750. Hruska, Thomas. "Henderson's Riches." *Journal of English
Studies* [India] 12.1 (1980): 779-84.

Illustrates the many critical models that can be applied to
the novel as a way of illustrating the immense richness of the
character of Henderson.

751. Hughes, Daniel J. "Reality and the Hero: *Lolita* and *Henderson
the Rain King*." *Modern Fiction Studies* 6.4 (1960-61): 345-64.
Rpt. *Saul Bellow and the Critics*. Ed. Irving Malin. New
York: New York UP, 1967. 69-91; *Saul Bellow*. Ed. Harold
Bloom. Modern Critical Views. New York: Chelsea, 1986.
25-43.

Hughes argues that both novels, if read in conjunction, throw
light on the problems of the contemporary novelist and the
much-heralded crisis in the novel. Both are novels about the
quest for reality on the part of protagonists who completely
fill the novels in which they appear, but who are not satis-
fied with such a role. Hughes goes on to make a series of
complex and enlightening comments on similarities and differences between the two novels.

752. Hull, Byron D. "*Henderson the Rain King* and William James."
Criticism 13.4 (1971): 402-14.

All of the chapters dealing with Henderson, Dahfu, and Atti
are explicable in terms of Jamesian psychology. In this light
the initiation process going on under the tutelage of Dahfu
becomes not only a part of the nature ritual allied to the
overall archetypal pattern, but directed therapy applied to
the ills of self which are Henderson's. Dahfu functions as

psychotherapist employing the ideas of James' psychology in
a program of rehabilitation.

753. Johnson, Lemuel. "Safaries in the Bush of Ghosts: Camara Laye,
Saul Bellow, and Ayi Kwei Armah." *Issue: Journal of Opinion*
13 (1984): 45-54. Cited in *MLA Bibliography*, 1985.

754. Kehler, Joel R. "Henderson's Sacred Science." *Centennial
Review* 24.2 (1980): 232-47.

In *HRK*, claims Kehler, Bellow draws many concepts from the
history of science in order to help define the hard-won but
provisional affirmation of his protagonist. The terms of
science interlock closely with those of romantic philosophy,
psychology, and cultural anthropology, to dramatize the
spiritual regeneration of a comically exaggerated twentieth-
century man.

755. Knight, Karl F. "Bellow's Henderson and Melville's Ishmael:
Their Mingled Worlds." *Studies in American Fiction* 12.1 (1984):
91-98.

Discusses the mingled and ambiguous nature of the world of
creatures as being the central theme of both works and the
common denominator they share. Carefully traces numerous
parallels between the two works. Concludes that at the end
of the respective quests neither quester is reconciled to
home and hearth.

756. Kruse, Horst. "Saul Bellow; *Henderson the Rain King*." *Schlussel-
motive der Amerikanischen Literatur*. Dusseldorf: Bagel, 1979.
184-201.

757. Leach, Elsie. "From Ritual to Romance Again: *Henderson the
Rain King*." *Western Humanities Review* 14.2 (1960): 223-24.

Certain important elements of the plot and situation of *HRK*
parallel components of Jesse L. Weston's *From Ritual to
Romance*. Leach points out that the fertility cult symbols of
the Grail Legend, the rain-making ceremonies, the propitiation
of the nature gods, the curse on the land, the dead body in

the dark sequences, strangulation for impotence, and many other similar motifs derive directly from Weston's book.

758. Majdiak, Daniel. "The Romantic Self and *Henderson the Rain King*." *Bucknell Review* 19.2 (1971): 125-46.

In *HRK* Bellow chooses to treat the growth of the spirit comically while he reaffirms the romantic assertion that spiritual growth is the end of existence even if, in the modern world, it manifests itself in strange and unexpected forms. Henderson, like the romantic poet, becomes the quester with his goal of expanded consciousness. Madjiak traces the development of this romantic quest for selfhood in considerable detail.

759. Markos, Donald W. "Life Against Death in *Henderson the Rain King*." *Modern Fiction Studies* 17.2 (1971): 193-205.

In the character of Henderson, writes Markos, we find both the destructive symptoms of alienation, and a potential vitality for regeneration. Bellow has made Henderson appear often larger than life, a mythical figure who embodies many of the fears and aspirations of a whole generation of Americans. Though grossly misdirected, the life instinct is strong in Henderson. The impulse toward renewal is at the heart of this novel; it is the source of motivation and symbolism, as well as incidental imagery. We have moved from the modernism typified by Eliot's listlessly questing Fisher King to the energy and vitality of post-modernism where significant positive action is once again possible.

760. Michelson, Bruce. "The Idea of *Henderson*." *Twentieth Century Literature* 27.4 (1981): 309-24.

Michelson sees this novel as lacking adequate critical treatment. In *HRK* Bellow explores and wages a kind of war against all the deceptive, fleeting seriousness of modern life, all those new ideas which demand such reverence and which wear out so quickly. It can defy seriousness even as it achieves it. Michelson goes on to explore a number of related themes in an effort to discern the structure of the book. States that his explicit intent is not to give the novel a reductive symbol hunters reading, but rather to examine a variety of themes without insisting on the primacy of any one. Its apparent disorder is its deliberate structure.

761. Moss, Judith. "The Body as Symbol in Saul Bellow's *Henderson the Rain King.*" *Literature and Psychology* 20.2 (1970): 51-61.

In *HRK*, Moss claims, the body of Eugene Henderson, viewed in the light of Freudian conversion symptomology, is a central dramatic symbol, "substantial" and unavoidable, which functions in characterization, shapes the narrative, and metaphorically generates the dual theme of regeneration and recovery.

762. Okeke-Ezigbo, Emeka. "The Frogs Incident in *Henderson the Rain King.*" *Notes on Contemporary Literature* 12.1 (1982): 7-8.

Argues that the difference between how Henderson views the frogs and how the Arnewi view them "sums up the opposition between Euro-American and the African world-views."

763. Pearce, Richard. "Harlequin: The Character of the Clown in Saul Bellow's *Henderson the Rain King* and John Hawkes' *Second Skin.*" *Stages of the Clown: Perspectives on Modern Fiction from Dostoevsky to Beckett.* Richard Pearce. Crosscurrents/Modern Critique. Carbondale, IL: Southern Illinois UP; London: Feffer, 1970. 102-16.

Pearce establishes that Bellow's Henderson is excellent for the purposes of exploring the modern manifestation of Harlequin, his situation, nature, and role, because of the emphasis on social reality. Henderson is a perfect Harlequin because he thrives in chaos, but to build rather than destroy. His creations are silly, precarious, evanescent; but they bring positive pleasure and are a source of positive values. The world this Harlequin inhabits is as menacing as the one left by the medieval demon or sottie fool. Harlequin has no illusions about this world, but nevertheless affirms the greatness of the human spirit that can not only endure but prevail.

764. Pearson, Carol. "Bellow's *Henderson the Rain King* and the Myth of the King, the Fool, and the Hero." *Notes on Contemporary Literature* 5.5 (1975): 8-11.

    HRK is a modern version of the myth of the king, the fool, and the hero. An examination of the novel from this perspective aids our understanding of it and shows how the myth has undergone changes to fit the conditions of the contemporary world. This article draws heavily on William Willeford's *The Fool and his Sceptor* for its basic argument.

765. Porter, M. Gilbert. "*Henderson the Rain King*: An Orchestration of Soul Music." *New England Review* 1.6 (1972): 24-33.

766. Pribanic, Victor. "The Monomyth and its Function in *Henderson the Rain King*." *Itinerary 3: Criticism*. Ed. Frank Baldanza. Bowling Green, OH: Bowling Green UP, 1977. 25-30.

    A brief application of the major features of the monomyth *a la* Joseph Campbell as they appear in *HRK*.

767. Rodrigues, Eusebio L. "Bellow's Africa." *American Literature* 43.2 (1971): 242-56.

    Rodrigues argues that Bellow's Africa is not just a geographical continent, but a strange land summoned into existence by Bellow's imagination. It is a metaphysical Africa--a paradigm of the modern world seen through a distorting and fantastic lens. Though Bellow did study African anthropology from the works of his teacher, Melville J. Herskovits, among others, nevertheless, Bellow transmutes these bare facts into a fictional and metaphysical landscape. Rodrigues traces Bellow's research borrowings very carefully in this article.

768. Rodrigues, Eusebio L. "The Reference to 'Joxi' in *Henderson the Rain King*." *Notes on Contemporary Literature* 8.4 (1978): 9-10.

    Rodrigues traces the references to Joxi or foot trampling massage to Richard F. Burton's *First Footsteps in East Africa*. He claims that though Bellow borrowed unashamedly

from Burton, he transformed what he took by changing spell-
ings, adding touches of color and detail and making it a
significant item in the overall Reichian pattern of *HRK*.

769. Rodrigues, Eusebio L. "Reichianism in *Henderson the Rain
      King*." *Criticism* 15.3 (1973): 212-33.

      The axis of the whirling world of *HRK*, according to Rodri-
      gues, is the Reichian thrust of Henderson's quest for
      humanness. A thorough analysis of the use Bellow makes of
      Reichian ideas in the novel.

770. Rodrigues, Eusebio L. "Saul Bellow's Henderson as America."
      Centennial Review 20.2 (1976): 189-95.

      Traces Bellow's deliberate references to Henderson as a Twain
      adventurer, a Whitmanlike poseur, another Ishmael and a new
      American Columbus, thus making him a symbol of America it-
      self. Gigantic, gargantuan, monumental, Henderson is endowed
      with huge, physical dimensions, suggesting he is not just an
      individual but a whole continent.

771. Rodrigues, Eusebio L. "Saul Bellow's Henderson as Mankind and
      Messiah." *Renascence* 35.4 (1983): 235-46.

      On the topmost level, gargantuan Henderson is both mankind
      itself and an extraordinary messiah who comes back from
      Africa (the original home of mankind) with tidings of hope
      and joy for his fellow man.

772. Sastri, P. S. "Bellow's *Henderson the Rain King*: A Quest for
      Being." *Panjab University Research Bulletin* (Arts) 3.1 (1972):
      9-18. Cited in *MLA Bibliography*, 1972.

773. Sieburth, Renee. "*Henderson the Rain King*: A Twentieth
      Century Don Quixote? " *Canadian Review of Comparative
      Literature* 5.1 (1978): 86-94.

      One of the main inspirations of *HRK* is Cervante's *Don
      Quixote*, which fact permeates the Henderson odyssey and

informs its deepest matter. Mostly traces the parallels
between the two characters, Don Quixote and Henderson.

774. Smelstor, Marjorie. "The Schlemiel as Father: A Study of
Yakov Bok and Eugene Henderson." *Studies in American Jewish
Literature* 4.1 (1978): 50-57.

Examines the contemporary use of the *schlemiel* as a useful
model for the modern bungling anti-hero. Proceeds to examine the *schlemiel* fathers, Bok and Henderson, as two Jewish
anti-heroes who are speaking to modern audiences about
their fears of fathering, being fathered, of giving and
receiving life.

775. Steig, Michael. "Bellow's *Henderson* and the Limits of Freudian
Criticism." *Paunch* 36-37 (1973): 39-46.

Asserts that Bellow's way of presenting Henderson is much
more compatible with a Reichian view of the relation between
psyche and soma, than with the Freudian concept of conversion hysteria.

776. Stout, Janis P. "Biblical Allusion in *Henderson the Rain King*."
South Central Bulletin 40.4 (1980): 165-67.

Stout establishes that though there are only direct allusions
to six books of the Bible, *HRK* abounds in indirect allusions,
knowledge of which enriches and extends the significance of
Henderson's journey to Africa by supporting its religious
dimension. But they also provide specific measures by which
to assess his changes in awareness and disposition during
the course of the journey.

777. Stout, Janis P. "The Possibility of Affirmation in *Heart of
Darkness* and *Henderson the Rain King*." *Philological
Quarterly* 57.1 (1978): 115-31.

Discusses the similarities between *Heart of Darkness* and
HRK. Stout concerns herself with the differences in tone,
the narrator's attitude and his response to the journey.
Attempts to answer the question of whether, within the
terms of the two novels, hope is feasible. Asserts that the

responses of both works to this question are more moderate, more qualified by reservations than commentators have generally allowed.

778. Tick, Stanley. "America Writes." *Meajin* [Australia] April 1961: 112-15.

779. Toliver, Harold E. "Bellow's Idyll of the Tribe." *Pastoral Forms and Attitudes*. Harold E. Toliver. Berkeley: U of California P, 1971. 323-25.

Deals with *HRK* in terms of the American pastoral dream of retreat.

780. Toth, Susan Allen. "*Henderson the Rain King*, Eliot and Browning." *Notes on Contemporary Literature* 1.5 (1971): 6-8.

Comments on Bellow's use of T.S. Eliot's "The Wasteland" and Robert Browning's "Childe Roland to the Dark Tower Came," both of which reverberate through the background of Bellow's novel.

781. Towner, Daniel. "Brill's Ruins and Henderson's Rain." *Critique* 17.3 (1976): 96-104.

Traces similarities between Vance Bourjaily's novel, *Brill Among the Ruins* (1970), and *HRK*. Explores also what can be learned from studying the dissimilarities between the novels.

782. Trachtenberg, Stanley. "Saul Bellow's *Luftmenschen*: The Compromise with Reality." *Critique* 9.3 (1967): 37-61.

783. Whittemore, Reed. "Safari Among the Wariri." *New Republic* 16 Mar. 1959: 17-18. Rpt. as "*Henderson the Rain King*." *The Critic as Artist: Essays on Books 1920-1970*. Ed. Gilbert A. Harrison. New York: Liveright, 1972. 382-87.

An interestingly testy essay on all the works of literature

to which *HRK* has been compared in the reviews. Complains of the lack of unity in the novel.

784. Winchell, Mark Roydon. "Bellow's Hero with a Thousand Faces: The Use of Folk Myth in *Henderson the Rain King*." *Mississippi Folklore Register* 14.2 (1980): 115-26.

Defines the Campbell monomyth in detail and then explicates the novel in light of it, showing how Bellow both borrows from and violates the structure of the myth. What makes this hero different from the traditional romantic hero of the monomyth is his unwillingness to "acknowledge a single, external source of meaning." Concludes that Bellow takes "an eclectic and utilitarian view of the folk myth."

Reviews

785. Baker, Carlos. "To the Dark." *New York Times Book Review* 22 Feb. 1959: 4-5.

786. Bradbury, Malcolm. "Saul Bellow's *Henderson the Rain King*." *Listener* 30 Jan. 1964: 187-88.

787. Cruttwell, Patrick. "Fiction Chronicle." *Hudson Review* 12.2 (1959): 286-95.

788. Curley, Thomas F. "A Clown Through and Through." *Commonweal* 17 Apr. 1959: 84.

789. Drabble, Margaret. "A Myth to Stump the Experts." *New Statesman* 26 Mar. 1971: 435.

790. "Dun Quixote." *Time* 23 Feb. 1959: 102.

791. Friedman, Joseph J. *Venture* 3.3 (1959): 71-73.

792. Gold, Herbert. "Giant of Cosmic Despair." *Nation* 21 Feb. 1959: 169-72.

793. Hardwick, Elizabeth. "A Fantastic Voyage." *Partisan Review* 26.2 (1959): 299-303.

794. Hicks, Granville. "The Search for Salvation." *Saturday Review* 21 Feb. 1959: 20.

795. Hogan, William. "Saul Bellow's Case Against Symbolism." *San Francisco Chronicle* 23 Feb. 1959: 25.

796. Jacobson, Dan. "The Solitariness of Saul Bellow." *Spectator* 22 May 1959: 735.

797. Knipp, Thomas R. "The Cost of Henderson's Quest." *Ball State University Forum* 10.2 (1969): 37-39.

798. Kogan, Herman. "Symbolism Beneath a Rushing Narrative." *Chicago Sunday Tribune* 22 Feb. 1959: 3.

799. Lemaire, Marcel. "Some Recent American Novels and Essays." *Revue des Langues Vivantes* 28 (1962): 70-78.

800. Levine, Paul. *Georgia Review* 14.2 (1960): 218-20.

801. Maddocks, Melvin. "In Search for Freedom and Salvation in New Novels." *Christian Science Monitor* 26 Feb. 1959: 11.

802. Malcolm, Donald. "Rider Haggard Rides Again." *New Yorker* 14 Mar. 1959: 171-73.

803. Miller, Karl. "Poet's Novels." *Listener* 25 June 1959: 1099-1100.

804. "Millionaire's Odyssey." *Newsweek* 23 Feb. 1959: 106-07.

805. Perrott, Roy. "Two Attempts at the Big American Novel." *Manchester Guardian* 29 May 1959: 6.

806. Pickrel, Paul. "Innocent Voyager." *Harper's* Mar. 1959: 104.

807. Podhoretz, Norman. "Saul Bellow's Power-Filled, Puzzling Novel of a Millionaire in Africa." *New York Herald Tribune Book Review* 22 Feb. 1959: 3.

808. Prescott, Orville. "Books of the Times." *New York Times* 23 Feb. 1959: 21.

809. Price, Martin. "Intelligence and Fiction: Some New Novels." *Yale Review* ns 48.3 (1959): 453-56.

810. Rolo, Charles J. "Reader's Choice." *Atlantic* Mar. 1959: 88.

811. Stern, Richard G. "Henderson's Bellow." *Kenyon Review* 21.4 (1959): 655-61.

812. Swados, Harvey. "Bellow's Adventures in Africa." *New Leader* 23 Mar. 1959: 23-24.

813. Thompson, Frank H., Jr. "I Want, I Want, I Want." *Prairie Schooner* 34.2 (1960): 174-75.

814. Wain, John. "American Allegory." *Observer* 24 May 1959: 21.

815. Waterhouse, Keith. *New Statesman and Nation* ns 6 June 1959: 805-06.

816. Weales, Gerald. "Comedy, Laughter and Fantasy." *Reporter* 19 Mar. 1959: 46-48.

817. Adams, Timothy Dow. "La Petite Madeleine: Proust and *Herzog*." *Notes on Contemporary Literature* 8.1 (1978): 11.

Links the name "Madeleine" with a reference in Proust's *Remembrance of Things Past*, in which a madeleine is a small cake which produces an intense inducement to memory in the protagonist who eats it.

818. Aldridge, John W. "The Complacency of Herzog." *Time to Murder and Create: The Contemporary Novel in Crisis.* John W. Aldridge. New York: McKay, 1966. 133-38. Rpt. in *The Devil and the Fire: Retrospective Essays on American Literature and Culture 1951-1971.* John W. Aldridge. New York: Harper's Magazine Press, 1972. 231-34; *Herzog: Text and Criticism.* Ed. Irving Howe. Viking Critical Library. New York: Viking, 1976. 440-44.

Sees Herzog's complacency as his badge of sainthood. "Herzog's suffering is right and admirable, and that suffering . . . is the very measure of his significance both as a person and as a dramatic figure."

819. Atkins, Anselm. "The Moderate Optimism of Saul Bellow's *Herzog*." *Personalist* 50.1 (1969): 117-29.

Postwar fictional heroes, including Bellow's early protagonists, are casualties of a disintegrating world who are often unable to rise above their fates. Many seem to be descendants of the "American Adam," innocents in paradise whose affirmative views have not been bought at a high enough price. Herzog, however, integrates and surpasses the simplicities of Bellow's earlier characters. His root stock is innocence, but onto

173

that innocence has been grafted a full emotional and intellectual awareness of the plight of contemporary man.

820. Axthelm, Peter M. "The Full Perception: Saul Bellow." *The
     Modern Confessional Novel*. Peter M. Axthelm. New Haven,
     CT: Yale UP, 1967. 128-79.

     Speaks of the modern confessional hero as seeking a state
     of full perception to make his consciousness less painful.
     Discusses *H* in detail from the perspective that "Herzog's
     perception amounted to nothing, in that it is a simple, quiet
     decision to stop his confession. . . . It contains nothing in
     the form of momentary vision or an affirmation of one speci〉
     value, but its development includes glimpses of almost every-
     thing in man's intellectual repertory." A major article on *H*.

821. Barasch, Frances K. "Faculty Images in Recent American
     Fiction." *College Literature* 10.1 (1983): 28-37.

     Perceives H as one of a developing genre of American "colleg〉
     professor novels." Criticizes such novelists for stereotyping
     their characters as Jews, whites, males and paranoids. Rarely
     seen at their academic work, the heroes are haunted by
     parental memories of pogrom and flight, the trauma of trans-
     plantation, the rigidity of old world patriarchy, the subver-
     siveness of Jewish mothers, and the amibivalence of wealthie〉
     well-married siblings toward a tribal member who has become
     learned in gentile ways. Herzog is depicted as preeminent
     among these neurotics.

822. Baruch, Franklin R. "Bellow and Milton: Professor Herzog in his
     Garden." *Critique* 9.3 (1967): 74-83.

     The anti-heroic frame into which Saul Bellow places the cen-
     tral figure of Herzog is given its final solidity and effect in
     the closing setting of the novel, a version of the ritual use
     of Eden that received its strongest traditional and classical
     expression in the epic context of Milton's *Paradise Lost*.

823. Bienen, Leigh Buchanan. "New American Fiction: Review of
     Herzog." *Transition: A Journal of the Arts, Culture and
     Society* 5.20 (1965): 46-51.

In *H* we perceive the fullest development of Bellow's and America's genuinely American style. This is because of its oblique style and generalized expression of American culture.

824. Bluefarb, Sam. "The Middle-Aged Man in Contemporary Literature: Bloom to Herzog." *College Language Association Journal* 20.1 (1976): 1-13.

Places Herzog in a long line of middle-aged heroes extending down through Anglo-American literature from Moses Bloom and Prufrock and Lambert Strether. Sees him as modeled on Bloom and possessing many traits in common with him and with many of the other middle-aged protagonists.

825. Boulger, James D. "Puritan Allegory in Four Modern Novels." *Thought* 174 (1969): 413-32.

Treats *H* along with three other novels as a work pervaded by an allegorical religious pattern that ultimately raises it above the ordinary level of the literal and the ephemeral. The allegorical pattern is a Puritan-Calvinist one. All four novelists use this mode because they are interested in American tradition and conflict, whether from the WASP standpoint or that of an aspiring minority.

826. Boulot, Elisabeth. "Rupture, revolte et harmonie dans *Herzog* de Saul Bellow." *Visages de l'harmonie dans la litterature Anglo-Americaine*. Reims: Centre de Recherche sur l'imaginaire dans le litterature de langue anglaise, University of Reims, 1982. 153-66.

Discusses rupture, revolt and harmony in *H* under the following headings: 1) Disintegration of the personality, 2) Chronicle of divorce and its consequences, 3) Philosophy of the rupture of the proclamation with the society which surrounds it, 4) Reconciliation of the Self--taking on the human condition, 5) Infancy and harmony.

827. Boyers, Robert T. "Attitudes Toward Sex in American 'High Culture'." *Annals of the American Academy of Political and Social Sciences* 376 (1968): 36-52.

828. Bradbury, Malcolm. "Saul Bellow's *Herzog*." *Critical Quarterly* 7.3 (1965): 269-78.

> Compares William Burrough's *The Naked Lunch*, a novel written out of deviance and celebrating it, with Saul Bellow's *H*, a novel which discusses the same questions and comes up with a much more positive and morally responsible answer. Likens Bellow's approach to Trilling's in his refusal to accept unquestioningly the views of Updike, Roth, Jones, Powers, Burroughs and Donleavy.

829. Brans, Jo. "The Balance Sheet of Love: Money and Its Meaning in Bellow's *Herzog*." *Notes on Modern American Literature* 2.4 (1978): Item 29.

> Money has symbolic significance in most Bellow novels but *HRK* seems indifferent to it. However, in *H* money becomes a credit item in a ledger of love. Financial depletion accompanies emotional bankruptcy, but love is generous and can afford to be. This dichotomy shows most clearly in the characters of the women in Herzog's life, Daisy, Sono, Madeleine, and Ramona.

830. Brezianu, Andrei. "Epistolarul lui Herzog sau Labirintul spre Adamville ["Herzog's Epistolary or the Labyrinth to Adamville"]." *Secolul* 20.9 (1970): 104-09.

831. Capon, Robert F. "Herzog and the Passion." *America* 27 Mar. 1965: 425-27.

> Capon questions whether *H* is really *Hamlet* with a happy ending. He also asks the Christian question of just what kind of freedom and repose it is that Herzog has brought himself at the end of the novel. What follows is primarily a discussion of how the Christian churches do and do not deal with the issues Bellow raises in the novel.

832. Casty, Alan. "Post-Loverly Love: A Comparative Report." *Antioch Review* 26.3 (1966): 399-411.

> While the dominant theme of modern literature has been the

search for love, the quest has moved in this latest Bellow novel beyond sentimentalism to a more sophisticated stage of posing a typical hero who does not naively discover love at the climax of his tale of misadventures, but who has known it all along. He finds it is more complex and subtle than he has thought, and now he has to struggle to live with it.

833. Chavkin, Allan. "Bellow's Alternative to the Wasteland: Romantic Theme and Form in *Herzog.*" *Studies in the Novel* 11.3 (1979): 326-37.

H is both a traditional novel and a radically experimental one. While Bellow urges a return to romantic values to overcome our contemporary spiritual one, he presents his romantic theme in a new form. This new theme is a radical alteration of the English romantic's early nineteenth-century invention, the discursive meditative mode. H has its roots in the English romantic tradition.

834. Chavkin, Allan. "Bellow's Investigation of the 'Social Meaning in Nothingness': Role Playing in *Herzog.*" *Yiddish* 4.4 (1982): 48-57.

Suggests that H be considered a vivid illustration of the Hobbesian view of life that would replace "the image of man as a romantic humanist with the 'mass man' who is self-centered, treacherous, and predatory." Demonstrates the extent to which Bellow's humanist roots lie in the romantic tradition and the extent to which he fights Hobbesian and nihilist estimates of human existence.

835. Chavkin, Allan. "The Unsuccessful Search for 'Pure Love' in Saul Bellow's *Herzog.*" *Notes on Modern American Literature* 2.4 (1978): Item 27.

Herzog's essential problem, the one that affects him most acutely and exacerbates his intellectual confusion, is his relationship with women. By the end of the novel he understands the inadequacy of his past attitude toward love that has resulted in dominating and being dominated by women.

836. Chyet, Stanley F. "Herzog's Folly: Or, A Discourse on History and Literature for American Jews." *American-Jewish History* 73.3 (1984): 286-95.

Discusses this novel in the context of a complex discussion of Jewish historiography.

837. Cixous, Helene. "Situation de Saul Bellow." *Les Lettres Nouvelles* 58 (Mar.-Apr. 1967): 130-45.

Sees Herzog as a character who has recognized the great complexity of the world he lives in and its power to constantly transform itself. Therefore he has an urgent need to discover what it truly means to be human and how to live this life. This is the struggle that lies at the heart of his thinking. It is a matter of survival as a member of the human species.

838. Colbert, Robert E. "Satiric Vision in *Herzog.*" *Studies in Contemporary Satire* 5 (1978): 22-33.

None of the present commentators on *H* have pointed out how important specifically satiric perspective and satirical portraiture are to the meaning of the novel. Bellow's vision, like that of his nineteenth-century Russian and English predecessors, is ultimately a humane and comic one; but, unlike the authors of *Dead Souls* and *Bleak House*, he has frequent recourse to satiric devices.

839. Contraire, A. U. "The Prufrock Corner: Herzog and Prufrock: Eyes that Fix You in a Formulated Phrase." *Windless Orchard* 38 (Spring-Summer 1981): 46-48.

Compares Prufrock and Herzog as men of sensibility whose antennae and levels of awareness enable them to interpret culture. They are archetypes of the era.

840. Coonley, Donald E. "To Cultivate, to Dread: The Concept of Death in *The Ginger Man* and *Herzog.*" *New Campus Review* [Metropolitan State College, Denver] 2 (1969): 7-12.

841. Cordesse, Gerard. "L'Unite de Herzog." *Caliban* 7 (1970): 99-113.

Sees this novel as both a psychological study and a philosophical debate. Concentrates primarily on the affirmative philosophical stance and the development of Herzog's character that goes along with it. Concludes that as a true artist Bellow eschews simplicities and goes on to espouse ambiguities and incongruities in his estimate of human nature.

842. Cronin, Gloria L. "*Herzog*: The Purgation of Twentieth Century Consciousness." *Interpretations: A Journal of Ideas, Analysis and Criticism* 16.1 (1985): 8-20.

Asserts that in *H* Bellow's primary intention was to demonstrate a hero ridding himself of all superfluous modernist ideas. The text is read as one of the century's major Anglo-American rejections of modernist ideas. Suppporting arguments are drawn both from the text and Bellow's interviews and essays. Illustrates the thoroughness of Herzog's and therefore Bellow's analysis of exactly what the effects on the contemporary sense of the Self have been of the works of all the great modernist thinkers.

843. de Rambures, Jean-Louis. "La Fin du Heros Muscle: *Herzog* de Saul Bellow." *Realities* Sept. 1966: 99-105. Cited in *Abstracts of English Studies*, 1969.

844. Elgin, Don D. "Order Out of Chaos: Bellow's Use of the Picaresque in *Herzog*." *Saul Bellow Journal* 3.2 (1984): 13-22.

It was not until *H* that Bellow was able to combine the traditional picaresque elements with the modifications necessary to make the American picaresque a logical alternative to the formlessness and despair of the stream-of-consciousness, experimental and/or historical novels that had previously seemed to be heralding their own imminent demise.

845. Ellmann, Richard. "Search for an Internal Sanctuary: *Herzog*." *Chicago Sun-Times Book Week* 27 Sept. 1964: 1-2.

Sees Herzog's search as more clearly focused than his
predecessors. Sees him fighting against the entire preoccupation with the ego, which he finds sinister in romantic
thought. "Against it he invokes a gregarious decency and
the moral realities that arise, incomprehensibly, from that."

846. Fisch, Harold. "The Hero as Jew: Reflections on *Herzog*."
     Judaism 17.1 (1968): 42-54.

Demonstrates the Jewishness of the novel in its depiction of
the Jew who becomes a representative American in the depic
tion of the modern dilemma in Western culture. Hence, all
are seen as outcasts pursuing "private intensities" in a state
of alienation and exile.

847. Flamm, Dudley. "Herzog--Victim and Hero." *Zeitschrift fur
     Anglistik und Amerikanistik* [East Berlin] 17.2 (1969): 174-88.

Examines the precise ways which, in a Jewish sense, Herzog
is both a victim and a hero. Concentrates largely on the
novel's Jewishness and Bellow's use of this means of
universalizing his material. Concludes by likening Herzog to
one of Andre-Schwartz-Bart's thirty-six "just men," each of
whom bears one thirty-sixth of the world's pain in order to
redeem mankind.

848. Franck, Jacques. "Saul Bellow: *Herzog*." *Revue General Belge*
     (Feb. 1967): 113-20. [In French]

849. Fuchs, Daniel. "*Herzog*: The Making of a Novel." *Critical
     Essays on Saul Bellow*. Ed. Stanley Trachtenberg. Critical
     Essays on American Literature. Boston: Hall, 1979. 101-21.
     Longer version rpt. in *Saul Bellow: Vision and Revision*.
     Daniel Fuchs. Durham, NC: Duke UP, 1984. 121-54.

Examines the early drafts of *H* and traces Bellow's revision
process with a view to discovering his methods and art.
Demonstrates Bellow's deliberate effort to show Herzog's
turning to God "as an act of the natural man recognizing
the limits of Nature. His quest has brought him to affirm
the primacy of moral authority of God." Major article.

850. Galloway, David D. "Moses-Bloom-Herzog: Bellow's Everyman." *Southern Review* 2.1 (1966): 61-76.

Identifies this novel as one in which Bellow has united two traditions: 1) that of meditative impotent victim, 2) that of comic rebel. Sees Joyce's *Ulysses*, and Bloom specifically, as the major source of the novel as well as the biblical prophet Moses. A major article.

851. Garcia Ponce, Juan. "A Hero of Our Time." *Entry Into Matter: Modern Literature and Reality.* Juan Garcia Ponce. Trans. David J. Parent and Bruce Novoa. Illinois Language and Culture Series 2. Normal, IL: Applied Literature Press, 1976. 18-24.

852. Garrett, George. "To Do Right in a Bad World: Saul Bellow's *Herzog.*" *Hollins Critic* 2.2 (1965): 1-12.

Primarily attempts to rescue Bellow from accusations of redundancy, Jewishness, urbaneness and mere intellectuality. Above all, praises him for escaping reductive estimates of his parameters and overcoming the "catastrophe of success."

853. Gerson, Steven M. "Paradise Sought: The Modern American Adam in Bellow's *Herzog.*" *McNeese Review* 24 (1977-78): 50-57.

Argues against R. W. B. Lewis's thesis that only nineteenth-century literature could produce an American Adam. Argues through an examination of Herzog that modern Adamism completely reverses the optimistic tenets of early Adamism. Concludes that Herzog finds the search for paradise futile and ends up adapting to life rather than fleeing from it.

854. Goldman, Liela H. "Bellow's Moses Herzog." *Explicator* 37.4 (1979): Item 26.

Describes the confusing information given by Bellow and by commentators on the origins of the name Moses Herzog. "By giving erroneous information, Bellow has not supported his

claims of 'coincidence,' nor has he elucidated the choice of
name to his readers. . . ."

855. Goldman, Liela H. "On the Character of Ravitch in Saul
Bellow's *Herzog.*" *American Notes and Queries* 19.7-8 (1981):
115-16.

Discusses the possibility that Ravitch was modeled on
Melech Ravitch, playwright, who was primarily famous for
his poetry and who lived in Montreal from 1941 until his
death in 1979. Convincing and detailed in its comparisons
between the real and the fictional counterpart.

856. Goldman, Liela H. "Saul Bellow's Misuse of Hebrew and Yiddish
in *Herzog.*" *Jewish Language Review* 2 (1982): 75-79.

Provides a detailed account of Bellow's actual use of Hebrew
and Yiddish in *H* with a commentary on the possible reasons
for the errors in the text.

857. Gross, Beverly. "Bellow's *Herzog.*" *Chicago Review* 17.2-3
(1964): 217-21.

Though Gross comments that this is a book with artistic
structure, she is reluctant to call that structure novelistic.
Rather, she complains that Bellow's books have become less
neat and reviewable but that Herzog is significant enough
fiction to compare with the experience of reading Henry
James or James Joyce.

858. Hermans, Rob. "The Mystical Element in Saul Bellow's *Herzog.*"
Dutch Quarterly Review of Anglo-American Letters 11.2 (1981):
104-17.

Hermans argues that what Herzog experiences at the end of
the novel is the unity of the phenomenal world to which he
naturally belongs. Behind this unity he senses a power he
calls God. The combination of these two aspects strongly
suggests a mystical element as the essence of experience.

859. Hicks, Granville. "Fragile Bits and Pieces of Life." *Saturday Review* 19 Sept. 1964: 37-38. Rpt. in *Literary Horizons: A Quarter Century of American Fiction.* Granville Hicks. New York: New York UP, 1970. 60-63.

860. Hill, John S. "The Letters of Moses Herzog: A Symbolic Mirror." *Studies in the Humanities* 2.2 (1971): 40-45.

Sees the epistolary structure of the novel as a mirror for Herzog's mind which, like his new manuscript, is a voluminous pile of "chaotic argument which never found its focus." Sees Bellow as re-creating environment to mean mental environment as he attempts to avoid Drieserian determinism and merely external environment. Through this manner, the hero is shown to be able to override the violence of nature and select his own course.

861. Hindus, Milton. "Herzog: Existentialist Jewish Hero." *Jewish Frontier* Dec. 1964: 11-14.

Examines the Jewishness of the novel and defends Bellow against charges that he has "exploited" Jewish materials. Sees the book aiming at a variant of the same kind of "fatalistic existentialism" found in *SD*. In the absence of traditional faith and belief, Bellow shows the neo-Freudian religion of sex as an ultimate value.

862. Hoffman, Michael J. "From Cohn to Herzog." *Yale Review* 58.3 (1969): 342-58.

Sees Herzog as the reincarnation of the spirit of Robert Cohn. Sees this merely as a shift from secularized white Protestant to secularized Jewish intellectual. Herzog is Cohn's "descendant and verbalizer." Both are naifs, both rationalize, both have mistresses, and so on.

863. Hogel, Rolf. "Gegenwart und Vergangenheit: Ihre synchrone Darstellung in Saul Bellows Roman *Herzog*." *Literatur in Wissenschaft und Unterricht* 14.2 (1981): 103-15.

864. Howe, Irving. "Odysseus Flat on His Back." *New Republic* 19
     Sept. 1964: 21-26. Rpt. as "Herzog." *The Critic as Artist:*
     Essays on Books 1920-1970. Ed. Gilbert A. Harrison. New
     York: Liveright, 1972. 181-91; as "Down and Out in New
     York and Chicago: Saul Bellow, Professor Herzog, and Mr.
     Sammler." *The Critical Point: On Literature and Culture.* Ed.
     Irving Howe. New York: Horizon, 1973. 121-36, and *Herzog:*
     Text and Criticism. Ed. Irving Howe. Viking Critical Library.
     New York: Viking, 1976. 391-400. Rpt. with original title in
     Saul Bellow. Ed. Harold Bloom. Modern Critical Views. New
     York: Chelsea, 1986. 45-51.

     Praises Bellow as one of the most powerful minds among con-
     temporary American writers and one "who best assimilates his
     intelligence to creative purpose." However, he has "become
     increasingly devoted to the idea of the novel as sheer spec-
     tacle." Howe sees *H* as Bellow's most remarkable and notably
     advanced novel in technique. Complains that instead of free-
     ing us from the image of the sick self we are still caught up
     with it in this novel. Howe sees the novel primarily as a
     remarkably animated performance combining both the despai
     ing and the comic.

865. Josipovici, Gabriel. "Bellow and Herzog." *Encounter* 37.5 (1971):
     49-55. Rpt. in *Herzog: Text and Critcism.* Ed. Irving Howe.
     Viking Critical Library. New York: Viking, 1976. 401-15; as
     "Herzog: Freedom and Wit" in *The World and the Book: A*
     Study of Modern Fiction. Ed. Gabriel Josipovici. London:
     Macmillan, 1971. 2nd ed., 1979. 221-35.

     Deals in depth with the themes of historicism, crisis ethics,
     existentialism, Rousseauistic notions of human possibilities
     and "potato love." Along with all these themes Bellow is
     actually writing a book "which is an attack on the structuring
     activity of the mind." Thus the sense of human mystery con-
     veyed by the book.

866. Kannan, Lakshmi. "Professor Herzog's Academy." *Journal of*
     English Studies [India] 12.1 (1980): 785-99.

     Kannan examines both the English and American "university
     novel" and concludes that *H* expands the genre thematically
     with its emphasis on moral and social ideals.

867. Kaplan, Harold. "The Second Fall of Man." *Salmagundi* 30
(Summer 1975): 66-89.

Sees Bellow negotiating some middle territory between the
"magnified human possibilities" posited by the classic
writers, and the inevitable American reaction to the failure
of such promises--failures that issue a challenge "to the
self-confidence of the species." Sees Bellow dealing with
existential naturalism and cults of "death and dread." A
major article.

868. Kemnitz, Charles. "Narration and Consciousness in *Herzog*."
Saul Bellow Journal 1.2 (1982): 1-6.

In *H* there is no distinction made between Herzog's voice
and that of the narrator. Discusses the relationship between Herzog and Bellow and between Herzog and Moses
Herzog. Applies Bakhtin's five stylistic unities. Describes
how Bellow carries on the "American poetics of subsuming
the narration in the consciousness of a character."

869. Kermode, Frank. "Books in General: *Herzog*." 5 Feb. 1965: 200-
01. Rpt. in *Continuities*. Frank Kermode. New York: Random,
1968. 222-27.

870. Kerneur, Marie-Pierre. "Herzog et les machiavels." *Delta* 19
(Oct. 1984): 109-29.

Provides an in-depth treatment on *H* as a representation of
Machiavellian ideology, society, and politics.

871. Kuehn, Robert E. "Fiction Chronicle." *Contemporary Literature*
6.1 (1965): 132-39.

Sees *H* in the "great tradition of the novel" but is surprised
that it is not better than it is.

872. Lamont, Rosette C. "The Confessions of Moses Herzog."
Massachusetts Review 6.3 (1965): 630-35.

Sees, in addition to its artistic appeal, that *H*'s appeal for

the reading public has largely to do with its curiosity over
Bellow's private intellectual and emotional safaris, many of
which are revealed in this novel as were Rousseau's in his
Confessions.

873. Lasater, Alice E. "The Breakdown in Communication in the
Twentieth-Century Novel." *Southern Quarterly* 12 (1973):
1-14.

874. Lemco, Gary. "Bellow's Herzog: A Flight of the Heart." *Saul
Bellow Journal* 3.1 (1983): 38-46.

Sees the pervasive pattern of bird imagery in the novel as
supporting symbolically the cyclical patterns of aspiration
and loss, yearning and disillusion that characterize the
protagonist's "alternating vision of human nature."

875. Lemco, Gary. "Theatrical Elements in *Herzog* or, An Act of the
Heart." *Studies in American Jewish Literature* [University
Park, PA] 3.1 (1977): 7-16.

Lemco argues that Herzog's dilemma concerning the relationship of learning and feeling lies at the heart of this novel.
Explores the theme of acting and theatrics in relation to
this dualism. The personalities, the authorities and the
courtroom in *H* are all symbolic of a form of social theatre.
There is also religious theatre in his stealing Madeleine
from the Monsignor. Like-wise, Moses' self-controlled role
playing has turned his personal life into a circus.

876. Lofroth, Erik. "Herzog's Predicament: Saul Bellow's View of
Modern Man." *Studia Neophilologica* 44.2 (1972): 315-25.

This writer examines the character of Herzog against the
backdrop of certain experiences he claims in the novel: 1)
his past experiences, 2) his Jewish background, 3) his
American environment, and 4) his studies.

877. Lucko, Peter. "Herzog--Modell der *acceptance* Eine Erwiderung."
Zeitschrift fur Anglistik und Amerikanistik [East Berlin] 17.2
(1969): 189-95.

Lucko's article is a response to Dudley Flamm's article in the same journal issue. Arguing from a formalist Marxist position, Lucko criticizes Flamm's concept of Herzog as reductionist and apologetic of capitalism, pointing out that Herzog's experience is not only a subjective minority view of a society distant to him but also a cybernetic model of alienation and passive acceptance within capitalistic American society at large.

878. Masinton, Martha, and Charles G. Masinton. "Second-Class Citizenship: The Status of Women in Contemporary American Fiction." *What Manner of Woman: Essays on English and American Life and Literature.* Ed. Marlene Springer. New York: New York UP, 1977. 297-315.

879. Maurocordato, Alexandre. *Les quatre dimensions du 'Herzog' de Saul Bellow.* Les Archives de Lettres Modernes 102. Paris: Minard, 1969.

880. Mellard, James M. "Consciousness Fills the Void: Herzog, History, and the Hero in the Modern World." *Modern Fiction Studies* 25.1 (1979): 75-91.

Examines the results of theories of the death of God and of the void as the epistemological basis of *H.* Hence, the interleaved themes explored in this novel become self and identity, reality and history. Sees these themes as more crucial in this novel than previously.

881. Mosher, Harold F., Jr. "Herzog's Quest." *Le Voyage dans la litterature anglo-saxonne.* Actes du Congres de Nice (1971). Paris: Didier, 1972. 169-79.

Explores the thematic significance of Herzog's profession as an historian, since it is through his examination of his own past and that of Western civilization that he both escapes and embraces his true Self. Hence, the book may be read as a dialogue between Herzog of the past (including other personages of the past) and the Herzog of the present.

882. Mosher, Harold F., Jr. "The Synthesis of Past and Present in
     Saul Bellow's Herzog." *Wascana Review* 6.1 (1971): 28-38.

     Almost identical in content to the previous article, number
     881. Written in English.

883. Mudrick, Marvin. "Who Killed Herzog? or, Three American
     Novelists." *Denver Quarterly* 1.1 (1966): 61-97.

884. Nassar, Joseph M. "The World Within: Image Clusters in
     Herzog." *Saul Bellow Journal* 2.2 (1983): 24-29.

     Discusses the confused perceptions in Herzog's mind
     of image clusters--colors, odors and natural phenomena (main-
     ly floral)--embedded in certain configurations in the novel.
     These clusters of color images accumulate symbolic value.
     Nassar attempts to account for this in terms of Herzog's
     hypersensitive mental condition.

885. Nathan, Monique. "Saul Bellow." *Esprit* 352 (1966): 363-70.

886. Newman, Judie. "*Herzog*: History as Neurosis." *Delta* 19 (1984):
     131-53.

     In *H* Bellow treats history, as well as Herzog the historian,
     as a study in neurosis. "In its central character the novel
     directs the reader's attention to the status of history, and
     in particular to the Freudian view of history." Quoting Rieff
     on history ("History, the memory of existence in time, is
     the flaw. Neurosis is the failure to escape the past, the
     burdens of history ") and proceeds to develop this thesis
     with regard to *H*.

887. Park, Sue S. "The Keystone and the Arch: Another Look at
     Structure in *Herzog*." *Notes on Modern American Literature*
     2.4 (1978): Item 30.

     Examines the book's chapter lengths in terms of a mathe-
     matical graph. The nine chapters, looked at this way,
     approximate an arch with chapter five forming a keystone in
     the middle.

888. Petillon, Pierre-Yves. "Le Heros de roman americain a pris de l'age." *Critique* [Paris] 236 (1967): 159-76.

889. Pinsker, Sanford. "Moses Herzog and the Modern Wasteland." *Reconstructionist* 20 Dec. 1968: 20-26.

Bellow is preoccupied with many of the same intellectual concerns that absorbed Eliot and other "wastelanders," but demonstrates there is "not much belief in wastelands." Traces Herzog's waverings between "highbrow literature" and *mammeloshen*, between "Heidegger" and *heimisch*.

890. Pinsker, Sanford. "Moses Herzog's Fall into the Quotidian." *Studies in the Twentieth Century* 14 (Fall 1974): 105-15.

Describes Herzog's loss of innocence and Hamlet-like madness as he encounters evil. Concentrates on his "fall into the quotidian."

891. Poirier, Richard. "Bellows to *Herzog*." *Partisan Review* 32.2 (1965): 264-71.

Criticizes Bellow for writing a smug book based on the assumption that "the life of the urban Jew, far from being something special, is assumed to be the life of the Modern American Everyman."

892. Poirier, Richard. "*Herzog*, or Bellow in Trouble." *Saul Bellow: A Collection of Critical Essays*. Ed. Earl Rovit. Twentieth Century Views. Englewood Cliffs, NJ: Prentice, 1975. 81-89.

Accuses Bellow of being more alienated than he knows. Though in *H* and *MSP* he is disparaging the wasteland tradition and testing some kind of "cultural conservatism," Bellow does so with the kind of "self-righteous victimization" that cripples his work. Sees Bellow retaliating against his alienation by "historical pontifications."

893. Porter, M. Gilbert. "*Herzog*: A Transcendental Solution to an Existential Problem." *Forum* [Houston] 7.2 (1969): 32-36.

Romantic, transcendental, and humanistic, Herzog finally affirms with Rousseau "*Je sens mon coeur et je connais les hommes.*" Skirting the void, he is finally true to the Emersonian text of his high school address and allows his life to be "open to ecstasy or a divine illumination."

894. Rahv, Philip. "Bellow the Brain King." *New York Herald Tribune Book Week* 20 Sept. 1964: 1, 14, 16. Rpt. in *The Myth and the Powerhouse*. Philip Rahv. New York: Farrar, 1965. 218-24; *Literature and the Sixth Sense*. Philip Rahv. Boston: Houghton, 1969. 392-97; *Essays on Literature and Politics 1932-1972*. Philip Rahv. Boston: Houghton, 1978. 62-64.

Praises *H* for its intelligence and style. Sees it as Bellow's most personal novel. Reviews several of its major themes and concludes that its deep sense is distinctly Jewish.

895. Raider, Ruth. "Saul Bellow." Rev. of *Herzog* and *Saul Bellow*, by Tony Tanner." *Cambridge Quarterly* 2.2 (1967): 172-83.

Sees Bellow as "a minor comic novelist whose style is more often like the heavy mud than heavy pigment and whose metaphysical garrulity . . . easily suffocates his insubstantial plots." Traces this thesis through the novels until, arriving at *H*, she accuses Bellow of "sentimentality," "empty bombast," and "false sophistication."

896. Read, Forrest. "Notes, Reviews, and Speculations." Rev. of *Herzog*." *Epoch* 14.1 (1964): 81-96. Rpt. in *Herzog: Text and Criticism*. Ed. Irving Howe. Viking Critical Library. New York: Viking, 1976. 416-39.

Sees *H* as a great comic novel and the most significant novel since *Ulysses*. "Herzog has the sense to respond, the emotions to care, and the mind to probe his surroundings, his people, and himself." Read goes on to praise the book for its vitality and humanity. Mostly concentrates on the picture of modern experience captured in the novel. Also points out Herzog's literary forebears. A major article.

897. Richter, David H. "Bellow's *Herzog*." *Fable's End: Completeness and Closure in Rhetorical Fiction.* David H. Richter. Chicago: U of Chicago P, 1974. 185-92.

Argues that Bellow's chief artistic problem in *H* was to keep the reader focused on the change in Herzog rather than on the other plot events. The reader must be made to understand the intricate twists in his dealings with others without expecting resolution in the relationships at the end of the novel.

898. Rodrigues, Eusebio L. "*Herzog* and Hegel." *Notes on Modern American Literature* 2.2 (1978): Item 16.

Notes the absence of any letters to Hegel in this novel and yet occupies himself centrally throughout the novel with many philosophical issues deriving from Hegel.

899. Rodrigues, Eusebio L. "The Two Manifestations of Jeremiah: Bellow's Creative Use of a Morsel of Experience." *Notes on Modern American Literature* 5.1 (1980): Item 6.

Points out that in *H* and *HG* there are two manifestations of the biblical character, Jeremiah. In *H* the character of Ravitch is built on this model and takes his contemporary characteristics from Bellow's personal childhood experience with one Jeremiah, a family boarder and friend. In *HG* the Jeremiah character is Menasha Klinger, a second reincarnation of the same childhood boarder-friend.

900. Rose, W. K. "The Suffering Joker." *Shenandoah* 16.2 (1965): 55-58.

Compares *H* with the flawed *Moby Dick* in terms of its scope, style and themes. Then discourses generally upon plot and theme.

901. Ross-Bryant, Lynn. "Literature as Dialogue." *Imagination and the Life of the Spirit: An Introduction to the Study of Religion and Literature.* Poleridge Books 2. Missoula, MT: Scholars, 1980. 123-57.

Ross-Bryant sees Herzog's "dialogue with himself as a
preparation for dialogue with others," making it possible for
him finally to "accept the otherness he cannot control, cannot
impose himself on, cannot fully comprehend."

902. Rovit, Earl. "Bellow in Occupancy." *American Scholar* 34.2
    (1965): 292, 94, 96, 98. Rpt. in *Saul Bellow and the Critics.*
    Ed. Irving Malin. New York: New York UP, 1967. 177-83.

    Praises the novel for its sane intelligence "acting upon and
    reacting to the imponderabilities of normal human existence
    in the vivid darknesses of the mid-twentieth-century." Then
    proceeds to discuss *H* as a comic novel, and the nature and
    characteristics of its hero.

903. Rovit, Earl. "Jewish Humor and American Life." *American
    Scholar* 36.2 (1967): 237-45. Rpt. in *Herzog: Text and
    Criticism.* Ed. Irving Howe. Viking Critical Library. New
    York: Viking, 1976. 510-19.

904. Rubenstein, Richard L. "The Philosophy of Saul Bellow."
    Reconstructionist 22 Jan. 1965: 7-12.

    Describes *H* as a story of "emotional catharsis through
    which [the hero] learns to accept and affirm himself as a
    man and a Jew." Deals also with Herzog's ideas and with
    Madeleine's self-rejection as a Jew and as a woman.

905. Rubin, Louis D., Jr. "Southerners and Jews." *Southern Review*
    2.3 (1966): 697-713.

    Compares some of the novels of the Southern literary regional
    genre with some novels considered part of the renaissance in
    Jewish-American literature. The rationale for comparing both
    groups seems to be that both are ancestor-conscious, strong
    on familial ties, and not yet thoroughly assimilated into the
    mainstream of American life. Discusses *H* in this comparative
    context.

906. Sale, Roger. "Now, and Then." *Literary Inheritance.* Roger Sale.
    Amherst, MA: U of Massachusetts P, 1984. 203-19.

907. Sale, Roger. "Provincial Champions and Grandmasters." *Hudson Review* 17.4 (1964-1965): 608-18.

Acclaims the novel as the least provincial and most contemporary novel on the current literary scene. Criticizes the novel for having "run down before the end." Sees *H* as the largest step taken beyond Lawrence and romanticism, but as a novel which buys this step at the price of fear and loathing of humankind. Concludes, nevertheless, that what Herzog ultimately finds is faith.

908. Samuel, Maurice. "My Friend, the Late Moses Herzog." *Midstream* Apr. 1966: 3-25. Rpt. in *The World of Maurice Samuels: Selected Writings*. Philadelphia: Jewish Publication Society of America, 1977. 409-45.

Sees *H*, along with *Ulysses*, as a major modern study of Jewish assimilation. Compares the two and discusses in narrative form his purported meeting with the real Moses Herzog. Readers frequently fail to realize that this latter material is a spoof.

909. Scheer-Schaezler, Brigitte. "Short Story and Modern Novel: A Comparative Analysis of Two Texts." *Orbis Litterarum* 25 (1970): 338-51.

910. Scheer-Schaezler, Brigitte. *A Taste for Metaphors: Die Bildersprache als Interpretationsgrundlage des modernen Romans dargestellt ausaul Bellows Herzog*. Modern Sprachen Schriftenreihe 11. Vienna: Vervand der Osterreichischen Neuphilologen, 1968.

911. Schraepen, Edmond. "*Herzog*: Disconnection and Connection." *Saul Bellow and His Work*. Ed. Edmond Schraepen. Brussels: Centrum voor Taal-en Literatuurwetenschap, Vrije Universiteit Brussel, 1978. 119-29. Proceedings of a symposium held at the Free University of Brussels (V.U.B.) on 10-11 Dec. 1977.

Investigates the network of images he finds underlying *H* in order to trace the structuring process of the novel--a process "towards order, towards self-reconstruction, a slow, shedding, purging process."

912. Schueler, Mary Dudley. "The Figure of Madeleine in *Herzog*."
     Notes on Contemporary Literature 1.3 (1971): 5-7.

     Sees Madeleine's name (derived from Magdalene) as placing
     her in the mainstream of two traditions--one beginning with
     the *New Testament* and the other beginning with Proust's *A
     la recherche du temps perdu.* Like the Proust character,
     Swann, who ate the madeleine, Herzog begins an examination
     of his own character.

913. Shulman, Robert. "Myth, Mr. Eliot, and the Comic Novel."
     Modern Fiction Studies 12.4 (1966-1967): 395-403.

914. Shulman, Robert. "The Style of Bellow's Comedy." *PMLA* 83.1
     (1968): 109-17. Rpt. in *Herzog: Text and Criticism.* Ed. Irving
     Howe. Viking Critical Library. New York: Viking, 1976.
     489-509.

     Sees *H* as demonstrating just how "fully Bellow has mastered
     his own version of an open style of ideological comedy."
     Sees the letter device as indicative of Bellow's impulse
     toward older literary forms. Analyzes in detail the nature
     and form of Bellow's comedy with specific reference to
     several novels and more detailed treatment of *H.*

915. Solotaroff, Theodore M. "Napolean Street and After." *Commentary*
     Dec. 1964: 63-66. Rpt. in *The Red Hot Vacuum and Other
     Pieces on the Writing of the Sixties.* Theodore Solotaroff.
     New York: Atheneum, 1970. 94-102; *Herzog: Text and
     Criticism.* Ed. Irving Howe. Viking Critical Library. New
     York: Viking, 1976. 472-80.

     Sees Herzog as a "high class" version of previous Bellow
     heroes. Reviews major themes, style and the general
     reflection of American society contained in the novel.

916. Sullivan, Quentin M. "The Downward Transcendence of Moses
     Herzog." *Gypsy Scholar* 3.1 (1975): 44-50.

     Herzog undergoes a downward transcendence during which he
     leaves an entire set of values behind, including cherished

images of himself. Traces the process by which he emerges
in possession of his "authentic self."

917. Tanner, Tony. "Saul Bellow: The Flight from Monologue."
     Encounter Feb. 1965: 58-70. Rpt. in *Herzog: Text and
     Criticism.* Ed. Irving Howe. Viking Critical Library. New
     York: Viking, 1976. 445-65.

918. Uphaus, Suzanne Henning. "From Innocence to Experience: A
     Study of *Herzog.*" *Dalhousie Review* 46.1 (1966): 67-78.

     Sees Moses Herzog leading modern man out of the wasteland
     into the promised land. Likens his progress to that re-
     counted in Blake's *Songs of Innocence and Experience.* A
     major article which develops its arguments meticulously as
     it traces the process of Herzog's search for self.

919. Van Egmond, Peter G. "Herzog's Quotation of Walt Whitman."
     Walt Whitman Review 13.2 (1967): 54-56.

     Traces the thematic implications of the key quotations from
     and references to Walt Whitman. Sees the whole letter
     writing habit as attributable to Whitman, who also did it in
     his waning years.

920. Vardaman, James M., Jr. "Herzog's Letters." *Journal of the
     English Institute* 9-10 (1979): 129-49.

     Provides a formalist and generalized analysis of the letters
     in *H.* Concludes that letters are the way Herzog orders reality
     for himself and discusses how they function in terms of point
     of view. As the final letters from the Berkshires appear, we
     see that Herzog is in the final stages of his mental
     housecleaning process.

921. Vogel, Dan. "Saul Bellow's Vision Beyond Absurdity: Jewishness
     in *Herzog.*" *Tradition* 9.4 (1968): 65-79.

     Sees Bellow, because of his Jewishness, as having achieved a
     vision beyond absurdity in this novel. "From [the] coalescence
     of the Jewish past and the American present emerges the fig-

ure of Moses Elkenah Herzog." Goes on to discuss Herzog in
light of Abraham Cahan's *The Rise of David Levinsky.*

922. Walker, Marshall. *"Herzog*: The Professor as Drop-Out?"
English Studies in Africa 15.1 (1972): 39-51.

Provides a generalized exegesis of Herzog's character and of
some of the thematic concerns of the novel. Deals briefly
with the issue of Herzog as urban Jew and representative
modern Everyman.

923. Weber, Ronald. "Bellow's Thinkers." *Western Humanities Review*
22.4 (1968): 305-13.

This article provides a loose discussion of the role of
intellect in the Bellow novel. The relationship of intellec-
tualism and the human discussion is elaborated most in the
brief section on *H.*

924. Weinstein, Norman. *"Herzog*, Order and Entropy." *English
Studies* 54.4 (1973): 336-46.

Shows *H* as an attempt to solve some of the same problems
Flaubert and Joyce worked on--particularly the problems of
order and unity as theme and as aesthetic concern in the
novel. Sees the earlier works as highly wrought artistically
and *H* as needing much critical exegesis before it can be
properly assessed.

925. Werner, Craig Hansen. "The Writer as Craftsman: Saul Bellow,
Ralph Ellison." *Paradoxical Resolutions: American Fiction Since
James Joyce.* Craig Hansen Werner. Urbana, IL: U of Illinois
P, 1982. 123-43.

Discusses *H* and *Invisible Man* in the wake of the tradition
of *Ulysses* as very major postwar novels. Discusses ironic
distance, ambivalence toward individuality, license with
regard to fact, and attempts to create representative
characters. A major explication of *H* that defies paraphrase.
Provides much comment on theme, style, character, philosophy
and structure. Werner's major thesis with regard to both

novels is that they are encyclopedic in their scope and achievement.

926. Young, James Dean. "Bellow's View of the Heart." *Critique* 7.3 (1965): 5-17.

Rejects considering the novel on any other terms than as a novel, i.e.,its inner structural relations. Admires Bellow's manipulation of his materials and particularly his handling of point of view. Concludes that this novel is Bellow's finest masterpiece.

Reviews

927. "The Altered Heart." *Newsweek* 21 Sept. 1964: 114.

928. Bailey, James W. *Social Education* 29.1 (1965): 49, 50, 52.

929. Barrett, William. "Reader's Choice." *Atlantic* Nov. 1964: 192, 196.

930. Boroff, David. "Mr. Bellow Achieves His 'Breakthrough.' " *National Observer* 5 Oct. 1964: 18.

931. Brodin, Pierre. "La litterature americaine." *Liberte* [Montreal] Nov.-Dec. 1964: 480-83.

932. Burns, Richard K. *Library Journal* 1 Sept. 1964: 3182.

933. Curley, Thomas. "Herzog in Front of a Mirror, the Reader Behind Him." *Commonweal* 23 Oct. 1964: 137-39.

934. Davenport, Guy. "Turn the Other Face." *National Review* 3 Nov. 1964: 978-79.

935. Elliott, George P. "Hurtsog, Hairtsog, Heart's Hog?" *Nation* 19
     Oct. 1964: 252-54.

936. Froncek, Tom. "Rising to Disaster." *Tablet: A Weekly Newspaper
     and Review* [London] 6 Feb. 1965: 154.

937. Geismar, Maxwell. "The Great Herzog Schande." *Minority of
     One* Dec. 1964: 29-30.

938. Gill, Brendan. "Surprised by Joy." *New Yorker* 3 Oct. 1964: 218,
     221-22.

939. Goldreich, Gloria. "Letters Never Sent." *Hadassah Magazine* Dec.
     1964: 14-15.

940. "The Good Guy." *Time* 25 Sept 1964: 105-06.

941. Goran, Lester. "Saul Bellow Makes It to the Top." *Chicago
     Sunday Tribune Books Today* 20 Sept. 1964: 1.

942. Grady, R. T., and S. J. Grady. *Best Sellers* 1 Nov. 1964: 309.

943. Gross, Beverly. *Chicago Review* 17.2-3 (1964): 217-21.

944. Hesla, David. "By Strength Shall No Man Prevail." *North
     American Review* ns 1.4 (1964): 90-91.

945. Hyman, Stanley Edgar. "Saul Bellow's Glittering Eye." *New
     Leader* 28 Sept. 1964: 16-17.

946. Isaac, Dan. "Orpheus Transcending." *Judaism* 14.1 (1965):
     125-27.

947. Klein, Marcus. "Holy Moses." *Reporter* 22 Oct. 1964: 53-54.

948. Lamott, Kenneth. "Books: Burgess and Bellow." *Show: The Magazine of the Arts* Dec. 1964: 80.

949. Lemon, Lee T. "A Simple Lesson." *Prairie Schooner* 39.2 (1965): 161-62.

950. Ludwig, Jack. "The Wayward Reader." *Holiday* Feb. 1965: 16, 18-19.

951. Maddocks, Melvin. "Saul Bellow--New Champ? *Christian Science Monitor* 24 Sept. 1964: 7.

952. Malin, Irving. "Herzog, the Jew." *Reconstructionist* 16 Oct. 1964: 28-30.

953. "Man Who Would Be Marvelous." *Times Literary Supplement* 4 Feb. 1965: 81. Rpt. in *T.L.S.: Essays and Reviews from the Times Literary Supplement*, 1965. London: Oxford UP, 1966. 31-34.

954. Moynahan, Julian. "The Way up from Rock Bottom. " *New York Times Book Review* 20 Sept. 1964: 1, 41.

955. Pickrel, Paul. "Testament of a Survivor." *Harper's* Oct. 1964: 128.

956. Prescott, Orville. "A Strange, Brilliant, New Bellow Novel." *San Francisco Sunday Chronicle This World Magazine* 27 Sept. 1964: 39.

957. Pritchett, V. S. "King Saul." *New York Review of Books* 22 Oct. 1964: 4-5.

958. Ribalow, Harold U. "The Woes of Herzog." *Congress Bi-Weekly* 18 Jan. 1965: 14.

959. Richler, Mordecai. "The Survivor." *Spectator* 29 Jan. 1965: 139.

960. Saporta, Par Marc. "Un roman d'antiamour." *Preuves* Nov. 1965:
     88-89.

961. Scott, Nathan A., Jr. "Transcendence Downwards." *Christian
     Century* 16 Dec. 1964: 1562-63.

962. Steiner, George. "Moses Breaks the Tablets." *Sunday Times* 31
     Jan. 1965: 48.

963. Taaffe, Gerald. *Montrealer* July 1965: 35-36.

964. Tijeras, Eduardo. "Saul Bellow." *Cuadernos Hispanoamericanos*
     274 (1973): 182-86. [In Spanish]

965. Trevor, William. "New Fiction." *Listener* 4 Feb. 1965: 201.

966. Weintroub, Benjamin. *Chicago Jewish Forum* 23.2 (1964-65):
     163-65.

967. Zinnes, Harriet. *Books Abroad* 39.4 (1965): 460-61.

968. Baker, Carlos. "Bellow's Gift." *Theology Today* Jan. 1976: 411-13.

   Contains a brief biographical sketch of Bellow and Delmore Schwartz at Princeton under R. P. Blackmur. Touches briefly on Citrine's character, the influence of George Steiner and assorted spiritual themes in *HG*.

969. Bartz, Fredrica K. "*Humboldt's Gift* and the Myth of the Artist in America." *South Carolina Review* 15.1 (1982): 79-83.

   HG has been identified as one more "artist-in-America-myth," but in this novel there is a new dimension--Steinerian thought. This thought adds a new dimension to the artist-in-American-myth by suggesting that Humboldt's tragedy is not caused just by materialistic America, but also by being a poet with too little strength of soul and too little concern for his mystic mission.

970. Bartz, Fredrica K. "The Role of Rudolph Steiner in the Dreams of *Humboldt's Gift*." *Ball State University Forum* 24.1 (1983): 27-29.

   Details the influence of Rudolph Steiner's thought on Bellow through an examination of Humboldt's dreams from the perspective of Steinerian dream theory. Identifies two dream motifs: 1) the unbeatable paddle ball champion and 2) the meeting with Humboldt. Claims Bellow has drawn very deeply on Steiner's anthroposophical thought in the entire novel.

971. Bell, Pearl K. "Bellow's Best and Worst." *New Leader* 1 Sept. 1975: 19, 20.

972. Bradbury, Malcolm. "The It & the We: Saul Bellow's New
     Novel." *Encounter* Nov. 1975: 61-67.

> Bellow novels now cover and record with an acute historical
> sense thirty years of stressful American history. But with
> *HG* Bellow has bounced back to the panoramic, picaresque,
> ebullient vein of some of his ealier novels, and back too, to
> his resilient registering of the contemporary consciousness.
> Bellow is one of the great novelists of the attempt to recon-
> cile the mind with all its wonderful inventiveness, with the
> burdensome body, the heavy weight of history, and the extra-
> vagant and absurd material of the modern environment.

973. Bragg, Melvyn. "'Off the Couch by Christmas': Saul Bellow on
     his New Novel." *Listener* 20 Nov. 1975: 675-76.

> This interview between Bellow and Bragg contains much
> valuable commentary from Bellow on the character of
> Humboldt and the major thematic issues in the novel.

974. Busby, Mark. "Castaways, Cannibals, and the Function of Art
     in Saul Bellow's *Humboldt's Gift*." *South Central Bulletin*
     41.4 (1981): 91-94.

> Examines the cannibalism motif as it relates to questions of
> nature, innocence, art, and society in *HG*, and particularly
> with respect to the relationship between Citrine and Cantabile.

975. Campbell, Jeff H. "The Artist as American Dreamer: *Humboldt's
     Gift*." *Journal of the American Studies Association of Texas*
     9 (1978): 3-10. Cited in *Annual Bibliography of English
     Language and Literature*, 1978.

> Argues that this is Bellow's most personal and most American
> novel. Concentrates on the character of the creative artist as
> explored by the novel.

976. Casey, Jane Barnes. "Bellow's Gift." *Virginia Quarterly Review*
     52.1 (1976): 150-54.

> Casey argues that in *HG* Bellow reacts to society's rational
> excesses by tossing his net over what has been the domain

of belief. By making the other world or afterworld a matter
of imaginativeness, he eludes the questions reason traditionally
raises about faith and God and heaven. Neither reason nor
faith are issues; it is whether or not people have the
imagination to conceive of life as more than the bodies it is
written on. *HG* is worth reading because Bellow treats the
task of raising people's moral estimation of themselves with
lavish inventiveness and tonal subtlety in probing the world
beyond the one we think we know.

977. Chavkin, Allan. "Baron Humboldt and Bellow's Von Humboldt
Fleisher: Success and Failure in *Humboldt's Gift.*" *Notes on
Contemporary Literature* 10.2 (1980): 11-12.

Points out that the name Von Humboldt Fleisher is derived
from Baron Alexander von Humboldt (1769-1859). Illustrates
how Bellow's intention was to contrast the careers of the
two men in order to reveal the source of Fleisher's failure--
a failure that is meant to serve as paradigm for the tragic
careers of so many American writers of promise.

978. Chavkin, Allan. "*Humboldt's Gift* and the Romantic Imagination."
Philological Quarterly 62.1 (1983): 1-19.

Chavkin illustrates that although no single ideology can be
relied on to provide an understanding of this ambivalent
novel, there is clearly at the core of the work a romantic
sensibility, a Wordsworthian faith in the power of the
imagination to renovate the individual who has lost the
visionary gleam and is suffering from boredom and fear of
the darkness of the grave. Wordsworth's "Ode: Intimations
of Immortality from Recollections of Early Childhood" must
have been very much in Bellow's mind as he wrote *HG*. The
novel is a discursive meditation upon the disturbing fact of
death and the reassuring possibility of immortality that
underlie the poem.

979. Clayton, John J. "*Humboldt's Gift*: Transcendence and the Flight
from Death." *Saul Bellow and His Work*. Ed. Edmond
Schraepen. Brussels: Centruum voor Taal-en Literatuurwetenschap Vrije Universiteit Brussel, 1978. 31- 48. Proceedings of a symposium held at the Free University of Brussels
(V.U.B.) on 10-11 Dec. 1977.

Clayton argues that this novel is built on the dichotomy
between the world of distraction and world of love, where
the soul--if not the absurd personality--is worth saving.
Other dichotomies include that of tough reality instructors
and innocents, the modern individual and the great chain of
being leading up to God, and the view of man as part of
the natural world against the view of man as part of a
supernatural world. Its ultimate question is "Can man be
saved?"

980. Cohen, Sarah Blacher. "Comedy and Guilt in *Humboldt's Gift*."
     Modern Fiction Studies 25.1 (1979): 47-57.

Guilt in *HG* derives from the protagonist's belief that there
is something wrong with having survived and prospered. This
is true of all of Bellow's Jewish protagonists. But in this
novel the precise wrongs are more elaborated, the condemna-
tion more harsh and the desire for atonement more earnest.
In addition, the self-confessed criminal, Charlie Citrine,
resorts to a more self-ironic humor to cope with his
transgression and remorse. Cohen examines the imaginative
transformation of Bellow's personal guilt and private
obsessions in *HG*.

981. Cronin, Gloria L. "Art vs. Anarchy: Citrine's Transcendental
     Experiment in *Humboldt's Gift*." *Indian Journal of American
     Studies* 15.1 (1985): 33-43.

A close textual reading of *HG* reveals a carefully structured
novel that derives its shape primarily from its concentration
on such themes as the ill effects of rationalism and naturalism, the exhaustion of the inner life, the failure of poetic
sensibility, the bankrupting of Western humanism, the diminishment of the private life by crises, and the Heraclitan
search for the essence of things. This is one more attempt by
Bellow to purge American intellectual life of the banalities
of historicism, the illogic of absurdism and the horror of
the void.

982. Epstein, Seymour. "Bellow's Gift." *Denver Quarterly* 10.4 (1975):
     35-50.

A central thematic concern in this novel arises early from th speech by Citrine on boredom and the response to it from Renata when she writes to explain her marriage to the mortician. The failures of Western civilization and the pleasures of it spin out the thematic thread that runs through the novels. Epstein details the falling short of a host of contemporary writers to deal effectively with this theme. He then traces Bellow's treatment of it through the earlier novels and concludes by developing it in relation to *HG*.

983. Estrin, Barbara L. "Recomposing Time: *Humboldt's Gift* and *Ragtime*." *Denver Quarterly* 17.1 (1982): 16-31.

Like the narrator of Delmore Schwartz's story "In Dreams Begin Responsibilities," who wants to stop his own conception and turn history back, the central characters of *Ragtime* and *HG* want to avert the crises of twentieth century history. *HG* inherits from the fictionalized Schwartz a certain sense of hysteria found in *Portnoy's Complaint* and *Fear of Flying*. The process of writing the novel enables the narrator to circumvent the tension dominating his life, to divest himself of the past by telling it, and to accept the gift of his friend.

984. Goldman, Mark. "*Humboldt's Gift* and the Case of the Split Protagonist." *Modern Language Studies* 11.2 (1981): 3- 16.

Argues that Bellow's use of Delmore Schwartz's character for Humboldt is more meaningful when viewed in terms of Bellow's characteristic use of subject and form. Discusses the dual point of view characters have in *HG* and shows how finally Humboldt serves as a mirror image embodying moral meaning for Citrine, but establishes that he is never given more depth and scope as a character because of his purpose as mere mirror to the actual protagonist, Charlie Citrine.

985. Grigorescu, Dan. "Adevaratul dar al lui Humboldt" [The True Gift of Humboldt]. *Darul lui Humboldt* [*Humboldt's Gift*]. Bucharest: Univers, 1979. v-xxxii. Cited in *Annual Bibliography of English Language and Literature*, 1979.

986. Gunn, Drewey Wayne. "The Followers of Humboldt." *American and British Writers in Mexico 1556-1973*. Drewey Wayne Gunn. Austin: U of Texas P, 14-36.

   A crucial chapter for background material on Alexander Von Humboldt. Has relevance for source studies in both *HG* and *AM*.

987. Kernan, Alvin B. "Mighty Poets in their Misery Dead: The Death of the Poet in Saul Bellow's *Humboldt's Gift*." *The Imaginary Library: An Essay on Literature and Society*. Alvin B. Kernan. Princeton, NJ: Princeton UP, 1982. 37-65. Abridged version rpt. in *Saul Bellow*. Ed. Harold Bloom. Modern Critical Views. New York: Chelsea, 1986. 179-93.

   Kernan spends considerable time tracing the historical evolution and devolution of the social role of the poet. Comments that in modern times poets within works are depicted as dismembered and demystified, not by philosophical and psychological anxieties, but by historical and social events generating those anxieties. Sees *HG* as a novel in which literature as a social institution is subject for its continued validity to the situation in the larger society. *HG* offers insights into the nature of the social changes that are unmaking that grand image of the poet and his powers that Petrarch constructed so long ago in Rome.

988. Kerner, David. "The Incomplete Dialectic of *Humboldt's Gift*." *Dalhousie Review* 62.1 (1982): 14-35. Rpt. in *Saul Bellow*. Ed. Harold Bloom. Modern Critical Views. New York: Chelsea, 1986. 161-77.

   HG centers on the theme of spiritual rebirth and escape from mortality, as evidenced by Humboldt's escape from madness and spiritual return seven years later. This irrepressibility establishes the connections between the self and the divine powers so that the reprieved Humboldt can claim we are "supernatural beings," but these divine powers are the "inner powers of nature, " which "art manifests." Yet Bellow knows that salvationist art cannot wish away rationalism. Bellow shows us Humboldt's box and chains from the outside only, as when a showman presenting an escape artist is afraid to let us examine the arrangements too closely.

989. Kistler, Suzanne F. "Bellow's Man-Eating Comedy: Cannibal Imagery in *Humboldt's Gift.*" *Notes on Modern American Literature* 2.1 (1977): Item 8.

In this article cannibalism is seen as the extended metaphor through which Bellow presents his vision of exploitative twentieth-century Western society. Kistler explores the references to the Cannibal Society of the Kwakiutl Indians found in *HG* and their subsequent thematic importance.

990. Mano, Keith. "Bellow's Dead Center." Rev. of *Humboldt's Gift.*" *National Review* 7 Nov. 1975: 1246-47.

Accuses Bellow of having produced a sloppy piece of work flawed by his preoccupation with the "so-what-ness" of mortality. Mano points out the weaknesses in the prose and characterization and the physical heaviness and imperfection of the protagonists. He does concede that while this is not Bellow's best book, it is his most significant.

991. McSweeney, Kerry. "Saul Bellow and the Life to Come." *Critical Quarterly* 18.1 (1976): 67-72.

Although Citrine is another incarnation of the traditional Romantic hero of the earlier novels, in HG he comes to a belief in the immortality of souls, and the ability to come close to and contact spirits of the dead. Unlike earlier novels in which transcendental postulates were a matter of choice, in this novel the task is really to penetrate eternity. McSweeney goes on to criticize the novel for its excesses, particularly when this causes the clumsy use of the crocus image at the end of the novel to be taken as evidence of Bellow's inability to incorporate satisfactorily in fictional form his new-found interest in the life to come.

992. Mowat, John. "*Humboldt's Gift*: Bellow's 'Dejection' Ode." *Dutch Quarterly Review of Anglo-American Letters* 8 (1978): 184-201. Cited in *MLA Bibliography*, 1978.

Mowat complains that Bellow has devised a manner and a prose that affront the reader. These he describes as didactic, knowing, and casual in the handling of prodigious generalities. It is a presumptuous book that makes a comedy of death, and whose language, instead of being the measure of value, acts as a solvent.

993. Nault, Marianne. "Saul Bellow's Humboldt the First." *American Notes and Queries* 15.6 (1977): 88-89.

Nault points out that there are several persons on whom Humboldt's character is based, as evident from examination of the various manuscript re-writings of both *H* and *HG*. Humboldt assumes a variety of identities: Vic Driver, Jonas Amilcar, and Abraham Hamilcar. Charlie Citrine appears as J. J. Orlansky, a Polish writer rather than a Jew. Contains several other tidbits of interest also.

994. Newman, Judie. "Bellow's 'Indian Givers': *Humboldt's Gift.*" *Journal of American Studies* 15.2 (1981): 231-38.

In this article Newman provides a sophisticated anthropologica account of gift-giving customs among the Kwakiutl Indians as she elucidates the thematic implications of Humboldt's gift giving in *HG*. She concludes that society functions as a web of obligations in which Citrine and Humboldt are trappee Yet Humboldt also uses this gift as an opportunity to avenge himself of Charlie's earlier betrayal of him.

995. Newman, Judie. "Saul Bellow: *Humboldt's Gift*--The Comedy of History." *Durham University Journal* 72 (Dec. 1979): 79-87.

This novel forces us again and again away from the celebration of order into chaos and contingency of history, forever demonstrating that wholeness of mind is merely an illusion of mind, and that patterns imposed upon events are arbitrary and even dangerous. In *HG* Bellow explores an encyclopedic assortment of different approaches to history, both in terms of literary stereotypes and of culture readings, thus parodying the hero's attempt to escape from time.

996. Novaceanu, Darie. "Balada din Chicago." *Romania Literara* 8 Nov. 1979: 20. Cited in *Annual Bibliography of English Language and Literature*, 1979.

997. Possler, Katherine E. "Cannibalism in *Humboldt's Gift*." *Gypsy Scholar: A Graduate Forum for Literary Criticism* 5.1 (1978): 18-21.

In Bellow's earlier books cannibalism has not the outstanding and direct expression it acquires in *HG*. Possler relates this metaphor to the issues of plagiarism, materialism and mutual aid in the novel. A brief but sophisticated treatment.

998. Radner, Sanford. "The Woman Savior in *Humboldt's Gift*." *Saul Bellow Newsletter* 1.1 (1981): 22-25.

Close study of the imagery of *HG* provides evidence of a shift in the consciousness of Charlie Citrine. In phase one women are the ultimate source of nourishment and comfort for men. In phase two women are deceitful depleters; men's succor must come from other men. Imagery that supports this shift centers on parts of the body to do with breathing and depleting, and with words and money used symbolically for all of the others.

999. Rodgers, Bernard F., Jr. "Apologia Pro Vita Sua: Biography and Autobiography in *Humboldt's Gift*." *Kwartalnik Neofilologiczny* 27.4 (1980): 439-54.

This article is an attempt to answer such questions as: 1) how autobiographical is the fiction? 2) what purposes dictated this approach? 3) where have the facts been altered? 4) what is the significance of the alterations? 5) how effectively does the author use the particulars of his experience to touch the universal elements in it? Rodgers confines himself primarily to *HG*. Concludes that Bellow has learned to use his preoccupations with self-consciousness, a practice which appeals to us because it touches our own habits.

1000. Rosenburg, Ruth. "Three Jewish Narrative Strategies in *Humboldt's Gift*." *Melus* 6.4 (1979): 59-66.

Rosenburg claims that there are three distinctly Jewish narrative strategies in *HG*: a characteristic narrative perspective, a characteristic mode of ordering events and a characteristic mode of closure.

1001. Rosenfeld, Alvin H. "Poet, Magician, and Anthroposophist: Saul
      Bellow's Latest Fiction." *Midstream* Dec. 1975: 62-67.

      Begins with some biographical material about Delmore
      Schwartz and then provides a long review essay on a
      variety of topics of general interest in *HG*.

1002. Ryan, Steven T. "The Soul's Husband: Money in *Humboldt's
      Gift*." *Money Talks: Language and Lucre in American Fiction.*
      Ed. Roy R. Male. Norman, OK: U of Oklahoma P, 1981. 111-21.
      Previously published as special topic issue of *Genre* 13.1
      (1980).

      Argues that Bellow's concern for wealth as a theme is
      unusual for a contemporary American writer. Traces this
      interest through several early short stories and shows how
      these ideas concerning money carry over into the novels and
      into HG in particular. Shows how Citrine ultimately makes his
      peace with the business world and how though money "has
      become a vital substance, an authentic shaper of worldly
      events," he permits only the "position of husband, the
      apparent power and provider."

1003. Sale, Roger. "The Realms of Gold." *Hudson Review* 28.4
      (1975-1976): 616-28.

      Reviews the major novels up to 1975 and feels that *HG* fails
      at the end, but "at a level no other American author tries to
      reach."

1004. Schraepen, Edmond. "*Humboldt's Gift*: A New Bellow." *English
      Studies* 62.2 (1981): 164-70.

      Schraepen claims two features in *HG* stand out: 1) the world
      of distraction, 2) the outspoken mystical strain. A closer
      look reveals thematic antitheses which are related to the
      basic opposition between the distracting world and the
      transcendental world. Examines how successfully Bellow
      attempts to integrate these experiences into his comic form
      for the novel.

1005. Siegel, Ben. "Artists and Opportunists in Saul Bellow's *Humboldt's Gift*." *Contemporary Literature* 19.2 (1978): 143-64. Rpt. *Critical Essays on Saul Bellow*. Ed. Stanley Trachtenberg. Critical Essays on American Literature. Boston: Hall, 1979. 158-74.

Centering on a live writer and a dead poet, Bellow tries to define the artist's role in a society lured away by its massive material substance from its cravings for the mind and beauty. He portrays the artist as one who, like his fellow Americans, frequently fails to consider moral and ethical--much less spiritual--aspects of his goals and behavior. His second major theme is the comic pathos of a vain intellectual's efforts to age with style and dignity. If Charlie's and Bellow's impressions and conlusions fail to convince totally, they can hardly be faulted for trying where no one else has succeeded. They do render the human journey more open and challenging than before.

1006. Simpson, Louis. "The Ghost of Delmore Schwartz." *New York Times Magazine* 7 Dec. 1975: 38, 40-43, 48, 52, 56.

Delmore Schwartz as model for Humboldt.

1007. Smith, Herbert J. "*Humboldt's Gift* and Rudolph Steiner." *Centennial Review* 22.4 (1978): 479-89.

HG, unlike other novels, explores the dialectical tension between human ideals and human actuality, between the spirit and the void, within the framework of Steiner's anthroposophy--a new influence on Bellow's fiction. Smith connects Steiner's thought with that of the American transcendentalists and with Goethe's World-Conception. Bellow uses Steiner's ideas to foster a more complete defense of man.

1008. Terakado, Yasuhiko. "Saul Bellow *Humboldt no Okurimono*: Jinchigaku to Cannibalism." *Bungaku to America: Ohashi Kenzaburo Kyoju Kanreki Kinen Ronbunshu*. Tokyo: Nanundo, 1980. 345-58. Vol. 2. Cited in *MLA Bibliography*, 1981.

1009. Toynbee, Philip. "Matter of Life and Death." *Observer* 5 Oct.
      1975: 23.

> Comments that the novel is overburdened with secondary
> characters. Also notes that he has transcended though not
> neglected the whole socio-political field in favor of a
> fervent look at the soul. Sees it as the nearest work to
> Dostoevsky's *The Idiot.*

1010. Updike, John. "Draping Radiance with a Worn Veil." *New
      Yorker* 15 Sept. 1975: 122, 125-30.

> Reviews character and content in *HG* and goes on to praise
> Bellow for his observance of the eccentric particulars of
> American life. Complains that he abandons a wonderful
> regional portrait of Chicago when he switches settings in the
> middle of the novel, and also of the tenuousness of the
> Madrid section. Finds that the novel has too many characters
> and exhibits a loss of stylistic verve. Concludes that "*HG*
> washed up on our drear cultural shore like some large,
> magnificently glistening but beached creature from another
> element."

1011. Vinoda. "Renewing Universal Connections: A Study of *Humboldt
      Gift.*" *Journal of English Studies* [India] 13.1 (1981): 876-80.

> *HG* probes the issue of what being human is, human ethics,
> and the issue of death. Citrine's interest in the life of the
> soul cannot be understood in light of moral concerns;
> however, it can be understood in light of his relationship
> with Humboldt.

1012. Weinstein, Mark. "Charles Citrine: Bellow's Holy Fool." *Saul
      Bellow Journal* 3.1 (1983): 28-37.

> Sees Charlie as one of the higher types of martyr the
> twentieth century has added--the farcical martyr, the artist.
> Reminds readers that Bellow has pointed to the amount of
> affection in this book. Comments on the numerous religious
> references throughout the book and its affirmative ending.

1013. Woelfel, James W. "Charlie Citrine and the Argument from Absurdity." *Religion in Life* 47.4 (1978): 460-76.

> Examines the character of Charlie Citrine "as a powerful and haunting contemporary literary expression of an old and many-faceted case for supernaturalism." Develops his thesis using Camus's idea of "incommensurability" or sense of nostalgia for meanings we can never attain.

1014. Yetman, Michael G. "Who Would Not Sing for Humboldt?" *ELH* 48.4 (1981): 935-51.

> Examines some parallel contributions of literary romanticism to 1) the author's use of one character in the creation of another and 2) his critique of the plight of the writer in contemporary America. In addition, he scrutinizes the way the book privileges a romantic interpretation of both the poet and the poetic imagination and concludes that, every bit as much as Steiner's ideas--indeed in concert with them--these novelistic preoccupations are central to our understanding of the complex thought of the narrator-main character.

Reviews

1015. Aaron, Daniel. "*Humboldt's Gift* by Saul Bellow." *New Republic* 20 Sept. 1975: 28-30.

1016. Aldridge, John W. "Saul Bellow at 60: A Turn to the Mystical." *Saturday Review* 6 Sept. 1975: 22-25. Rpt. in *Critical Essays on Saul Bellow.* Ed. Stanley Trachtenberg. Critical Essays on American Literature. Boston: Hall, 1979. 49-57.

1017. Cushman, Keith. "Discriminating Gusto." *Chicago Review* 27 (1975-76): 145-48.

1018. Dame, Enid. "Bellow & Potok: The Saving Force." *Congress Monthly* Apr. 1976: 20-22.

1019. Gilman, Richard. "*Humboldt's Gift.*" *New York Times Book Review* 17 Aug. 1975: 1-3.

1020. Lodge, David. "Dead Reckoning." *Times Literary Supplement* 10 Oct. 1975: 1173.

1021. Mayne, Richard. "A Long Cool Summa." *Listener* 9 Oct. 1975: 484-85.

1022. Newman, Charles. "Lives of the Artists." *Harper's* Oct. 1975: 82-83, 85.

1023. Pritchett, V. S. "Potato Pie." *New Statesman* 10 Oct. 1975: 442-43.

1024. Raphael, Frederic. "Mr. Bellow's Big Idea." *Sunday Times* 5 Oct. 1975: 35.

1025. Rhodes, Richard. "In Bellow's Work the Talk Is All and Marvelous Talk It Is." *Chicago Tribune Book World* 24 Aug. 1975: 1.

1026. Richardson, Jack. "A Burnt-Out Case." *Commentary* Nov. 1975: 74, 76-78.

1027. Sarotte, Georges-Michel. "Le plus grand peut-etre." *Quinzaine Litteraire* 283 (1978): 7.

1028. Shattuck, Roger. "A Higher Selfishness." *New York Review of Books* 18 Sept. 1975: 21-25.

1029. Sheppard, R. Z. "Scribbler on the Roof." *Time* 25 Aug. 1975: 62.

1030. Sire, James W. "Saul Bellow: Higher-Thought Clown." *Christianity Today* 12 Mar. 1976: 26-27.

1031. Stern, Daniel. "The Bellow-ing of the Culture." *Commonweal* 24 Oct. 1975: 502-04.

Mr. Sammler's Planet

1032. Alexander, Edward. "Imagining the Holocaust: *Mr. Sammler's Planet* and Others." *Judaism* 22.3 (1973): 288-300.

Alexander argues persuasively that the central intent of *MSP* is an examination and denunciation of the Holocaust. Beginning with Sammler's attack on ideas of Hannah Arendt's thesis on Eichmann and moving through Sammler's gradual awareness of the insanity of the twentieth-century, the reader reaches the bedrock of Sammler's experience--the death camp sojourn that constantly rises to the surface of his mind and asserts itself as the chief determinant of such life as is left to him.

1033. Alter, Robert. "A Fever of Ethnicity." *Commentary* June 1972: 68-73.

Comments briefly on *MSP* in the context of a broad discussion of the history of the American identity crisis issue and the two major alternatives of identity developed in the dissident movements of the late 1960's--submergence of individuality in the paramilitary collective and a flamboyant antinomianism among the proponents of the counter-culture. Sees *MSP* as a compassionately sad comment on how the programmatic abandonment of modes of self leads to the unwitting imitation of lesser models.

1034. Atchity, Kenneth John. "Bellow's Mr. Sammler: 'The Last Man Given for Epitome.'" *Research Studies* 38.1 (1970): 46-54.

Complains that *MSP* is "a plotless, interminable interior monologue, starkly naked in its insufficiency as a structuring agent." The focus of the novel is the implications of the Apollo moon landing. Sammler is "the last man given for

217

epitome" because he straddles two worlds, one dying and
one struggling to be born--of the past and the future."

1035. Bayley, John. "By Way of Mr. Sammler." *Salmagundi* 30
(Summer 1975): 24-33. Rpt. in *Salmagundi Reader*. Eds.
Robert T. Boyers and Peggy Boyers. Bloomington, IN: Indiana
UP, 1983. 384-93.

Sees Sammler and Gruner as nineteenth-century bourgeois
recreated to see if they can acclimatize to our times. Sees the
American-Jewish novel as optimal for the experiment, given
its roots in the traditions of the Victorian novel. Yet the
modern reader probably cannot take its premises about nobil
seriously. Hence *MSP* functions partly as a parody on the
techniques, symbolism and egocentric premises of the modern
novel. *MSP* succeeds by being partial and incomplete, by
rejecting the modern novel's paradigm of totality in the act
of consciousness.

1036. Bell, Pearl K. "American Fiction: Forgetting the Ordinary
Truths." *Dissent* 20 (1973): 26-34.

1037. Berger, Alan L. "Holocaust Survivors in *Anya* and *Mr. Sammler's
Planet*." *Modern Language Studies* 16.1 (1986): 81-87.

Deals with the psycho-social catastrophe of the Holocaust as
Berger traces the Holocaustal reactions of Anya, Ninka, Shul
and Mr. Sammler in terms of survivor missions intended to
clarify identity and recreate a moral universe.

1038. Berryman, Charles. "Saul Bellow: Mr. Sammler and King Lear."
Essays in Literature 10.1 (1983): 81-92.

Calls in question criticism that has lauded Bellow for his
affirmations. Reviews major opinions on Bellow's work gene
ally and sees criticism reaching "its uncritical height" with
the publication of *MSP*. Sammler is very possibly mad and h
bitter views are not those of the author. Sammler is presente
with considerable irony and is an unreliable seer and
prophet. The plot follows the outline of *King Lear*. Bellow's
version of the play does not reach a full, tragic conclusion

because Sammler, though lunatic, eccentric and endearing, is still alive.

1039. Bilik, Dorothy Seidman. "Bellow's Worldly 'Tsadik'." *Immigrant Survivors: Post Holocaust Consciousness in Recent Jewish-American Literature.* Dorothy Seidman Bilik. New York: Wesleyan UP, 1981. 137-66.

Sammler as a worldy *tsadik* whose history is synchronous with that of the twentieth-century in its endowment of Western, Eastern, Christian and Jewish thought. He is a man without a real home who has lived as a Jew, as a European intellectual, as a victim of the holocaust and as an American. His mental world may be seen as a metaphoric *diaspora* wherein he attempts to see possible relationships between universal and particular, past and present, God and man, in order to find tentative answers as to how one should prepare for death, or conversely, how one should live.

1040. Bolling, Douglass. "Intellectual and Aesthetic Dimensions of *Mr. Sammler's Planet.*" *Journal of Narrative Technique* 4.3 (1974): 188-203.

Defends *MSP* as a novel whose unreconciled duality is a deliberate artistic invention. Two major patterns inform the novel; and these generate the substance of the work less as plot and subplot or as polarities orchestrated within a culminant vision than as equally demanding, equally important tensions. One of these controlling patterns is Mr. Sammler's involvement in ethical and philosophical concerns at a primarily speculative and intellectualized level. The second controlling rhythm is the protagonist's efforts to recover Govinda Lal's purloined manuscript. The view of the protagonist as lofty contemplator and farcical fool is deliberate. *MSP* evinces a highly disciplined artistry.

1041. Boyers, Robert T. "Nature and Social Reality in Saul Bellow's *Sammler.*" *Critical Quarterly* 15.3 (1973): 251-71. Rpt. in *Salmagundi* 30 (Summer 1975): 34-56; *Excursions: Selected Literary Essays.* Port Washington, NY: Kennikat, 1977. 25-46.

Examines the idea of nature in Bellow and its relation to two

others--the idea of social reality, and the idea of character
conceived both in its moral and aesthetic dimensions.

1042. Bus, Heiner. "Saul Bellow: *Mr. Sammler's Planet.*" *Amerikanische
Erzahlliteratur 1950-1970.* Ed. Frieder Bush and Renate
Schmidt-von Bardeleben. Kritische Information 28. Munich:
Fink, 1975. 170-85. Cited in *MLA Bibliography*, 1975.

1043. Cronin, Gloria L. "Faith and Futurity: The Case for Survival
in *Mr. Sammler's Planet.*" *Literature and Belief* 3 (1983):
97-108.

Cronin argues that *MSP*, while it minimizes external action,
employs what R.S. Crane has called the "plot of thought."
Far from exhibiting a failure of moral energy or faltering
design, the novel is centered on a three-way debate between
three radically opposed contemporary philosophies: 1) traditional humanism, 2) modernist scientific rationalism, 3)
bizarre late romantic individualism. However, instead of
focusing on the modernist literary legacy of Joyce, Lawrence
and Eliot, his indictment of modernism targets the unleashing
of radicalism, perverted individualism, liberalism and
hedonism--in short the Nietzschean Dionysiac spirit.

1044. Cushman, Keith. "Mr. Bellow's *Sammler*: The Evolution of a
Contemporary Text." *Studies in the Novel* 7.3 (1975): 425-44.

This is the only article on *MSP* whose author has attempted
to describe the evolution of the novel with the benefit of
all the various holograph, typescript and galley materials
available in the Special Collections Department at the
University of Chicago Regenstein Library. It is a detailed
textual analysis of considerable sophistication.

1045. DeMott, Benjamin. "Saul Bellow and the Dogmas of Possibility."
Saturday Review 7 Feb. 1970: 25-28, 37.

Discusses the narrative action, history and character of
Sammler, humorous episodes like the flooding of the Gruner
household, and Bellow's informing humanity. Criticizes
Bellow for overprotecting his sage and for his gratuitous
optimism.

1046. Ertel, Rachel. "*Mr. Sammler's Planet*--Roman de memoire et d'Histoire." *Delta* 19 (Oct. 1984): 155-69.

Discusses *MSP* as taking a place apart among Bellow's works as a novel of memory and history.

1047. Finkelstein, Sidney. "The Anti-Hero of Updike, Bellow and Malamud." *American Dialogue* 7.2 (1972): 12-14, 30.

1048. Galloway, David D. "*Mr. Sammler's Planet*: Bellow's Failure of Nerve." *Modern Fiction Studies* 19.1 (1973): 17-28.

MSP, argues Galloway, shows the bankruptcy of Bellow's novelistic imagination. After admitting that the novel is beautifully written, and that its avuncular hero is its greatest asset, Galloway criticizes the novel for its lack of discrimination in what Sammler calls the "sovereign youth-style." Mr. Sammler himself is full of contradictions. He is forced to assume a burden of meaning he cannot bear. The dialogue with Lal is terribly contrived. Sammler ends up as a ventrioloquist's dummy. Galloway also condemns the facile formula of the typical Bellovian ending found in *MSP*, and criticizes the clumsy handling of symbols.

1049. Gelfant, Blanche. "In Terror of the Sublime: Mr. Sammler and Odin." *Notes on Modern American Literature* 2.4 (1978): Item 25.

Traces some rather interesting archetypal patterns in *MSP* by comparing those same patterns as they appear in the mythology surrounding Odin. Particularly convincing in its tracing of several parallel motifs.

1050. Gittleman, Sol. "*Mr. Sammler's Planet* Ten Years Later: Looking Back on Crises of 'Mishpocha.'" *Judaism* 30 (Fall 1981): 480-83.

Represents, as does no other work of American literature, the confrontation between Jewish children of the 1960's generation and their parents. It climaxes a century of Jewish writing about the father who fails.

1051. Glickman, Susan. "The World as Will and Idea: A Comparative Study of *An American Dream* and *Mr. Sammler's Planet.*" *Modern Fiction Studies* 28.4 (1982-83): 569-82.

Discusses the distance Bellow creates between himself and his persona. Describes the distance between actuality and the American dream. Makes a variety of comparative references to other works of contemporary American literature.

1052. Goldman, Liela H. "The Source for Saul Bellow's *Mr. Sammler's Planet.*" *American Notes and Queries* 20.7-8 (1982): 117-19.

Examines the novel as a tribute to Isaac Rosenfeld whose masterpiece short story "King Solomon" provided Bellow with the idea of a satirical King Solomon. Traces the influence of Ecclesiastes generally.

1053. Graff, Gerald. "Babbitt at the Abyss." *Literature Against Itself: Literary Ideas in Modern Society.* Chicago: U of Chicago P, 1979. 207-39.

1054. Greenstone, Maryann D. "Saul Bellow and Isaac Babel: A Review of *Mr. Sammler's Planet.*" *Jewish Spectator* Nov. 1970: 10-12.

Provides a general discussion of theme in MSP based on a comparison between Babel and Bellow. Claims that both are writing about the nature of man's heart and his future.

1055. Gross, Beverly. "Dark Side of the Moon." *Nation* 9 Feb. 1970: 153-55.

Gross writes that this book has not earned its perspective as a secular *summa.* Sammler is dismissed as crotchety, ruminative and passive. Morally and artistically the book too easily dismisses its own life. The novel is rich with ideas about life but poor in life itself.

1056. Grubb, Daniel S. "Another Gulliver?" *Studies in the Humanities* 4.1 (1974): 3-9.

Compares Sammler and Gulliver as subjective-objective observers, as moralists, as travelers, and as collectors. Both are associated with animal imagery and scatological references; both note the sexual madness of the world, and both are mystical and empirical. Concludes that having described the world in these terms, neither of the men feels a part of it.

1057. Guthridge, George. "The Structure of Twentieth-Century Society: The Concept of the Intellectual in Bellow's *Mr. Sammler's Planet.*" *Saul Bellow Newsletter* 1.1 (1981): 6-10.

Unlike the situation in *H*, Mr. Sammler's philosophizing "is coordinated with the novel's physical action, and subordinate to it." Bellow protagonists do nothing and their attempts to understand their experiences are more important to them than the experiences themselves. Yet Mr. Sammler is more than acted upon. The meeting ground between intellectuals and actors is a sexual one. Concludes with a series of loosely connected general observations.

1058. Guttman, Allen. "Saul Bellow's *Mr. Sammler.*" *Contemporary Literature* 14.2 (1973): 157-66.

Guttman defends the negative critical reception of *MSP* by insisting on the ironic distance that exists between the author and his protagonist. He finds many parallels between the two but concludes that Sammler is older, narrower, more crotchety, and opinionated than Bellow. Guttman provides a detailed examination of Sammler's character as a means of refuting much of the initial criticism of the novel. Concludes that Bellow has created an extraordinary character and not a mouthpiece for the radical right.

1059. Haber, Leo. "Saul Bellow's Discourse." *Jewish Frontier* June 1970: 24-26.

Sees Mr. Sammler as a seventy-year-old *luftmensch* who, after several lifetimes of experience that have culminated in his confrontation with Black Power, sexuality and psychosis in friend and foe, finds himself out of the frying pan and into the fire. Criticizes the novel's lack of real action, and concludes by asking if this is a novel or the "stenographic record of Talmudic debate."

1060. Hadari, Amnon. "Ha-professor Eino Me'uban; *Cohav Ha-lekhet
      Shel Mar Sammler* Me'et Saul Bellow." *Shdemot* 44 (1971):
      102-13. Cited in *MLA Bibliography*, 1971.

1061. Harris, James Neil. "One Critical Approach to *Mr. Sammler's
      Planet.*" *Twentieth Century Literature* 18.4 (1972): 235-50.

      Harris finds *MSP* a profoundly religious work concerned with
      the process of acquiring faith. It attempts to show that Mr.
      Sammler's quest, that finally culminates in epiphany, in-
      volves a struggle which seems to be the use of irony to
      finally destroy irony, and, to reconcile the paradoxical
      nature of religious faith through the paradox of the novel's
      dianoia. The faith finally acquired is an ethical faith.
      Sammler finally eschews "mere explanation hunting" for the
      higher activity of distinguishing as a means toward religious
      faith.

1062. Held, George. "Men on the Moon: American Novelists Explore
      Lunar Space." *Michigan Quarterly Review* 18.2 (1979): 318-42.

      Discusses the idea that from the beginning the ability of
      America to absorb infinite space has gripped the American
      imagination. Sees the American imagination now projecting
      itself beyond consideration of frontier and into outer space
      itself. Traces this in many writers, including Bellow, where
      the discussion centers mainly on *MSP.*

1063. Hirsch, David H. "Jewish Identity and Jewish Suffering in
      Bellow, Malamud and Philip Roth." *Jewish Book Annual.* 29th.
      ed. New York: Jewish Book Council, 1971. 12-22.

1064. Howe, Irving. "Fiction: Bellow, O'Hara, Litwak." *Harper's* Feb.
      1970: 106, 108, 112, 114, 116-118.

1065. Jones, Roger. "Artistry and the Depth of Life: Aspects of
      Attitude and Technique in *Mr. Sammler's Planet.*" *Anglo-Welsh
      Review* 25 (1975): 138-53.

      This is a discursive introductory article arranged under such
      headings as "Organization and Meaning," "Toward Meaning,"

"Living with all Combinations of the Facts," "Form and
Material," and "The Failure of Artistry."

1066. Kar, Prafulla C. "What it Means to Be Exactly Human: A
Study of *Mr. Sammler's Planet.*" *Studies in American
Literature: Essays in Honour of William Mulder.* Eds. Jagdish
Chander and Pradhan S. Narindar. Delhi: Oxford UP, 1976.
97-109.

Kar argues that his novel defines what it means to be
human in a society that tries to destroy all traces of
humanity. It is built upon tensions between society and the
individual. Through his historical consciousness, Sammler sifts
the world for evidence of the human and humanizing.

1067. Kistler, Suzanne F. "Epic Structure and Statement in *Mr.
Sammler's Planet.*" *Notes on Modern American Literature* 2.4
(1978): Item 28.

Sees *MSP* as a literary epic in the Bowra sense, a pattern
exemplified in the *Aenied* and *Paradise Lost.* Sammler as
epic hero undertakes an Odyssean journey from nineteenth-
century blindness to illumination and wisdom. MSP is a
modern epic because of its magnitude, its consecrated hero,
and its positive vision of man's potential.

1068. Kremer, S. Lillian. "The Holocaust in *Mr. Sammler's Planet.*
Saul Bellow Journal 4.1 (1985): 19-32.

Claims that in Bellow's pre-1970's novels the Holocaust was
evoked symbolically and allusively, but that in *MSP* he deals
with the subject by recording the haunting recollections of
survivors, and studies the current behavioral and emotional
disorders stemming from wartime brutality. Provides a
detailed examination of *MSP* from this perspective.

1069. Kumar, P. Shiv. "Yahudim and Ostjude: Social Stratification in
Mr. Sammler's Planet." *Literary Half-Yearly* 21.2 (1980):
53-67.

Examines the pattern of immigration into the USA that
brought *Yahudim* and *Ostjude* into sociological conflict.

Applies these observations to *MSP*, a novel that tries to
vindicate the *Ostjude* ethic over against the ethic of the
Yahudim, which, as the novel sees, is undifferentiated from
the WASP code. The novel projects the social stratification
through Elya Gruner and his wife Hilda.

1070. Kuna, F. M. "The European Culture Game: Mr. Bellow's Planet."
English Studies 53.6 (1972): 531-44.

Provides a general overview of the plot and some of the
formal elements of the novel. Sees the novel as a vendetta
against the "Schopenhauerian-Nietzschean legacy in modernism." Condemns it for its unsuccessful attempt to blend art
and philosophy.

1071. Loris, Michelle Carbone. "*Mr. Sammler's Planet*: The Terms of
the Covenant." *Renascence* 30.4 (1978): 217-23.

Asserts that for Bellow the essential quest is the spiritual
search for humanness in a world that daily assaults and
denies such a search. This search informs every novel and
MSP is no exception.

1072. Maloney, Stephen R. "Half-Way to Byzantium: *Mr. Sammler's
Planet* and the Modern Tradition." *South Carolina Review* 6.1
(1973): 31-40.

Defines Bellow's anti-modernism not as a reaction against the
Eliot-Pound-Joyce movement, but against liberalism, progres-
sivism, and relativism. Traces similarities between Mr.
Sammler and the personna of Yeats' "Sailing to Byzantium."

1073. Manning, Gerald F. "The Humanizing Imagination: A Theme in
Mr. Sammler's Planet." *English Studies in Canada* 3.2 (1977):
216-22.

MSP displays Bellow's characteristic preoccupation with the
relationship between individual and environment, as well as
extensive social and cultural criticism. However, this novel
also develops some ideas with aesthetic as well as moral
dimensions.

1074. Mesher, David R. "Three Men on the Moon: Friedman, Updike, Bellow, and Apollo Eleven." *Research Studies* 47.2 (1979): 67-75.

> Mesher comments on the responses to space travel of three contemporary novelists, including Bellow. With particular reference to *MSP*, he discusses what the Apollo Eleven flight symbolized to the human imagination. Sammler rejects Lal's idea that landing a colony on the moon might solve metaphysical problems. The moon becomes a symbol for Sammler of all the deaths and escapes he has known. Yet it does not solve the problem of death or morality.

1075. Murty, M. S. Rama. "The Creative Intransigent: A Study of *Mr. Sammler's Planet*." *Journal of English Studies* [India] 12.1 (November 1980): 800-11.

> Comments that the central quest for Sammler is not personal, nor is it to question the limitations of the self, but rather it is to fulfill the terms of one's contract and to know life. Provides a general exposition of theme and intent in the novel, and concludes that the novel is more concerned with values than with individual adjustment.

1076. Newman, Judie. "*Mr. Sammler's Planet*: Wells, Hitler and the World State." *Dutch Quarterly Review of Anglo-American Letters* 13.1 (1983): 55-71.

> Newman establishes that in *MSP* Bellow's primary interest lies in two historical events governing the action, the Holocaust, in the past, and the Apollo moonshot, in the immediate future of the novel. Both are governed by a planetary metaphor. The world of the death camps is another planet, as is the world of the future that lies beyond man's comprehension. The novel is structured around the infinite poles of optimistic and pessimistic ideas of history, with the middle gound of the present defined in ethical imperatives. Only one fixed pole emerges from this--the moral imperative. Sees the novel as profoundly moral and carrying both aesthetic and intellectual conviction. A major article.

1077. O'Brien, Maureen S. N. D. "Seeing and Knowing in *Mr. Sammler's Planet.*" *Chu-Shikoku Studies in American Literature* [Japan] 12 (1976): 1-8. Cited in *MLA Bibliography,* 1979.

1078. Overton, Harvey. "Sharing Mr. Sammler's Planet: Intellect and Conscience in Science and Technology." *Journal of General Education* 32.4 (1981): 309-19.

This article uses a brief passage from *MSP* as a preface to a worthwhile and erudite article on the subject of science, technology and moral issues. Its text elucidates a subject that Bellow has discussed fictionally for a long time.

1079. Pifer, Ellen. "'Two Different Speeches': Mystery and Knowledge in *Mr. Sammler's Planet.*" *Mosaic* 18.2 (1985): 17-32.

Descibes a rift in Sammler's consciousness that author identifies as "the polarization of two modes of consciousness, the analytic and the intuitive." Sammler perceives reality in radically opposing terms. At times he attempts to disengage himself from the world and the claims he intuitively knows it has upon him. These shifting modes of apprehension unfold a continuous dialectic between two modes of speech in his consciousness.

1080. Russell, Mariann. "White Man's Black Man: Three Views." *College Language Association Journal* 17 (1973): 93-100.

Russell examines *MSP* and several other novels of the 1960's and 1970's with regard to what their white authors have made of black characters within the novels. It illustrates the complexity of Bellow's black character and establishes how far Bellow reaches beyond the traditional stereotypes initially invoked in the novel to develop his character as a meaningful aspect of Mr. Sammler's humanity.

1081. Salter, D. P. M. "Optimism and Reaction in Saul Bellow's Recent Work." *Critical Quarterly* 14.1 (1972): 57-66.

Sees this novel as an extension of *H* with a new departure into a sense of affirmation and wisdom embodied in the hero, Arthur Sammler. Sammler is a person who has the

kind of sanctity or wholeness which Herzog is beginning to
grope for at the end of the book. In this book Bellow more
openly functions as a writer with a moral function.

1082. Samuels, Charles T. "Bellow on Modernism." *New Republic* 7
Feb. 1970: 27-30.

Sees the book as intelligent and beautifully written, but
imperfect in its failure to connect between action and idea.

1083. Satyanarayana, M. R. "The Reality Teacher as Hero: A Study of
Saul Bellow's *Mr. Sammler's Planet.*" *Osmania Journal of
English Studies* [India] 8.2 (1971): 55-68.

Unlike previous novels, *MSP* has a hero who instead of
having a separate reality instructor is his own reality
instructor. Sensing that the world is mad, Sammler confronts
it with disinterestedness. He tries to keep his counsel, to
avoid involvement, but the outside world pulls him into its
whirlpool.

1084. Scheick, William J. "Circle Sailing in Bellow's *Mr. Sammler's
Planet.*" *Essays in Literature* 5.1 (1978): 95-101.

Scheick describes Mr. Sammler as possessing an imaginary axis
comprised of the emotional extremities of attraction and
repulsion, around which axis the self, as it were, rotates,
experiencing a cyclic affirmation and despair equivalent to
the planetary manifestations of day and night. This is
indicated in the lunar symbolism and Sammler's light and
dark eyes.

1085. Schneider, Joseph L. "The Immigrant Experience in *Prin* and
Mr. Sammler's Planet." *On Poets and Poetry: Second Series.*
Salzburg Studies in English Literature 27. Salzburg: Institut
fur Anglistik und Amerikanistik, Universitat Salzburg, 1980.
37-40.

1086. Schulz, Max F. "Mr. Bellow's Perigree, Or, The Lowered
Horizon of *Mr. Sammler's Planet.*" *Contemporary American-
Jewish Literature: Critical Essays.* Ed. Irving Malin. Blooming-
ton: Indiana UP, 1973. 117-33.

In *MSP* Bellow unveils a central character who, unlike previous Bellow characters, is analytical rather than generous
and somehow less optimistic. His vision is essentially more
earth-centered than visionary. This novel represents Bellow
in retreat. Sammler is a collector of dour prognostications
of the imminent collapse of civilization. This philosophical
shift may be temporary or permanent.

1087. Sharma, D. R. "*Mr. Sammler's Planet*: Another 'Passage' to
    India." *Panjab University Research Bulletin* (Arts) 4.1 (April
    1973): 97-104.

    Provides an overall analysis of the socio-cultural critique in
    the novel and an explanation of its basic value structure.
    Clearly sees the novel in terms of E. M. Forster's *A Passage
    to India*. Concentrates largely on the exchange between Samm-
    ler and Lal in the latter part of the novel. Also expands on
    the theme of India found in earlier American literature.

1088. Siegel, Ben. "Saul Bellow and Mr. Sammler: Absurd Seekers of
    High Qualities." *Saul Bellow: A Collection of Critical Essays.*
    Ed. Earl Rovit. Twentieth Century Views. Englewood Cliffs,
    NJ: Prentice, 1975. 122-34.

    Siegal traces carefully the intellectual climate of the late
    1950's and early 1960's that produced cries that the old
    novel was dead, that a generation of apocalyptic young
    novelists had arrived, and that post-modernism had triumphed
    in such radicalism as that advocated by hipster and hippy
    alike. Against this socio-intellectual background, Siegal shows
    MSP as an unpopular comment on the failure of this movement
    to be "more dishevelled than revolutionary." The article
    illustrates the book's value as a social commentary of the
    times and as a protest against the failure of 1960's radi-
    calism to produce values, ideas and a lifestyle that can
    stand the test of history. Siegal is careful to point out how
    Bellow distinguishes in the novel between true radicalism and
    misused, phony radicalism. A major article.

1089. Sire, James W. "Mr. Sammler and the God of Our Fathers."
    Christianity Today 4 June 1971: 6-9.

    Sees *MSP* as an almost Christian novel, a piece of work that

stands out like an oasis in the desert of postwar American
literature. Sees the character, Mr. Sammler, as an analogue
of seventy years of Jewish experience. Documents Sammler's
intellectual and spiritual strength and his eventual escape from
reason. Criticizes Bellow for taking the last step that would
make this a truly Christian novel--belief in the teachings of
Meister Eckhart.

1090. Sloss, Henry. "Europe's Last Gasp." *Shenandoah* 22.1 (1970):
82-86.

Quarrels with the premises behind Sammler's lifestyle
described as being comprised of the wisdom of Europe and
of American schools. This wisdom counts the world as
something to be understood, given to us to interpret,
analyze, and perceive. With this goes hopelessness and a
recognition of unresponsive necessity as signs of intelligence.
This is what Sloss's article warns against. Sammler is a lost
man--a troglodyte.

1091. Stafford, W. T. "The Black/White Continuum: Some Recent
Examples in Bellow, Malamud, and Updike." *Books Speaking
to Books: A Contextual Approach to American Fiction.* W. T.
Stafford. Chapel Hill, NC: U of North Carolina P, 1981.
71-102.

1092. Trilling, Lionel, et al. "Sincerity and Authenticity: A Symposium."
Salmagundi 41 (1977): 87-110.

1093. Vernier, Jean-Pierre. "Mr. Sammler's Lesson." *Les Americanistes:
New French Criticism on Modern American Fiction.* Eds. Ira
D. Johnson and Christiane Johnson. Port Washington, NY:
Kennikat, 1978. 16-36.

Provides a thorough analysis of the value system implicit in
the text through an examination of narrative technique.
Establishes that Bellow's fiction is extremely sophisticated and
extremely modern in that it questions the capacity of
literature to convey truth and stresses the autonomous
quality of the world of the imagination. But, on the other
hand, Bellow apparently refuses to be concerned with the
various problems connected with the creation of artistic

illusion by means of writing. His ontological quest bypasses
the level of fictional representation in order to refer
directly to a metaphysical question. Bellow is not unaware
of or uninterested in the problems raised by his own medium:
for him no novel can find itself sufficient justification and
raison d'etre. Ultimately the novel is a lesson to the reader
that each reader must decipher for himself.

1094. Weber, Ronald. "The View from Space: Notes on Space
      Exploration and Recent Writing." *Georgia Review* 33.2 (1979):
      280-96.

      Weber finds that both serious and popular contemporary
      fiction that use space exploration in significant ways do so,
      as Bellow does in *MSP*, to explore its "triumphs and
      possibilities . . . in ironic counterpoint to the messy yet
      human concerns of the earthbound."

1095. Weinstein, Mark A. "The Fundamental Elements in *Mr. Sammler's
      Planet*." *Saul Bellow Journal* 1.2 (1982): 18-26.

      Weinstein demonstrates that the fundamentals with which *MSP*
      concerns itself are communicated by means of elaborate image
      patterns from the four basic elements: earth, air, fire, and
      water. The article analyzes these patterns in considerable
      depth.

1096. Wirth-Nesher, Hana, and Andrea Cohen Malamut. "Jewish and
      Human Survival on Bellow's Planet." *Modern Fiction Studies*
      25.1 (1979): 59-74.

      Sees *MSP* as Bellow's best Jewish novel because it deals
      directly with the Holocaust, the state of Israel, and
      American Jewry's relation to both. The value system in the
      novel also is essentially Jewish, with its unwavering belief in
      survival under any circumstances, an emphasis on reason and
      human intellect. It is part of a long tradition of interpretation
      and commentary on scripture; a preference for good deeds
      and actions over contemplation; the concept of *mitzvoth*. All
      of these values constitute a rejection of despair. Applies all
      these values to an examination of *MSP*.

Reviews

1097. Bayley, John. "More Familiar than Novel." *Listener* 9 July 1970: 51-52.

1098. Braine, John. "Bellow's Planet." *National Review* 10 Mar. 1970: 264-66.

1099. Broyard, Anatole. "*Mr. Sammler's Planet.*" *New York Times Book Review* 1 Feb. 1970: 1, 40.

1100. Edelman, Lily. "Saul Bellow's Planet--and Ours." *Jewish Heritage* Sept. 1970: 3-4, 67.

1101. Epstein, Joseph. "Saul Bellow's Messenger of Ill-Tiding." *Chicago Tribune Book Week* 1 Feb. 1970: 1, 3.

1102. Fein, Richard J. "Bellow's Turf." *Judaism* Sept. 1970: 252-54.

1103. Fletcher, Janet. "*Mr. Sammler's Planet.*" *Library Journal* Feb. 1970: 511.

1104. Frank, Mike. "The Travail of Being Human." *American Zionist* Dec. 1970: 41-42.

1105. Gray, Paul Edward. "New Novels in Review." *Yale Review* 59.3 (1970): 430-38.

1106. "In Search of Order." *Times Literary Supplement* 9 July 1970: 749. Rpt. in *T.L.S., Essays and Reviews from The Times Literary Supplement.* London: Oxford U P, 1971. 38-43.

1107. Katz, Phyllis R. *Best Sellers* 1 Feb 1970: 409-10.

1108. Kazin, Alfred. "Though He Slay Me. . ." *New York Review of Books* 3 Dec. 1970: 3-4.

1109. Kiely, Robert. "Saul Bellow's Balanced Man." *Christian Science Monitor* 5 Feb. 1970: 11A.

1110. Lindroth, James R. "The Proper Study of Mankind Is. . ." *America* 21 Feb. 1970: 190.

1111. Lurie, Alison. "The View From the Moon." *New Statesman* 10 July 1970: 19.

1112. Oates, Joyce Carol. "Articulations." *Critic: A Catholic Review of Books and the Arts* May-June 1970: 68-69.

1113. Opdahl, Keith M. "An Honorable Old Man in a World of Obsessed Young Adults." *Commonweal* 13 Feb. 1970: 535-36.

1114. Pinsker, Sanford. "Few Real Surprises." *Reconstructionist* 29 May 1970: 20-22.

1115. Pritchard, William H. "Senses of Reality." *Hudson Review* 23.1 (1970): 169-70.

1116. "Saul Bellow: Seer with a Civil Heart." *Time* 9 Feb. 1970: 81-84.

1117. Sissman, L. E. "Uptight." *New Yorker* 31 Jan. 1970: 82, 85-87.

1118. Sokolov, Raymond A. "West Side Lear." *Newsweek* 2 Feb. 1970: 77.

1119. Stock, Irvin. "Man in Culture." *Commentary* May 1970: 89-94.

1120. Sullivan, Walter. "Where Have All the Flowers Gone?" *Sewanee Review* 78.4 (1970): 654-64.

1121. Wohlgelernter, Maurice. "Don't Stop the World: Sammler Wants to Stay On." *Congress Bi-Weekly* 25 Dec. 1970: 17-21.

Plays

1122. Anderson, David D. "The Novelist as Playwright: Saul Bellow on Broadway." *Saul Bellow Journal* 5.1 (1986): 48-62.

Reviews briefly Bellow's history of involvement with the theatre and his writings both for it and about it. Discusses several dramatic pieces including *The Wrecker* and *The Last Analysis*. Discusses the textual evolution of *LA* and the character of Bummidge. Concludes with Bellow's responses concerning his broadway career.

1123. Bigsby, C. W. E. "The New Surrealism." *Confrontation and Commitment: A Study of Contemporary American Drama 1959-66.* C. W. E. Bigsby. Columbia, MO: U of Missouri P, 1968. 93-99.

Bigsby discusses the thematic content of *LA* in the context of a discussion of experimentalism and surrealism on the drama of the period.

1124. Brustein, Robert. "Saul Bellow on the Drag Strip." *New Republic* 24 Oct. 1964: 25-26. Rpt. in *Seasons of Discontent: Dramatic Opinions 1959-1965.* Robert Brustein. New York: Simon and Schuster, 1965. 172-75.

Brustein complains of sprawling structure and lack of integrated theme and form. The farce is too serious and dark for theater farce. Provides good plot summary of the play. Sees the piece as anarchic to the theater itself. Sees that Bellow has potential as a playwright and condemns those of lesser talent who may have permanently exiled him from attempting theater again.

1125. Clurman, Harold. "Theatre." Rev. of *The Last Analysis*. *Nation*
      19 Oct. 1964: 256-57.

      Contains a review of *Oh What a Lovely War* and Bellow's
      LA. Complains that farce is the wrong mode for the serious
      business the play concerns itself with. Bummidge never
      becomes real. He remains a "figure of verbiage." There is
      little logic in his process. The play remains unfulfilled. Also
      condemns the producer for his lack of style.

1126. Clurman, Harold. "Theatre." Rev. of *Under the Weather*. *Nation*
      14 Nov. 1966) 523-24. Rpt. in *The Naked Image: Observations
      on the Modern Theatre*. Harold Clurman. New York: Macmillan
      1966. 45-47.

      Clurman categorizes Bellow's plays as one act farces.
      Provides a detailed account of the content and structure of
      UW. Claims that the final result of the play is to stimulate
      curiosity rather than gratify. Sees the play as more likely to
      succeed as a commercial venture than as an artistic one.

1127. Cohn, Ruby. "Saul Bellow." *Dialogue in American Drama*. Ruby
      Cohn. Bloomington, IN: Indiana UP, 1971. 192-97.

      Cohn discusses Bellow's play *The Wrecker*, 1954. One of the
      few references to this play in the literature. Complains of its
      brevity and lack of farcical savagery. Claims the play lacks
      focus. Goes on to discuss *LA*, giving a succinct plot and
      character summary. Claims that the optimistic ending lacks
      conviction and that the audience balks at farce containing
      redemption themes. Describes the chief character, Bummidge,
      as "a pygmy" compared to the heroes of the novels.

1128. Corrigan, Robert W. "Engagement/Disengagement in the
      Contemporary Theatre." *The Theatre in Search of a Fix*.
      Robert W. Corrigan. New York: Delacorte, 1973. 282-84.

      Corrigan calls Bellow a great comic artist like Chekov. Deals
      with Bummidge in *LA* as a modern-day Hamlet. He concen-
      trates on the spoof, farce and burlesque in the play.

1129. "From Womb to Gloom." Rev. of *The Last Analysis*. *Time* 9

Oct. 1964: 92.

A brief statement of the content of *LA* that refuses even to discuss it as drama. The review is essentially a dismissal of the play.

1130. Gilman, Richard. "Bellow on Broadway." Rev. of *Under the Weather*. *Common and Uncommon Masks: Writings on Theatre 1961-1970*. Richard Gilman. New York: Random, 1971. 242-44.

1131. Hewes, Henry. "A Muse of Fire." Rev. of *The Last Analysis*. *Saturday Review* 17 Oct. 1964: 29.

A brief derogatory review of *LA* that condemns it for its lack of focus and "depressingly domestic discord."

1132. Malin, Irving. "Bummy's Analysis." *Saul Bellow: A Collection of Critical Essays*. Ed. Earl Rovit. Twentieth Century Views. Englewood Cliffs, NJ: Prentice, 1975. 115-21.

Discusses Bummidge as one more of Bellow's "autodidacts." Provides an intensive and theoretical analysis of the play and its central protagonist. Concludes that the final effect of the play is mixed and that "we dangle between different worlds--ours and his, Bellow's and ours." Calls it a powerful, shrewd and funny play. A major article on this play.

1133. McCarten, John. "Look, Ma, I'm Playwriting." Rev. of *Under the Weather*. *New Yorker* 5 Nov. 1966: 127-28.

Comments on *LA* as a disaster and complains that *UW* is another example of Bellow's "getting an education in public" and earning as he gets one. Critiques the female characters in the play disparagingly but does give a fairly thorough plot summary. Concludes that Bellow never persuaded him that the participants were "worth a second thought."

1134. "Out of Sync." Rev. of *The Last Analysis*. *Newsweek* 12 Oct. 1964: 105.

Condemns the production of *LA* and then condemns the play

saying that "it committed suicide before its assassination."
Bellow fails to dramatize his ideas. "The play's soliloquies
and dialogue are not in coherence with its ostensibly farcical
action." The play is full of "thick, clotted, unrealized
ambitions."

1135. Philips, Louis. "The Novelist as Playwright: Baldwin, McCullers,
and Bellow." *Modern American Drama: Essays in Criticism.* Ed.
William E. Taylor. Deland, FL: Everett/Edwards, 1968.
145-62.

Reviews the critics' comments on Bellow as playwright.
Provides a character analysis of Bummidge in *LA* and a short
production account. Deals primarily with Bellow's literary
ideas in the play. Concludes his critique of the play qua
play with the comment that Bellow as satirist is defeated by
his own earnestness.

1136. Prideaux, Tom. "Don't Let Bellow Get Scared Off." Rev. of
The Last Analysis. Life 30 Oct. 1964: 17.

Accuses Bellow of failing to recognize some of the almost
childish truths of the theater--a play cannot ever meander
like passages in a novel. Sees Bellow as one of the long line
of American novelists who give the theater one try and give
up. Claims that one can never really sympathize with
Bummidge because he is never really in trouble.

1137. "Sex as Punishment." Rev. of *Under the Weather. Time* 4 Nov.
1966: 85.

A brief dismissal of the play that disparages Bellow's
assessment of women in *UW*.

1138. Sheed, Wilfred. "Weathering the Folly." Rev. of *Under the
Weather. Commonweal* 18 Nov. 1966: 199-201.

1139. Weales, Gerald. "Saul Bellow and Some Others." *The Jumping
Off Place: American Drama in the 1960's.* Gerald Weales.
New York: Macmillan; London: Collier-Macmillan, 1969.
195-223.

Weales provides a detailed account of Bellow's interest in the theater and a production history of *LA*. Describes it as one of the "most fascinating and funniest plays to turn up in the 1960's." This is followed by a detailed and intelligent critical analysis of the play far beyond the scope of any other published source.

1140. Alhadeff, Barbara. "The Divided Self: A Laingian Interpretation of *Seize the Day*." *Studies in American Jewish Literature* 3.1 (1977): 16-20.

Tommy Wilhelm so fills the mold R. D. Laing delineates in his work *The Divided Self* that his character becomes the literary embodiment of the notion of the "divided self." Laing's approach to schizophrenia also shows a high degree of correlation with the existential condition of Tommy Wilhelm.

1141. Baker, Robert. "Bellow Comes of Age." *Chicago Review* 11.1 (Spring 1957): 107-10.

Reviews the novel briefly and develops the view that it culminates a line of development begun with *DM*. Traces the ideational development across the four novels and concludes that *SD* constitutes a major coup.

1142. Bordewyk, Gordon. "Nathanael West and *Seize the Day*." *English Studies* 64.2 (1983): 153-59.

Traces the direct influence of West's *Miss Lonely Hearts* and *Day of the Locust* on *SD*. Detailed and convincing.

1143. Bordewyk, Gordon. "Saul Bellow's Death of a Salesman." *Saul Bellow Newsletter* 1.1 (1981): 18-21.

Argues that Bellow relies heavily on Miller's plays for the themes and characters of *SD*. Bordewyck traces similarities in names, occupational fortunes, problems with insurance companies, similar post-war backdrop, alienation of the middle-class, family break-down, a strong pastoral nostalgia,

urban misery and other shared material between the two
playwrights.

1144. Bouson, J. Brooks. "The Narcissistic Self-Drama of Wilhelm
      Adler: A Kohutian Reading of Bellow's *Seize the Day*." *Saul
      Bellow Journal* 5.2 (1986): 3-14.

      Bellow, through his character Wilhelm Adler, anticipates
      recent psychoanalytic investigations into the dynamics of the
      narcissistic personality disorder. Wilhelm Adler provides an
      artistic anticipation of what psychoanalyst Heinz Kohut
      describes as "tragic," "broken" man, the narcissistically
      defective individual "who suffers from an enfeebled,
      crumbling sense of self."

1145. Bowen, Robert O. "Bagels, Sour Cream and the Heart of the
      Current Novel." *Northwest Review* 1.2 (1957): 52-56.

      Bowen complains that *SD* is the third in the "mopery series"
      and is of interest as morbid social pathology insofar as it
      deals with the surface of a current American phenomenon:
      the middle-age adolescent. The ending of the novel is pure
      self-pity of the most saccharine order. There is no turning
      outward to humanity. This is not literature; it is a *tour de
      force* based on subject matter dear to the urban book
      reviewer.

1146. Chavkin, Allan. "'The Hollywood Thread' and the First Draft of
      Saul Bellow's *Seize the Day*." *Studies in the Novel* 14.1
      (1982): 82-94.

      Demonstrates Bellow's primary concerns in *SD* by discussing
      his examination of the earliest draft of the book entitled
      One of Those Days. A technical, detailed and essential article
      since it is the only study of the early manuscript and its
      relationship to the published novel. Deals primarily with the
      evolution of the characters and particularly that of Tommy
      Wilhelm.

1147. Chavkin, Allan. "Suffering and Wilhelm Reich's Theory of
      Character-Armoring in Saul Bellow's *Seize the Day*." *Essays
      in Literature* 9.1 (1982): 133-37.

Demonstrates that the early manuscript copy of the novel
entitled *One of Those Days* contains the specific notions of
character-armoring as elucidated originally by Wilhelm Reich
in his book *Character Analysis*. Goes on to add to the
previous discussions of this by Eusebio Rodrigues and John
J. Clayton.

1148. Ciancio, Ralph. "The Achievement of Saul Bellow's *Seize the
    Day*." *Literature and Theology*. Eds. Thomas F. Staley and
    Lester F. Zimmerman. The University of Tulsa Department
    of English Monograph Series 7. Tulsa, OK: U of Tulsa, 1969.
    49-80.

What begins as the schizoid estrangement of the individual
and his authentic self begets the estrangement of father and
son, the individual and contemporary urban world, the Jew
and his spiritual heritage, the individual and humanity--
issues that Bellow manages to encompass in the short breadth
of this novel by focusing squarely on the plight of his
protagonist and expanding centrifugally the antagonism
between the real and the pretender souls. Makes much of
Wilhelm's radical adolescence and radical innocence.
Develops a sophisticated explanation of the intimated
relationship between Wilhelm and Tamkin. Defines a *zaddick*
in historical terms and demonstrates Tamkin's role with
regard to Wilhelm's salvation.

1149. Clayton, John J. "Alienation and Masochism." *Saul Bellow: In
    Defense of Man*. John J. Clayton. Bloomington, IN: Indiana
    UP, 1968. 2nd ed. 1979. 49-76. Rpt. in *Saul Bellow*. Ed.
    Harold Bloom. Modern Critical Views. New York: Chelsea,
    1986. 65-85.

Discusses the paradox of Bellow's personal despair and
romantic idealism, not to mention his Jewish humanism and
Jewish guilt and self-hatred. Details evidences of Bellow's
personal despair creeping into his fiction. Concludes that
Bellow, like his heroes, is "life-affirming, love-affirming,
individual-affirming. But underneath the 'yea' is a deep,
persuasive 'nay'--underneath belief in the individual and in
the possibility of community is alienation, masochism, despair."

1150. Clayton, John J. "Saul Bellow's *Seize the Day*: A Study in

Mid-Life Transition." *Saul Bellow Journal* 5.1 (1986): 34-47.

Argues that the ending of the novel is based on the study of
Wilhelm as an infantile regressive who, while in the midst
of a mid-life crisis, takes steps toward true maturity as he
mourns the corpse (the casting off of his old self) and
emerges from the experience more maturely and deeply
connected with the world of human beings.

1151. Cronin, Gloria L. "The Seduction of Tommy Wilhelm: A
      Post-Modernist Appraisal of *Seize the Day*." *Saul Bellow
      Journal* 3.1 (1983): 18-27.

      The surface world of *SD* is deceptively modern in construc-
      tion, comprised as it is of urban alienation materials such as
      its nightmare urban landscape, pathetic hero and carefully
      constructed patterns of descent, sickness, decay, impotence
      and drowning imagery. However, Bellow is actually making
      clever ironic use of such materials, and particularly with
      such shopworn materials as absurdist and Freudian estimates
      of man. *SD* is actually a drama of seduction in which
      Wilhelm is forced to faith through having to resist the
      appealing modernist notions of Tamkin, the espouser of
      alienation ethics and nihilism. Provoked finally to examine
      such modernist estimates of life, Wilhelm rediscovers his
      faith in the human enterprise.

1152. Giannone, Richard. "Saul Bellow's Idea of Self: A Reading of
      Seize the Day." *Renascence* 27.4 (1975): 193-205.

      Unlike previous novels dealing with fallen characters like
      Tommy Wilhelm, this novel embodies the quest for personal
      light in deliberately romantic structural forms. Like the
      romantic sun gods, Apollo and Hyperion, Tommy must be
      schooled in suffering before he can reach his "humanness." In
      the modern materialistic world, this is a process of losing--
      not acquiring. Only at this point is true creative energy
      released. A sophisticated explication in which Tommy Wilhelm
      is seen as an inadvertent aspirant to romantic ambition.

1153. Gordon, Andrew. "Shakespeare's *The Tempest* and Yeats'
      'Sailing to Byzantium' in *Seize the Day*. *Saul Bellow Journal*
      4.1 (1985): 45-51.

1154. Handy, William J. "Bellow's *Seize the Day.*" *Modern Fiction: A Formalist Approach.* William J. Handy. Crosscurrents/Modern Critiques. Carbondale, IL: Southern Illinois UP, 1971. 119-30.

Claims that in *SD* it is the image of mid-century American man that is most significant in the novel. Describes the narrative line of the story and the relationship of the characters within the plot, treats the father-son theme and the failure of modern man implied in Dr. Tamkin.

1155. Handy, William J. "Saul Bellow and the Naturalistic Hero." *Texas Studies in Literature and Language* 5.4 (1964): 538-45.

Describes Bellow's break with the Dreiserian and Hemingwayesque naturalistic hero struggling and being defeated in an ultimately malevolent world. Indicates briefly Bellow's affirmative modifications on the naturalistic formula and its premises.

1156. Howe, Irving. Introduction. *Seize the Day. Classics of Modern Fiction: Ten Short Novels.* Ed. Irving Howe. New York: Harcourt Brace and World, 1968. 457-66; 2nd ed. 1972. 511-20; 3rd ed. 1980. 457-66.

Introduces the work under the headings: The Setting, Poetry, The Hero, Minor Characters, and Style. A useful overview of major issues in the novel for the beginning student.

1157. Jefchak, Andrew. "Family Struggles in *Seize the Day.*" *Studies in Short Fiction* 11.3 (1974): 297-302.

In *SD* we see that family relationships, not church, army, or big business, form the psychocenter of the novel. Traces convincingly the destructive dynamics and values that govern the failed familial relationships in the novel. The ending of the novel suggests the improbability of twentieth-century familial closeness and indicates that true feeling can only be generated both within and toward one's own self. The unshared life is depicted as a permanent condition.

1158. Kremer, S. Lillian. "*Seize the Day*: Intimations of Anti-Hasidic
      Satire." *Yiddish* 4.4 (1982): 32-40.

      Intelligent application of the materials and techniques of
      Jewish literature infuses the content and style in *SD*. Set in
      New York City's decaying West Side, the narrative deals
      with a multilevel conflict, including, on an allusive plane,
      the historic antagonism between the Hasidim and their Jewish
      opponents. Bellow's use of the historic *misnagdic* and
      maskilic opposition to the Hasidic way justifies the dramatic
      function of the novella's minor actors and, more importantly,
      clarifies the paradoxical nature of Tamkin's character.

1159. Kulshreshtha, Chirantan. "*Seize the Day* and the Bellow
      Chronology." *Literary Criterion* 13.3 (1978): 29-33. Cited in
      Annual Bibliography of English Language and Literature,
      1978.

1160. Lister, Paul A. "The 'Compleat Fool' in *Seize the Day*." *Saul
      Bellow Journal* 3.2 (1984): 32-59.

      Bellow leads Wilhelm through a complete progression from
      foolishness to wisdom. Suggests a relationship to I. B.
      Singer's "Gimpel the Fool" that Bellow translated just three
      years before. Suggests *Proverbs* as an influence. Claims
      Wilhelm arrives at the heart of his maturity in the funeral
      parlor.

1161. Marotti, Maria Ornella. "Concealment and Revelation: The
      Binary Structure of *Seize the Day*." *Saul Bellow Journal* 5.2
      (1986): 46-51.

      Discusses the idea that though the novel is centered on a
      central character facing a moment of deep crisis and self-
      discovery, the novella is organized through the principle of
      a shifting center of consciousness that is functional to the
      deep structure of the text, that is, to the underlying binary
      pattern of concealment and revelation. Not only is the
      reader allowed to penetrate the true emotional roots of the
      protagonist's personality through his thoughts, delusions, and
      memories, but also he or she is able to see the impact of
      his appearance on the world both through his father's

thoughts and the narrator's grotesque descriptions of his discordant physical traits.

1162. Mathis, James C. "The Theme of *Seize the Day.*" *Critique* 7.3 (1965): 43-45.

Traces the complex strands of meaning and associations set off in the novel by the unconventional use of the *carpe diem* theme from Shakespeare's Sonnet 73.

1163. Morahg, Gilead. "The Art of Dr. Tamkin: Matter and Manner in *Seize the Day.*" *Modern Fiction Studies* 25.1 (1979): 103-16. Rpt. in *Saul Bellow.* Ed. Harold Bloom. Modern Critical Views. New York: Chelsea, 1986. 147-59.

SD is problematic in that its intellectual values depend heavily on the enigmatic character of Dr. Tamkin, who, through seemingly negative ideas, communicates positive healing effects. Morahg provides a good review of critical assessments of Tamkin. Tamkin uses his imaginative vision to communicate cogent visions of human reality. These are generally analogous to a developing vision postulated in Bellow's later novels. Like Bellow, he is dedicated to a cultural and spiritual mission he believes can be carried out through his art. Moragh traces these ideas throughout this and later novels.

1164. Mukerji, Nirmal. "A Note on the Animal Imagery in *Seize the Day.*" *Asian Response to American Literature.* Ed. C. D. Narasimhaiah. New York: Barnes, 1972. 313-15.

Provides a general overview of the theme and style in the novel. Develops a slightly more detailed analysis of its patterns of animal and water imagery.

1165. Mukerji, Nirmal. "A Reading of Saul Bellow's *Seize the Day.*" *Literary Criterion* 9.1 (1969): 48-53.

Provides a general overview of the theme and style and develops a slightly more detailed analysis of patterns of animal and water imagery in the novel (See item 1164).

1166. Nelson, Gerald B. "Tommy Wilhelm." *Ten Versions of America.*
Gerald B. Nelson. New York: Knopf, 1972. 129-45.

A general discussion detailing the exact dimensions of
Tommy's defeat in modern America. Concludes that the
journey was simply too rigorous for him, that he really
didn't have what it takes to negotiate modern America and
that Tommy cannot "protect himself from the savages" by
building any kind of a fence. He doesn't really want to die,
he just doesn't want to be a man.

1167. Pinsker, Sanford. "Bellow's *Seize the Day.*" *Explicator* 41.3
(1983): 60-61.

Pinsker argues that the poem "Eyes and Tears" by Andrew
Marvell provides a striking analogue of Tommy's situation.
Pinsker goes on to document the large number of water
images in the novel and to conclude that weeping in the
novel, as in the poem, is a sign of strength, not of weakness.

1168. Porter, M. Gilbert. "The Scene as Image: A Reading of *Seize
the Day.*" *Saul Bellow: A Collection of Critical Essays.* Ed.
Earl Rovit. Twentieth Century Views. Englewood Cliffs, NJ:
Prentice, 1975. 52-71.

1169. Raper, J. R. "Running Contrary Ways: Saul Bellow's *Seize the
Day.*" *Southern Humanities Review* 10.2 (1976): 157-68.

Develops the thesis that there is no longer a unitary
personality in the novel that emerged after the hardboiled
era of Hemingway. True identity of the real self is always
compounded in part of the "Spirit of Alternatives" that
appears in many of Bellow's novels. Interest in this stems
from Bellow's interest in psychoanalysis and Jungian psychology. Believes a man's character runs "contrary ways"
and that "none has as broad and immediate application to
American society as the change in Tommy Wilhelm's personality in *SD.*"

1170. Richmond, Lee J. "The Maladroit, the Medico, and the Magician:
Saul Bellow's *Seize the Day.*" *Twentieth Century Literature*
19.1 (1973): 15-25.

Dr. Adler functions as a failed medico and father. Tommy fulfills the role of the maladroit. He is the deluded inheritor of a bogus mythology of commerce like Jay Gatsby, Willy Loman and others before him. Tamkin the magician, however, is the archetypal shaman who has a special form of medicine power. His is, in fact, the trickster-transformer. He is a master at exorcising tormented souls of evil things. Kin to Tommy as his name suggests, he becomes Tommy's elected father and finally his savior, only to disappear magically as Tommy takes possession of himself in the funeral parlor.

1171. Rodrigues, Eusebio L. "Bellow's Confidence Man." *Notes on Contemporary Literature* 3.1 (1973): 6-8.

Traces the evolution of Tamkin from a variety of sources: Reich, the American literary con man, and the con men of Chicago who inhabit Bughouse Square, Hyde Park, and particularly Yellow Kid Weil.

1172. Rodrigues, Eusebio L. "Reichianism in *Seize the Day*." *Critical Essays on Saul Bellow*. Ed. Stanley Trachtenberg. Critical Essays on American Literature. Boston: Hall, 1979. 89-100.

1173. Sharma, J. N. "*Seize the Day*: An Existentialist Look." *Existentialism in American Literature*. Ed. Ruby Chatterji. Atlantic Highlands, NJ: Humanities Press, 1983. 121-33.

Examines *SD* as an existentialist novel emphasizing the aspect of individual choice as the chief criterion. Explores the relationship of this novel to its two predecessors. Mines several of Bellow's essays and interviews for supporting arguments.

1174. Shear, Walter. "*Steppenwolf* and *Seize the Day*." *Saul Bellow Newsletter* 1.1 (1981): 32-34.

Likenesses between *Steppenwolf* and *SD* point to some shared concerns of both Herman Hesse and Saul Bellow. Such concerns include suffering, the dual nature of the individual, adult isolation, the human meaning of finality, and "the heart's ultimate need." Bellow finally reverses Hesse's isolating duality and supplants it with evidence of man's tendency toward inclusiveness.

1175. Sicherman, Carol M. "Bellow's Seize the Day: Reverberations and Hollow Sounds." *Studies in the Twentieth Century* 15 (1975): 1-31.

SD presents an analysis of human isolation in mid-twentieth-century New York through ironic play on the central *carpe diem* motif. Hence, Bellow is able to detail the manifold discordances between Wilhelm's world and the literary world evoked by the book's title. A sophisticated treatment of Bellow's inversions and uses of the traditional associations suggested by the *carpe diem* cannon of literature.

1176. Teodorescu, Anda. "Introduction." *Traieste-ti clipa* [*Seize the Day*]. Saul Bellow. Bucuresti: Univers., 5-11. Cited in *Annual Bibliography of English Language and Literature*, 1972.

1177. Trowbridge, Clinton W. "Water Imagery in *Seize the Day*." *Critique* 9.3 (1967): 62-73.

SD is an essentially positive work depicting the birth of Tommy Wilhelm's soul through a pervasive pattern of drowning and other water imagery. Traces Tommy's ironic passage from apparent despair to a rebirth through drowning. Water imagery is especially significant since it is an emotional birth which is occurring. Argues that SD demonstrates the use of the symbolist technique at its best.

1178. Tuerk, Richard. "Tommy Wilhelm--Wilhelm Adler: Names in *Seize the Day*." *Naughty Names*. Ed. Fred Tarpley. Commerce, Texas: Names Institute Press, 1975. 27-33.

Sees the central theme of the novel as being Tommy Wilhelm's identity--a problem intimately tied up with his confusing number of names. Reviews all of the phases of Wilhelm's search for identity in relation to names he is currently using and their particular cultural and symbolic significance.

1179. Weiss, Daniel. "Caliban on Prospero: A Psychoanalytic Study of the Novel *Seize the Day* by Saul Bellow." *American Imago* 19.3 (1962): 277-306. Rpt. in *Saul Bellow and the Critics*. Ed. Irving Malin. New York: New York UP, 1967. 114-141; *Psychoanalysis and American Fiction*. Ed. Irving Malin. New York: Dutton, 1965. 279-307.

> *SD* concentrates on the father-son relationship that proceeds with unceasing conflict toward ultimate atonement. In this novel it stems from neurotic conflict between instinctual cravings and outwardly determined frustrations. The pattern of repression and its eventual shattering suggests close parallels with the situation revealed in Kafka's "Letter to His Father." Sees Tommy as a moral masochist who hates his father and adopts Tamkin as a substitute for his dead mother. The actual day of the novel's action is a day of traumatophilia that induces, among other neurotic reactions, conversion hysteria in the suffocation episodes. All resolves itself with Tommy's eventual healing through Tamkin, the surrogate and psychoanalyst.

1180. West, Ray B., Jr. "Six Authors in Search of a Hero." *Sewanee Review* 65.3 (1957): 498-508.

> Sees Tommy Wilhelm as perversely unheroic. Despite its pathos the novel is really a comic case study in mediocrity. Criticizes the book for being small and for returning to the themes of the earlier fiction, rather than moving out toward those suggested by *AM*.

Reviews

1181. Allen, Walter. *New Statesman and Nation* ns 27 Apr. 1957: 547-48.

1182. Alpert, Hollis. "Uptown Dilemmas." *Saturday Review* 24 Nov. 1956: 18, 34.

1183. Crane, Milton. *Chicago Sunday Tribune Magazine of Books* 30 Dec. 1956: 7.

1184. Fiedler, Leslie A. "Some Footnotes on the Fiction of '56."
      Reporter 13 Dec. 1956: 44-46.

1185. Flint, Robert W. "The Undying Apocalypse." *Partisan Review*
      24.1 (1957): 139-45.

1186. Gill, Brendan. "Long and Short." *New Yorker* 5 Jan. 1957:
      69-70.

1187. Gilman, Richard. "The Stage: Novelists in the Theater."
      Commonweal 29 Mar. 1963: 20-22.

1188. Gold, Herbert. "The Discovered Self." *Nation* 17 Nov. 1956:
      435-36.

1189. Hicks, Granville. "Collections of New and Classic Works by
      Saul Bellow, Orwell and Wilder." *New Leader* 26 Nov. 1956:
      24-25.

1190. Kazin, Alfred. "In Search of Light." *New York Times Book
      Review* 18 Nov. 1956: 5, 36.

1191. Lynch, John A. "Prelude to Accomplishment." *Commonweal* 30
      Nov. 1956: 238-39.

1192. Rolo, Charles J. "Reader's Choice." *Atlantic* Jan. 1957: 86-87.

1193. Rugoff, Milton. "A Saul Bellow Miscellany." *New York
      Herald Tribune Book Week* 18 Nov. 1956: Part I, 3.

1194. Schwartz, Edward. "Chronicle of the City." *New Republic* 3
      Dec. 1956: 20-21.

1195. Schwartz, Nils. "Forlorarens underbara tarar." *Bonniers
      Litterara Magasin* 51.1 (1982): 73-74.

1196. Swados, Harvey. "A Breather from Saul Bellow." *New York Post Weekend Magazine* 18 Nov. 1956: 11.

1197. Swados, Harvey. "The Long and the Short of It." *Hudson Review* 10.1 (1957): 155-60.

1198. "Upper West Side." *Newsweek* 19 Nov. 1956: 142-43.

Short Fiction

1199. Alter, Robert. "Kafka's Father, Agnon's Mother, Bellow's Cousins." *Commentary* Feb. 1986: 46-52.

1200. Alter, Robert. "Mr. Bellow's Planet." Rev. of *Him with His Foot in His Mouth and Other Stories. New Republic* 11 June 1984: 33-37.

These stories read more like brilliant fragments than well-made wholes, says Alter. Each story is like a small vignette that captures the essential issues of the novels. Discusses Bellow's work in general terms, commending him for his "mantic" vision, which vision extends to the short stories in this collection.

1201. Conant, Oliver. "Burlesquing Intellectuals." Rev. of *Him with His Foot in His Mouth and Other Stories. New Leader* 11 June 1984: 16-17.

Argues that this collection is not as powerful or as even as the previous collection, but goes on to praise it for its ease, boldness, language and carnival of ideas. Deals primarily with how Bellow treats intellectuals in the collection as a whole.

1202. Demarest, David P., Jr. "The Theme of Discontinuity in Saul Bellow's Fiction: 'Looking for Mr. Green' and 'A Father-to-Be.'" *Studies in Short Fiction* 6.2 (1969): 175- 86.

Sees these stories as excellent introductions to Bellow's views generally. Suggests that the polar issues are seeking for intellectual order or taking life as it is. Provides an excellent comparative and formalistic treatment of the two stories.

1203. Dietrich, Richard F. "The Biological Draft Dodger in Bellow's 'A Father-to-Be.'" *Studies in the Humanities* 9.1 (1981): 45-51.

An exhaustive exegesis of the story showing how irrational and human a scientist like Rogin can be in face of inner psychological issues. Shows the central concern of the story to be Rogin's relationship with his fiancee, Joan. The psychological nexus is Rogin's refusal of fatherhood after marriage. What and who Rogin is, and why he must avoid the future in the form of children, becomes the burden of the story. Hence, we see the supposedly rational scientist behaving like anything but a rational being as he attempts to cope with sex, love and mature adult responses to his impending marriage. He evades clear thinking, philosophizes and rationalizes as he tries to reconcile his infantilism and oedipal urges. He ends in total regression.

1204. Donoghue, Denis. "Bellow in Short." Rev. of *Mosby's Memoirs and Other Stories. Art International* 13 (1969): 59-60, 64.

Provides a general discussion of the stories in light of the novels. Neither detailed nor stystematic.

1205. Galloway, David D. "Saul Bellow: 'The Gonzaga Manuscripts.'" *Die Amerikanishe Short Story der Gegenwart: Interpretationen.* Ed. Peter Freese. Berlin: Schmidt, 1976. 175-83. Cited in *MLA Bibliography,* 1976.

Galloway views this short story as a forerunner to HRK. Describes the parallels between the two works.

1206. Geismar, Maxwell. "The American Short Story Today." *Studies on the Left* 4.2 (1964): 21-27.

1207. Gray, Paul. "The Naysayer to Nihilism." Rev. of *Him with His Foot in His Mouth and Other Stories. Time* 14 May 1984: 84.

Provides mainly a content summary of the stories in the collection. No critical opinion offered except in conclusion. "Faithful readers will welcome this book as an addendum, a chance to watch the old master fiddling with themes and variations."

1208. Kindilien, Glenn A. "The Meaning of the Name 'Green' in Saul Bellow's 'Looking for Mr. Green.'" *Studies in Short Fiction* 15.1 (1978): 104-07.

Makes a creative and detailed attempt to explore the implications of the name "Green" and relates this to thematic issues in the story.

1209. Knight, Karl F. "Bellow's 'Cousins': The Suspense of Playing It to the End." *Saul Bellow Journal* 5.2 (1986): 32-35.

The principal theme in Saul Bellow's "Cousins" is the effort to hold things together against the forces of dissolution. Ijah Brodsky, the protagonist, has an apocalpytic sense of the struggle, but avoids despair by working for continuity within his family, by being a responsive and responsible cousin. But the story suggests that responsibility to the larger society may at times take precedence over loyalty to a particular cousin; indeed, the term "cousins" comes to mean the universal human family.

1210. Lemon, Lee T. "A Browningesque Protrait." Rev. of *Him with His Foot in His Mouth and Other Stories. Prairie Schooner* 58.4 (1984): 110.

Concentrates on a brief discussion of character in each of the stories. Lemon is generally appreciative and unsurprised by the collection.

1211. Lippit, Noriko M. "A Perennial Survivor: Saul Bellow's Heroine in the Desert." *Studies in Short Fiction* 12.3 (1975): 281-83.

1212. McQuade, Molly. Rev. of *Him with His Foot in His Mouth and Other Stories. Chicago* 33.2 (1984): 108.

Commends the book for its "skill, tenderness and authority." Calls the stories "rhythmically personal talk," and admires their concrete detail and successful texture and characterization. Provides semi-detailed exegesis of the title story.

1213. Mizener, Arthur. "Saul Bellow: 'Looking for Mr. Green.'"
Handbook for Analyses, Questions, and a Discussion of Technique for Use with Modern Short Stories: The Uses of the Imagination. Arthur Mizener. 4th ed. New York: Norton, 1979. 50-53.

Provides a useful social and character analysis of the story, plus a series of study questions.

1214. Nakajima, Kenji. "A Study of Saul Bellow's 'A Sermon by Dr. Pep.'" *Kyushu American Literature* 17 (1976): 12-19. Cited in *MLA Bibliography*, 1976.

1215. Nakajima, Kenji. "A Study of Saul Bellow's 'Looking for Mr. Green.'" *Kyushu American Literature* 18 (1977): 5-18. Cited in *MLA Bibliography*, 1978.

Provides a fairly detailed formalistic exegesis of the story under the headings: Idea in the Structure, Initiation Theme, Green: The Namer of the Unnameable, and Looking for Mr. Green.

1216. Newman, Judie. "Saul Bellow and Trotsky: 'The Mexican General.'" *Saul Bellow Newsletter* 1.1 (1981): 26-31.

This story, like all the novels, is formally located in the contingency of historical process. Bellow is actively engaged in analysis of the dynamics of history. In this story one of the questions raised is whether man makes history or history makes man. The indirection of this story forces the reader to question his principal focus. The final question the story forces the reader to ask is whether all the characters, important or not so important, really are of any significance to history. Is history the record of public acts of great men, or is it made by men in the grip of secret desires, swayed by forces beyond their control? Newman also discusses nature as a counterforce to history.

1217. O'Connell, Shaun. "Bellow: Logic's Limits." Rev. of *Mosby's Memoirs and Other Stories. Massachusetts Review* 10.1 (1969): 182-87.

Provides a brief critical overview of the stories published in *MM*. Praises the stories for their taut style, their emphasis on intellectual life and their awareness.

1218. Ozik, Cynthia. "Farcical Combat in a Busy World." Rev. of *Him with His Foot in His Mouth and Other Stories. New York Times Book Review* 20 May 1984: 3. Rpt. in *Saul Bellow*. Ed. Harold Bloom. Modern Critical Views. New York: Chelsea, 1986. 235-41.

Calls the volume *HWFIM* "a concordance, a reprise, a summary, all the old themes and obsessions hauled up by a single tough rope." Praises the work further as a "cumulative art concentrated, so to speak, in a vial." Sees the stories as the long-awaited personal decoding process for Bellow. Comments on each story and places Bellow in his twentieth-century American and international context. A major review essay.

1219. Pinsker, Sanford. Rev. of *Him with His Foot in His Mouth and Other Stories. Studies in Short Fiction* 21.4 (1984): 404-05.

A brief review commenting on the emphasis in the collection on style, voice, and memory. Condemns earlier fiction for its preachiness and sighs with relief that the short stories are not as bad in this respect. Identifies *HWFIM* as a collection of short stories that helps decode the earlier fiction. Asserts that the voice of the stories is finally "demonized by the right questions." No in-depth analysis; only a brief review of each story.

1220. Prescott, Peter S. "Him at His Most Impressive." Rev. of *Him with His Foot in His Mouth and Other Stories. Newsweek* 14 May 1984: 76.

Laments that Bellow has written so few short stories. Sees the form as a natural curb on his "didacticism." Sees the stories as "well-crafted and thickly textured." Provides a brief introduction to each story.

1221. Rodrigues, Eusebio L. "Koheleth in Chicago: Quest for the Real
    in 'Looking for Mr. Green.'" *Studies in Short Fiction* 11.4
    (1974): 387-93.

> Sees the story as a *bildungsroman* that uses the quest
> pattern. Sees it as a species of Drieserian metaphysical
> parable. Commends it as one of the great short stories of
> our time.

1222. Rodrigues, Eusebio L. "A Rough-Hewn Heroine of Our Time:
    Saul Bellow's 'Leaving the Yellow House.'" *Saul Bellow
    Newsletter* 1.1 (1981): 11-17.

> Suggests that previous critics have failed to properly explain
> Bellow's short stories, which are by-products of his fictional
> talents, when they fail to see them in terms of the analogous
> themes and characters in the novels. Gives a highly
> sophisticated critique of this short story, and particularly of
> the character of Hatti Waggoner. Draws parallels between
> Hattie and Joseph, Charlie and Herzog. Interprets the story
> as pointing up the failure of human love, isolation, and the
> failure of the American dream of the Edenic West. Also
> discusses the themes of inertia, identity and death contained
> in the story, all in terms of the novels.

1223. Rooke, Constance. "Saul Bellow's 'Leaving the Yellow House':
    The Trouble with Women." *Studies in Short Fiction* 14.2 (1977):
    184-87.

> Discusses Hattie in detail, comparing her predicament and
> personality to those of Bellow's male protagonists. Yet Bellow
> fails to distinguish her as he should and give her both
> intellectual dimension or his full sympathy. She fails to
> wake from her living sleep and achieve salvation through
> confronting death, as do the male protagonists. Concludes
> that although Bellow's notorious sexism is less apparent in
> this story than in most other works, there are textual
> evidences of authorial sexism.

1224. Roudane, Matthew C. "Discordant Timbre: Saul Bellow's 'Him
    with His Foot in His Mouth.'" *Saul Bellow Journal* 4.1 (1985):
    52-61.

Examines the manner in which "Shawmut's present recollections of his past irresponsible and comic outbursts shape not
only his life, but Bellow's structural and thematic concerns
within the short story." Roudane concludes that what
emerges is an extension of Bellow's philosophical conviction
that the individual can take an affirmative essentially
romantic stance towards both an internal world that, for
Shawmut at least, is complicated by his "hysterical syndrome"
which causes him "to put his foot in his mouth."

1225. Solotaroff, Theodore M. "Saul Bellow: Lines of Resistance."
Rev. of Mosby's Memoirs and Other Stories. *The Red Hot
Vacuum and Other Pieces of Writing of the Sixties.* Theodore
Solotaroff. New York: Atheneum, 1970. 298-305.

1226. Stevick, Philip. "The Rhetoric of Bellow's Short Fiction."
Critical Essays on Saul Bellow. Ed. Stanley Trachtenberg.
Critical Essays on American Literature. Boston: Hall, 1979.
73-82.

Argues that Bellow's short fiction carries power and integrity.
Claims that like other writers of the period he deals in the
"ludic, the fabulous, and the linguistic." Provides a
historical overview of the various stories and collections.
Comments that the implications of such rhetorical fiction as
these stories are 1) special verbal effects and grammar, 2)
the invention of a grammar of resistance, 3) certain kinds
of valuations of the human community. What follows is a
detailed account of the kind of grammar being spoken of with
specific reference to individual stories. A major article.

1227. Walsh, Thomas. "Heroism in Bellow's 'The Mexican General.'"
Saul Bellow Journal 1.2 (1982): 31-33.

Shows how in this story Bellow "laments history's sordidness,
but shows that the General's ignorance and opportunism that
seem to undermine the old man's greatness ultimately serve
to sharpen it."

1228. Weinstein, Ann. "A Toast to Life, L'Chayim: Saul Bellow's 'A
Father-to-Be.'" *Saul Bellow Journal* 2.1 (1982): 32-35.

Discusses the story as a veritable seedbed of ideas, characters and themes used by Bellow later in the novels. In particular shows the relationship between Rogin and the later Herzog.

Reviews

1229. Adams, Robert M. "Winter's Tale." Rev. of *Him with His Foot in His Mouth and Other Stories. New York Review of Books* 19 July 1984: 28-29.

1230. Bloom, Alice. "Recent Fiction II." Rev. of *Him with His Foot in His Mouth and Other Stories. Hudson Review* 37.4 (1984-85): 621-30.

1231. Enright, D. J. "Exuberance-Hoarding." Rev. of *Him with His Foot in His Mouth and Other Stories. Times Literary Supplement* 22 June 1984: 688.

1232. Gilbert, Harriett. Rev. of *Him with His Foot in His Mouth and Other Stories. New Statesman* 29 June 1984: 26.

1233. Goodheart, Eugene. "Parables of the Artist." Rev. of *Him with His Foot in His Mouth and Other Stories. Partisan Review* 52.2 (1985): 149-53.

1234. Halperin, Irving. "Therefore Choose Life." Rev. of "Mosby's Memoirs." *Jewish Affairs* Mar. 1976: 65, 67, 69.

1235. Klausler, Alfred P. Rev. of *Him with His Foot in His Mouth and Other Stories. Christian Century* 12-19 Sept. 1984: 848.

1236. LaSalle, Peter. "Sumer is icumen in, Llude sing cuccu!" Rev. of *Him with His Foot in His Mouth and Other Stories. America* 14 July 1984: 16-17.

1237. Mano, D. Keith. "In Suspense." Rev. of *Him with His Foot in His Mouth and Other Stories. National Review* 10 Aug. 1984: 48.

1238. Mudrick, Marvin. Rev. of *Mosby's Memoirs & Other Stories. Hudson Review* 21.4 (1968-69): 751-63.

1239. Rev. of *Him with His Foot in His Mouth and Other Stories. New York Times* 27 Oct. 1985: 50.

1240. Peden, William. "Recent Fiction: Some of the Best." Rev. of *Him with His Foot in His Mouth and Other Stories. Western Humanities Review* 39.3 (1985): 267-74.

1241. Richardson, Jack. "Chasing Reality." Rev. of *Mosby's Memoirs and Other Stories. New York Review of Books* 13 Mar. 1969: 12-14.

1242. Samuels, Charles Thomas. "Action and Idea in Saul Bellow." Rev. of *Mosby's Memoirs and Other Stories. Atlantic* Nov. 1968: 126-28, 130.

1243. Tanner, Tony. "Tony Tanner Writes about the American Novelist, Saul Bellow." Rev. of *Mosby's Memoirs and Other Stories. Listener* 23 Jan. 1969: 113-14.

1244. Tobias, Richard. Rev. of *Him with His Foot in His Mouth and Other Stories. World Literature Today* 59.1 (1985): 90-91.

To Jerusalem and Back

1245. Baker, Carlos. "Bellow in the Holy Land." *Theology Today* Jan. 1977: 407-08.

Provides a brief summary of events mentioned in the book. Briefly discusses Bellow's political stance toward Israel.

1246. Bellman, Samuel Irving. "Rambling Scenario of Life." *Southwest Review* 62.2 (1977): 202-05.

Provides a brief synopsis of contents of the book with commentary on Bellow as activist and contemporary.

1247. Bird, Christine M. "The Return Journey in *To Jerusalem and Back*." *Melus* 6.4 (1979): 51-57.

Concentrates on the promise implied in the title that before the book ends Bellow will make sense of America and his return home. Discusses Bellow's sense of being an American in Israel and a Jew in America.

1248. Chomsky, Noam. "Bellow's Israel." *New York Arts Journal* (Spring 1977): 29-32. Rpt. as "Bellow, *To Jerusalem and Back*." *Towards a New Cold War: Essays on the Current Crisis and How We Got There*. Noam Chomsky. New York: Pantheon, 1982. 299-307.

Complains that in *TJ* Bellow is a propagandist who has produced a book of what every good American should believe about Israel according to the Israeli Information Ministry. Complains also of simplistic political analyses, biases and even misinformation in the book. Finally accuses

Bellow of possessing merely an engaging ability to skim the surface of ideas.

1249. Cohen, Sarah Blacher. "Saul Bellow's Jerusalem." *Studies in American Jewish Literature* [University Park, PA] 5.2 (1979): 16-23. Joint issue with *Yiddish* 4.1 (1979).

Likens the Bellow who travels to Jerusalem, and into his Jewish past, to the mental travelers in his own fiction. Takes parts of the book and compares them to scenes and episodes in Bellow's fiction.

1250. Dahlin, Robert. "Bellow's Nonfiction Debut, on Jerusalem, Coming From Viking in the Fall." *Publishers Weekly* 19 Apr. 1976: 40.

Provides a general overview of the contents of the book.

1251. Duchovnay, Gerald. "The Urgency of Survival." *CEA Critic* 43.1 (1980): 20-24.

Sees *TJB* as an awakening or a reassessment by Bellow of his attitude toward Israel and his own Jewishness. Recounts Bellow's comments on the subject of such categorizations as Jewish-American writer. Sees the major theme of the book as survival. Describes Bellow's mixed feelings on his return to America. Portrays him as man trying to retain a footing on a tottering world.

1252. Ehrenkrantz, Louis. "Bellow in Jerusalem." *Midstream* Nov. 1977: 87-90.

Predicts the book will disturb Middle East partisans because it fails to endorse one position entirely. Sees this in light of Bellow's disavowal of being labeled "Jewish." Commends the book for the quality of the character portraits it achieves. Discusses Bellow's assessment of Sartre's critique of the issues at stake in Israel, and yet condemns Bellow's lack of commitment, likening it to the lack of commitment found in all of his fictional creations.

1253. Grossman, Edward. "Unsentimental Journey." *Commentary* Nov. 1976: 80, 82-84.

> Grossman provides an account of the reading Bellow did in preparation for the book. Admires his hard-headed appraisal of the situation in Israel. Delineates Bellow's own political response to Zionism. Critiques the book by examining tone and content.

1254. Hollander, John. "Return to the Source." *Harper's* Dec. 1976: 82, 84-85. Rpt. as "*To Jerusalem and Back*." *Saul Bellow*. Ed. Harold Bloom. Modern Critical Views. New York: Chelsea, 1986. 97-100.

> Hollander describes the trip depicted in the book as an inward and backward, as well as an outward and onward, journey. Suggests the book has as much to do with the *diaspora* Jew traveling to a lately marked-out center and home again to exile as it has to do with Israel itself. Describes the book as being as full of talk as encounter and of asking one central question about the survival of Israel. Discusses the "grotesque awkwardness" with which Bellow depicts the Israeli political experiment. Describes also the shadow of Russia that falls across the pages of the book, both through Bellow's personal acquaintance with Russian literature and through the history of the Middle East itself. Concludes that what gives the book unity is the author's fierce personality as referee. A major article.

1255. Lavine, Steven David. "In Defiance of Reason: Saul Bellow's *To Jerusalem and Back*." *Studies in American Jewish Literature* [University Park, PA] 4.2 (1978): 72-83. Joint issue with *Yiddish* 3.3 (1978).

> Lavine criticizes the book for a "want of hard thought, of ideas engaged, analyzed, and judged." Discusses the recurring themes of the threat of annihilation, incessant talking as a means to solution, the loss of purpose of the democratic West, Western naivete in face of the USSR and several others. Claims that though the book fails as social analysis, perhaps its primary objective is rather to dramatize, in a non-fictional context, the primary concerns of the fiction with regard to humanity and modern existence. By looking at the problems of men like Teddy Kollek and Meyer Weisgal, "Bellow

has come closer to presenting good men in action than in
any of his fiction."

1256. Lavine, Steven David. "On the Road to Jerusalem: Bellow
Now." *Studies in American Jewish Literature* [University
Park, PA] 3.1 (1977): 1-6.

A general and rather unfavorable review of the book in which
Lavine begins to formulate ideas that will form the substance
of his more developed article in the 1978 issue of *Studies in
American-Jewish Literature*. (See item 1255).

1257. Libowitz, Richard. "Of Sights and Vision." *Reconstructionist*
Mar. 1977: 24.

Predicts that the book will be a best seller because of its
concrete detail. Notes Bellow's discomfiture at the end of
the work that there are no easy solutions to the problem of
Israel. "Declaration of these findings makes the reader privy
to a learned man's despair," he concludes. Sees the book as
both Jewish and Catholic in its scope.

1258. Pinsker, Sanford. "Jerusalem Without Fictions." *Jewish Spectator*
42.1 (1977): 36-37.

Commends Bellow for having produced an engrossing and intelligent view of Israeli life and spirit. Describes the various
dimensions of Bellow's response to Zionism.

1259. Saposnik, Irving S. "Bellow's Jerusalem: The Road Not Taken."
Judaism 28.1 (1979): 42-50.

Describes how the mystique of Chicago is translated into the
account of Jerusalem. Shows both the biblical Jerusalem and
the modern Jerusalem as the geo-political center of modern
Israel. Sees Israel--like Henderson's Africa--as a place of
spiritual renascence. Also comments on the circular structure
of the book, characters, tone and personal biographical
elements.

1260. Siskin, Edgar E. "Saul Bellow in Search of Himself." *CCAR Journal* 25.2 (1978): 89-93.

1261. Willson, Robert F., Jr. "The Politics of Massage: Moshe the Masseur in *To Jerusalem and Back.*" *Notes on Modern American Literature* 2.4 (1978): Item 26.

Moshe, by laying hands on the author, "takes on a somewhat priestly role; his philosophy of dedication to principle approximates that of the typical Bellow hero." Ultimately he becomes a suitable symbol "for the balance of mood Bellow hopes will prevail in the Middle East." His character reaffirms a faith in reason and a mature love "that is central to the acts of self-discovery of such heroes as Herzog and Charlie Citrine."

Reviews

1262. Agress, H. *"To Jerusalem and Back: A Personal Account."* *Contemporary Judaism* 31 (1976-1977): 101-03.

1263. Burgess, Anthony. "A Resonant Bellow." *Spectator* 27 Nov. 1976: 26.

1264. Howe, Irving. "People on the Edge of History--Saul Bellow's Vivid Report on Israel." *New York Times Book Review* 17 Oct. 1976: 1-2.

1265. Johnson, Paul. "The Issue of Israel." *Times Literary Supplement* 3 Dec. 1976: 1509.

The Victim

1266. Aharoni, Ada. "*The Victim*: Freedom of Choice." *Saul Bellow Journal* 4.1 (1985): 33-44.

> Explicates the metaphysical issue of whether a man might choose his own fate or whether it is chosen for him. Traces Bellow's handling of these ideas through his early short stories and through *DM*. Proceeds then to examine Asa Leventhal's problem in *TV*. Concludes that in *TV* he treats the subject simultaneously at two different levels--the realistic and the symbolic.

1267. Baumbach, Jonathan. "The Double Vision: *The Victim* by Saul Bellow." *The Landscape of Nightmare: Studies in the Contemporary American Novel*. Jonathan Baumbach. New York: New York UP, 1965. 35-54.

> An exemplary nightmare novel in the Jamesian tradition of the well-made novel. Leventhal emerges in this critique as a complex and ambiguous protagonist in whom Bellow invests all the mystery of the victim-victimizer syndrome. Baumbach also develops in great depth the complex relationship between Allbee and Leventhal. Part of this focuses on the redemptive implications of it for Leventhal as he learns compassion and experiences redemption. Baumbach also accounts very effectively for the Mickey and Elena subplot. A major article.

1268. Bradbury, Malcolm. "Saul Bellow's *The Victim*." *Critical Quarterly* 5.2 (1963): 119-28.

> Sees the Bellow hero as intellectual, uncertain of his nature, remote from traditional faith and concerned to discover his proper relationship to his fellowman. Leventhal is typical of the Bellow hero in his individual assertion of will against a

273

deterministic environment. Bradbury carefully traces the
nature of Leventhal's moral development through nightmare
and anarchy into social complicity. Believes Bellow has
extended himself far beyond realism into the larger sphere
of the poetic, the lyrical and the psychological, thus
rivalling the best of the French existentialist writers.

1269. Chavkin, Allan. "Ivan Karamazov's Rebellion and Bellow's *The
Victim.*" *Papers on Language and Literature: A Journal for
Scholars and Critics of Language and Literature* 16.3 (1980):
316-20.

Discusses the influence of Dostoevsky's *The Brothers
Karamzov* and *TV*. Traces the possible influences incident by
incident. Both novels develop the theme of who is responsible
for accidental suffering and both radiate an eloquent protest
against this. Ultimately, Leventhal fails to make the kind of
growth Ivan is capable of. He remains a passive victim being
led to a seat in a darkened theatre by an unknown usher.
He is the typically weak-willed twentieth-century hero unable
to engage with higher reality.

1270. Clayton, John J. "*The Victim.*" *Saul Bellow: In Defense of Man.*
Bloomington, IN: Indiana UP, 1968. 139-65. Rpt. in *Saul
Bellow: A Collection of Critical Essays.* Ed. Earl Rovit.
Twentieth Century Views. Englewood Cliffs, NJ: Prentice,
1975. 31-51.

1271. Dittmar, Kurt. "Realitat und Fiktion in der zeitgenossischen
amerikanischen Erzahlliteratur." *Literarische Ansichten der
Wirklichkeit: Studien zur Wirklichkeitskonstitution in
englischsprachiger Literatur.* Eds. Hans-Heinrich Freitag and
Peter Huhn. Anglo-American Forum 12. Frankfurt aM: Lang,
1980. 401-27.

1272. Downer, Alan S. "Skulduggery in Chungking and Manhattan."
New York Times Book Review 30 Nov. 1947: 29.

Accuses *TV* of being contrived and unclear in its meaning.
Sees Levanthal as deriving from Oeidipus, Leopold Bloom
and Joseph K. Decries the ending of the novel for its
timidity.

1273. Farrelly, John. "Among the Fallen." *New Republic* 8 Dec. 1947:
27-28.

Placed in relation to one another, the victim victimizing the
victimizer, their opposite problems define their characters and
contain their solution. Concludes that the book contains much
wit and wisdom. Hails Bellow as a major writer.

1274. Fiedler, Leslie. "The Fate of the Novel." *Kenyon Review* 10.3
(1948): 519-27.

Sees Leventhal as Jew both particularized and universal. He
is Leopold Bloom, the urban man, the sojourner, the bastard
artist, infinite in feeling and limited in expression. Fiedler
commends the book for the tension sustained between its palpable realistic surfaces, its symbolic implications and its
achieved ideas.

1275. Gilmore, Thomas B. "Allbee's Drinking." *Twentieth Century
Literature* 28.4 (1982): 381-96.

TV affords a rich commentary on drinking, attitudes toward
it and reasons for it. Asa Leventhal furnishes many of the
attitudes and reactions, but Kirby Allbee, supposed problem
drinker, also has much to say. Discusses in depth Leventhal's
antipathy, fear and stereotyping of Allbee, thus limiting
Allbee's humanity and revealing his own character and
Jewish attitudes toward drinking. Likewise, Allbee has his
own stereotypical ideas on Jews that he delivers to the hostile
Leventhal. A sophisticated study of how these attitudes
reveal the inner characters and relational attitudes of these
two men.

1276. Glicksberg, Charles I. "The Theme of Alienation in the
American Jewish Novel." *Reconstructionist* 29 Nov. 1957:
8-13.

1277. Gordon, Andrew. "Pushy Jew: Leventhal in *The Victim.*" *Modern
Fiction Studies* 25.1 (1979): 129-38.

Gordon argues that Leventhal's emotional problem is finding
a balance between his aggressive and passive impulses,

between being pushy and being pushed around. Isolated and
tested during an unbearably hot summer, he is forced to
come to terms with himself. Gordon analyzes Leventhal's
psychological background, then traces his difficulties with
these two aspects of his personality. Typically, he manifests
the push of the second generation Jew to find a place in an
upwardly mobile society, yet he suffers from lack of
self-worth. Life for him is a crowded, hostile race. Gordon
also explains his ambivalence toward women. Pursues
convincingly the theme of "pushing" throughout the novel. A
major article.

1278. Greenberg, Martin. "Modern Man as Jew." *Commentary* Jan.
1948: 86-87.

Argues that *TV* is the first American novel to see Jewishness
not in its singularity, not as constitutive of a special world
of experience, but as a quality that informs all of modern
life, as the quality of modernity itself. All that stamps
Leventhal as Jew also stamps him as representative *homo
urbis*. Bellow captures the malaise of the megalopolis very
skillfully. Allbee the anti-Semite is the materialization of all
the real threats that surround Leventhal. He is also a negative
inversion of Leventhal. Jewishness in the story is what
gives it its radical depth. Criticizes the typically American
spareness and abruptness of the genre compared to its
European counterparts.

1279. Hardwick, Elizabeth. "Fiction Chronicle." *Partisan Review* 15.1
(1948): 108-17.

Hardwick describes the novel as thoroughly and exquisitely
honest. Less episodic than *DM*, this novel is more objective,
less cramped and uncertain, and equally vigorous intellectually
The prose is both unpretentious and fine.

1280. Kremer, S. Lillian. "Acquiescence to Anti-Semitism in *The
Victim*: An Alternate Reading of Bellow's Daniel Harkavy."
Saul Bellow Journal 1.2 (1982): 27-30.

In *TV* Bellow probes not only the pathology of anti-Semitism,
but polar Jewish responses to anti-Semitism. Harkavy functions
as a healthy foil to Leventhal's paranoia. Both are finally

seen as fellow victims of an historic evil. Asa chooses to
see enemies everywhere while Harkavy chooses to be blind.
Harkavy finally offers not an antidote to anti-Semitic
poison, but a placebo.

1281. Kremer, S. Lillian. "The Holocaust in *The Victim.*" *Saul Bellow
Journal* 2.2 (1983): 15-23.

Bellow's fiction both subordinates and confronts the Holocaust.
Though absent from the dramatic center of Bellow's works,
his characters are haunted by its specter. Centering on the
dynamics of anti-Semitism, *TV* abounds in Holocaust symbolism.
In this reading Leventhal, a first generation American Jew,
and Allbee, who represents the old order traditionally bred to
rule, demonstrate allegorically the intricate and diverse
nature of anti-Semitism and the dynamics of the Holocaust.
There are echoes of Nazi propaganda and values in the
speech of Allbee. Bellow uses many archetypal images of the
Holocaust centering on the associations with the color
yellow, claustrophobic air pressure, heat, bad smells, gas,
fire, the color orange, train images, dream sequences,
suffocation and dislocation.

1282. Miller, Karl. "Leventhal." *New Statesman* 10 Sept. 1965: 360-61.

Denies the accusations by Fiedler that there is an homoerotic
relationship between Leventhal and Allbee. However, much
in this novel is mad, part of the psychopathology of everyday
life. Criticizes Bellow for not providing an adequate diagnosis
of the relationship and comments that all along it has seemed
finite. Allbee is a type who comes and goes in any life.

1283. Murai, Mami. "A Study of *The Victim* by Saul Bellow--Human
Mortality and Chain of Life." *Kyushu American Literature* 23
(1982): 85-88.

1284. Nilsen, Helge N. "Anti-Semitism and Persecution Complex: A
Comment on Saul Bellow's *The Victim.*" *English Studies* 60.2
(1979): 183-91.

TV treats the problem of anti-Semitism as being sustained by
Jew and Gentile alike. It can only be created by two willing

parties. Leventhal is the eternal Jew accepting moral responsibility for a world he has not created. Traces in detail the paranoia and ghetto psychology of the Jew and the hostility and prejudices of the displaced WASP. These twin responses deny the common humanity of all people as evidenced by the recurring images of faceless throngs of people throughout the novel. Though Leventhal is able to deal with Allbee in the last scene of the novel, new stresses would probably induce the old traumas.

1285. Le Pellec, Yves. "New York in Summer: Its Symbolic Function in *The Victim.*" *Caliban* 8 (1971): 101-10.

Throughout *TV* we are made to feel the oppressive weight of the crowd, the environment and the suffocating heat of the city summer in order to symbolize Asa Leventhal's inner psychic states. These elements are always contrapuntal to the hero's feelings. His New York is depicted as a jungle because he is trying to reduce raw existence to its very essentials.

1286. Shastri, N. R. "Self and Society in Saul Bellow's *The Victim.*" *Osmania Journal of English Studies* 8.2 (1971): 105-12.

Analyzes the basic dichotomy in the Bellow novel as that between the demands of self and the demands of society. *TV* explores how far the individual can accept the demands of the world and how soon he is likely to be alienated from it. The novel is about the spectacle of man seeking resolution. The hero moves from alienation to accommodation and from denial to acceptance. However, in this novel Allbee has made his peace with a paranoiac vision of the world and Leventhal is finally seen groping in the dark with the problem of choice despite the choices before him.

1287. Trilling, Diana. "Fiction in Review." *Nation* 3 Jan. 1948: 24-25.

Trilling sees the strength of *TV* in its physical descriptions of domestic detail and landscape. The novel contains many levels of meaning and is hard to match in recent fiction for skill and brilliance. Poses the question "Who is the victim?" Through these two protagonists Bellow explores the whole issue of guilt. What emerges is the notion that no man is without responsibility for either himself or his neighbor. More impressive is the fact that this is done in an inter-racial context. Bellow establishes the unpleasant fact that minority victims themselves contribute to victimization.

Reviews

1288. Coleman, John. "Bellow at His Blackest." *Observer* 12 Sept. 1965: 26.

1289. Coren, Alan. "Manhattan Agony." *Punch* 27 Oct. 1965: 624.

1290. Hale, Lionel. *Observer* 13 June 1948: 3.

1291. Match, Richard. "Anti-Semitism Hits a Jew." *New York Herald Tribune Weekly Book Review* 23 Nov. 1947: 10.

1292. Poore, Charles. "Books of the Times." *New York Times* 22 Nov. 1947: 13.

1293. Rago, Henry. "The Discomforts of Storytelling." *Sewanee Review* 56.3 (1948): 514-21.

1294. Richler, Mordecai. "Number One." *Spectator* 1 Oct. 1965: 425.

1295. Smith, R. D. "Fiction." *Spectator* 4 June 1948: 686, 688.

1296. "Suffering for Nothing." *Time* 1 Dec. 1947: 111-112.

1297. Winegarten, Renee. "Victim of Alternatives." *Jewish Observer and Middle East Review* 15 Oct. 1965: 21-22.

Doctoral Dissertations

1298. Allen, Mary Lee. "The Flower and the Chalk: The Comic Sense of Saul Bellow." Diss. Stanford University, 1968.

1299. Andres, Richard John. "Self-Consciousness and the 'Heart's Ultimate Need': A Reading of Saul Bellow's Novels." Diss. Fordham University, 1977.

1300. Blanch, Mable. "Variations on a Picaresque Theme: A Study of Two Twentieth-Century Treatments of Picaresque Form." Diss. University of Colorado, 1966.

1301. Borrus, Bruce Joseph. "Thoughts Informed Against Me: The Fiction of Saul Bellow." Diss. University of Washington, 1978.

1302. Brackenhoff, Mary Guess. "Saul Bellow's Myth of the Picaro." Diss. The University of Nebraska-Lincoln, 1984.

1303. Braham, Jeanne. "A Sort of Columbus: An Investigation of the American Voyages of Saul Bellow's Major Fiction." Diss. Carnegie-Mellon University, 1975.

1304. Browne, Phiefer L. "Men and Women, Africa and Civilization: A Study of the African Novels of Haggard, Greene, and Bellow." Diss. Rutgers University, 1979.

1305. Buckton, R. J. "Novels of Saul Bellow." Diss. University of Leicester, 1976.

1306. Bullock, C. J. "The Self and the World: A Study of Form and Theme in the Novels of Saul Bellow." Diss. University of Leeds, 1975.

1307. Buranarom, Nantana Yunibandhu. "Saul Bellow's Anatomy of Love: A Study of the Theme of Love in *The Adventures of Augie March, Herzog*, and *Humboldt's Gift*." Diss. Ohio University, 1979.

1308. Cagan, Anita P. "Sons and Misogynists: A Study of the Protagonists in Saul Bellow's Novels." Diss. New York University, 1983.

1309. Chavkin, Allan. "The Secular Imagination: The Continuity of the Secular Romantic Tradition of Wordsworth and Keats in Stevens, Faulkner, Roethke, and Bellow." Diss. University of Illinois, 1977.

1310. Clayton, John J. "Saul Bellow: In Defense of Human Dignity." Diss. Indiana University, 1966.

1311. Cohen, Sarah Blacher. "The Comic Elements in the Novels of Saul Bellow." Diss. Northwestern University, 1969.

1312. Crabtree, Ursula Margot. "Facing the Bogeyman: A Comparative Study of the Motif of the Double in the Novels of Saul Bellow and Gunter Grass." Diss. University of California, Davis, 1978.

1313. Craig, Harry Edward. "The Affirmation of the Heroes in the Novels of Saul Bellow." Diss. University of Pittsburgh, 1967.

1314. Cronin, Gloria L. "Saul Bellow's Rejection of Modernism." Diss. Brigham Young University, 1980.

1315. Dickstein, Felice Witztum. "The Role of the City in the Works of Theodore Dreiser, Thomas Wolfe, James T. Farrell, and Saul Bellow." Diss. City University of New York, 1973.

1316. DiGennaro, Michael William. "The Primitive and the Civilized: The Dialectical Nature of Saul Bellow's Art." Diss. Fordham University, 1978.

1317. Dutton, Robert R. "The Subangelic Vision of Saul Bellow: A Study of His First Six Novels, 1944-1964." Diss. University of the Pacific, 1966.

1318. Edelstein, Mark Gerson. "Saul Bellow: Columbus of the Near-at-Hand." Diss. State University of New York at Stony Brook, 1982.

1319. Feuer, Diana Marcus. "The Rehumanization of Art: Secondary Characterization in the Novels of Saul Bellow." Diss. Wayne State University, 1974.

1320. Fortson, Kay Kenney. "Saul Bellow's Use of Imagery as Metaphor in *Herzog*, *Mr. Sammler's Planet*, and *Humboldt's Gift*." Diss. Oklahoma State University, 1979.

1321. Galloway, David D. "The Absurd Hero in Contemporary American Fiction: The Works of John Updike, William Styron, Saul Bellow, and J. D. Salinger." Diss. State University of New York at Buffalo, 1962.

1322. Gerson, Steven M. "Paradise Sought: Adamic Imagery in Selected Novels by Saul Bellow and Kurt Vonnegut, Jr." Diss. Texas Tech University, 1977.

1323. Gitenstein, Rose Barbara. "Versions of the Yiddish Literary Tradition in Jewish-American Literature: Isaac Bashevis Singer, Abraham Cahan, and Saul Bellow." Diss. The University of North Carolina at Chapel Hill, 1975.

1324. Gold, R. Michael. "The Influence of Emerson, Thoreau, and Whitman on the Novels of Saul Bellow." Diss. New York University, 1979.

1325. Golden, Daniel. "Shapes and Strategies: Forms of Modern American Fiction in the Novels of Robert Penn Warren, Saul Bellow, and John Barth." Diss. Indiana University, 1972.

1326. Golden, Susan Landau. "The Novels of Saul Bellow: A Study in Development." Diss. Duke University, 1975.

1327. Goldman, Liela H. "Affirmation and Equivocation: Judaism in the Novels of Saul Bellow." Diss. Wayne State University, 1980.

1328. Hammond, John Francis. "The Monomythic Quest: Visions of Heroism in Malamud, Bellow, Barth, and Percy." Diss. Lehigh University, 1979.

1329. Harper, Howard Morrall. "Concepts of Human Destiny in Five American Novelists: Bellow, Salinger, Mailer, Baldwin, Updike." Diss. Pennsylvania State University, 1965.

1330. Hartman, Hugh Callow. "Character, Theme and Tradition in the Novels of Saul Bellow." Diss. University of Washington, 1968.

1331. Hulley, Kathleen. "Disintegration as Symbol of Community: A Study of *The Rainbow, Women in Love, Light in August, Prisoner of Grace, Except the Lord, Not Honour More,* and *Herzog.*" Diss. University of California, Davis, 1973.

1332. Huq, Abi Mohammad Nizamul. "The Pattern of Family Relationships in Four Selected Novels of Saul Bellow." Diss. Oklahoma State University, 1983.

1333. Hux, Samuel Holland. "American Myth and Existential Vision: The Indigenous Existentialism of Mailer, Bellow, Styron, and Ellison." Diss. University of Connecticut, 1965.

1334. Inglehart, Babette. "Drama as Reality and Metaphor in the Work of Saul Bellow." Diss. The University of Chicago, 1972.

1335. Johnson, Gregory Allen. "'Creatures and More': Codes of Nonverbal Dialogue in the Canon of Bellow." Diss. University of Washington, 1981.

1336. Johnson, Lee Richard. "The Novels of Saul Bellow and Norman Mailer: A Study of Their Polar Perceptions of American Reality." Diss. University of Minnesota, 1979.

1337. Kar, Prafulla Chandra. "Saul Bellow: A Defense of the Self." Diss. University of Utah, 1973.

1338. Kathe, Barbara Ann. "Self Realization: The Jungian Process of Individuation in the Novels of Saul Bellow." Diss. Drew University, 1979.

1339. Kelly, W. J. "Viewpoint and Vision: A Study of Perspective in the Novels of Saul Bellow." Diss. National University of Ireland, 1979.

1340. Kirstein, Ruth Gabriela. "The Dual Vision: Reality and Transcendence in Saul Bellow's Fiction." Diss. State University of New York at Buffalo, 1980.

1341. Kreiger, Barbara Sue. "The Fiction of Saul Bellow." Diss. Brandeis University, 1978.

1342. Kremer, S. Lillian. "Bellow and the Inherited Tradition: A Study of Judaic Influence on Form and Content in Saul Bellow's Fiction." Diss. Kansas State University, 1979.

1343. Leese, David Allen. "Laughter in the Ghetto: A Study of Form in Saul Bellow's Comedy." Diss. Brandeis University, 1975.

1344. Lewin, Lois Symons. "The Theme of Suffering in the Work of Bernard Malamud and Saul Bellow." Diss. University of Pittsburgh, 1967.

1345. Mackintosh, Esther Marie. "The Women Characters in the Novels of Saul Bellow." Diss. Kansas State University, 1979.

1346. Manning, James Brewster. "Craters of the Spirit: Saul Bellow's Novels of Entrapment." Diss. Columbia University, 1978.

1347. Marin, Daniel Barbour. "Voice and Structure in Saul Bellow's Novels." Diss. The University of Iowa, 1972.

1348. Markos, Donald W. "The Humanism of Saul Bellow." Diss. University of Illinois at Urbana-Champaign, 1966.

1349. Marney, Elizabeth Ann Bingham. "Six Patterns of Imagery in Three of Saul Bellow's Novels." Diss. The University of Texas at Austin, 1977.

1350. McCadden, Joseph F. "The Hero's Flight from Women in the Novels of Saul Bellow." Diss. Fordham University, 1979.

1351. Melbourne, Lucy Lauretta. "The Nested Structure of Unreliable First-Person Narrative: Explicit and Implicit Texts in Saul Bellow's *Dangling Man*, Albert Camus's *La Chute* and Franz Kafka's *Ein Landarzt*." Diss. The University of North Carolina at Chapel Hill, 1984.

1352. Merkowitz, David Robert. "Bellow's Early Phase: Self and Society in *Dangling Man*, *The Victim*, and *The Adventures of Augie March*." Diss. University of Michigan, 1971.

1353. Michael, Bessie. "What's the Best Way to Live? A Study of the Novels of Saul Bellow." Diss. Lehigh University, 1969.

1354. Morahg, Gilead. "Ideas as a Thematic Element in Saul Bellow's 'Victim' Novels." Diss. The University of Wisconsin-Madison, 1973.

1355. Nadon, Robert Joseph. "Urban Values in Recent American Fiction: A Study of the City in the Fiction of Saul Bellow, John Updike, Philip Roth, Bernard Malamud, and Norman Mailer." Diss. University of Minnesota, 1969.

1356. Nault, Marianne. "Women Characters in the Fiction of Saul Bellow." Diss. University of Birmingham, 1978-79.

1357. Noreen, Robert G. "Bearing Witness To Life: The Novels of Saul Bellow." Diss. The University of Chicago, 1970.

1358. Offutt, John Corydon. "A Study of Adult Developmental Stages of Behavior in Saul Bellow's Literary Characters." Diss. George Peabody College for Teachers, 1980.

1359. Opdahl, Keith M. "'The Crab and the Butterfly': The Themes of Saul Bellow." Diss. University of Illionis at Urbana-Champaign, 1961.

1360. O'Sullivan, Liam. "Saul Bellow's 'Man Thinking'." Diss. St. John's University, 1978.

1361. Pally, Erwin. "From Realism to Romance in Six Novels by Bellow, Updike and Malamud." Diss. University of Massachusetts, 1977.

1362. Peontek, Louana L. "Images of Women in Saul Bellow's Novels." Diss. Saint Louis University, 1980.

1363. Porter, M. Gilbert. "The Novels of Saul Bellow: A Formalist Reading." Diss. University of Oregon, 1969.

1364. Price, Nancy Laine. "The Serious Self in a Rhetorical World: Affirmative Ambiguity Toward Language in Six Novels of Sa Bellow." Diss. Texas Christian University, 1985.

1365. Quart, Barbara. "The Treatment of Women in the Work of Three Contemporary Jewish-American Writers: Mailer, Bellow, and Roth." Diss. New York University, 1979.

1366. Rader, Barbara A. "Rite of Passage: The Quest of the Hero in Saul Bellow's Novels." Diss. Rice University, 1985.

1367. Reiner, Sherry Levy. "'It's Love That Makes Reality Reality': Women Through the Eyes of Saul Bellow's Protagonists." Diss. University of Cincinnati, 1980.

1368. Riehl, Betty Ann Jones. "Narrative Structures in Saul Bellow's Novels." Diss. The University of Texas at Austin, 1975.

1369. Rodrigues, Eusebio L. "Quest for the Human: Theme and Structure in the Novels of Saul Bellow." Diss. University of Pennsylvania, 1970.

1370. Rosenthal, Melvyn. "The American Writer and His Society: The Response to Estrangement in the Works of Nathaniel Hawthorne, Randolph Bourne, Edmund Wilson, Norman Mailer, Saul Bellow." Diss. The University of Connecticut, 1968.

1371. Sanders, Margaret Moran. "Romantic Elements in the Criticism and Fiction of Saul Bellow." Diss. George Washington University, 1979.

1372. Schraepen, Edmond. "Comedy in Saul Bellow's Work." Diss. University of Liege, 1975.

1373. Sewell, William Jacob. "Literary Structure and Value Judgment in the Novels of Saul Bellow." Diss. Duke University, 1974.

1374. Sheres, Ita G. "Prophetic and Mystical Manifestations of Exile and Redemption in the Novels of Henry Roth, Bernard Malamud, and Saul Bellow." Diss. The University of Wisconsin-Madison, 1972.

1375. Sheridan, Judith Rinde. "Beyond the Imprisoning Self: Mystical Influences on Singer, Bellow and Malamud." Diss. State University of New York at Binghamton, 1979.

1376. Singh, Yashoda Nandan. "The City as Metaphor in Selected Novels of James Purdy and Saul Bellow." Diss. Loyola University of Chicago, 1979.

1377. Svore, Judy Lee. "An Ontological Perspective Applied to the Interpretation of Saul Bellow's *Henderson the Rain King.*" Diss. The University of Arizona, 1977.

1378. Tajima, Junko. "The Role of Intellection in Saul Bellow's Fiction." Diss. Indiana University, 1981.

1379. Tajuddin, Mohammad. "The Tragicomic Novel: Camus, Malamud, Hawkes, Bellow." Diss. Indiana University, 1967.

1380. Tewarie, Bhoendradatt. "A Comparative Study of Ethnicity in the Novels of Saul Bellow and V. S. Naipaul." Diss. Pennsylvania State University, 1983.

1381. Thomas, Jesse James. "The Image of Man in the Literary Heroes of Jean-Paul Sartre and Three American Novelists: Saul Bellow, John Barth, and Ken Kesey--A Theological Evaluation." Diss. Northwestern University, 1967.

1382. Tudish, Catherine Louise. "The Schlemiel and the Reality Instructor: Moral Tension in the Novels of Saul Bellow." Diss. Saint Louis University, 1979.

1383. Walker, Kent Woodward. "The Balancing Perspective: The Paradox of Alienation and Accommodation in the 'Victim' Novels of Saul Bellow." Diss. York University [Canada], 1981.

1384. Wallach, Judith Dana Lowenthal. "The Quest for Selfhood in Saul Bellow's Novels: A Jungian Interpretation." Diss. University of Victoria, 1975.

1385. Warner, Stephen Douglas. "Representative Studies in the American Picaresque: Investigation of *Modern Chivalry*, *Adventures of Huckleberry Finn*, and *The Adventures of Augie March*." Diss. Indiana University, 1971.

1386. Weissman, Maryjo Kores. "Saul Bellow: A Reputation Study." Diss. University of Maryland, 1978.

1387. Wieting, Molly Stark. "A Quest for Order: The Novels of Saul Bellow." Diss. The University of Texas at Austin, 1969.

1388. Williams, Patricia Whelan. "Saul Bellow's Fiction: A Critical Question." Diss. Texas A & M University, 1972.

AUTHOR AND SUBJECT INDEX

Author and Subject Index

Aaron, Daniel, 1015
Abbott, H. Porter, 249
Abeltina, Renate, 727
Absurdism, 332, 336, 337, 354, 370, 388, 624, 630, 739, 981, 1151
Accommodation, 436
Acting, 875
Adam, 819
Adams, Henry, 255
Adams, Robert M., 1229
Adams, Timothy Dow, 817
"Address by Gooley Macdowell . . .," 10
The Adventures of Augie March, 1, 255, 269, 275, 283, 294, 336, 342, 356, 387, 411, 439, 456, 540, 557, 558, 559, 560, 561, 562, 563, 564, 565, 566, 567, 568, 569, 570, 571, 572, 573, 574, 575, 576, 577, 578, 579, 580, 581, 582, 583, 584, 585, 586, 587, 588, 589, 590, 591, 592, 593, 626, 737, 986
Aeneid, 1067
Aesthetics, 442
Affirmation, 354, 629
Agress, H., 1262
Ahab, 461
Aharoni, Ada, 250, 251, 252, 621, 1266
Aithal, S. Krishnamoorthy, 557
Alam, Fakrul, 558
Alcoholism, 1275
Aldridge, John W., 253, 559, 818, 1016

Alexander, Edward, 254, 1032
Alger, Horatio, 590
Alhadeff, Barbara, 1140
Alienation, 264, 315, 324, 394, 428, 487, 524, 588, 627, 630, 631, 736, 739, 821, 877, 892, 1054, 1090, 1142, 1143, 1149, 1151, 1152, 1174, 1276, 1282, 1286
Allegory, 736, 740, 767, 771, 780, 825
Allen, Mary Lee, 1298
Allen, Michael, 255
Allen, Walter, 1181
Alpert, Hollis, 1182
Alter egos, 280
Alter, Robert, 256, 560, 728, 1033, 1199, 1200
Alvarez, Carmen Gago, 257
American Adam, 447, 570, 853
Amis, Kingsley, 594
Anders, Jaroslaw, 258
Anderson, David D., 259, 622, 654, 1122
Anderson, Jon, 214
Anderson, Sherwood, 622
Andres, Richard John, 1299
Anthroposophy, 312, 1001, 1007
Anti-hero, 379, 624
Anti-Semitism, 291, 354, 1267, 1280, 1281, 1282, 1284, 1286
Apollo, Hyperion, 1157
Archetypes, 740, 752, 763, 819, 847, 853
Arendt, Hannah, 1032
Armah, Ayi Kewi, 753